THE ATOMIC SECRET
OF HUEMUL ISLAND

A history of the origins of atomic energy in Argentina

Mario A. J. Mariscotti

The Atomic Secret of Huemul Island. A history of the origins of atomic energy in Argentina

© 2017 Mario Mariscotti
mario.mariscotti@gmail.com

.

Cover design: Miur
Cover image: The author is grateful to Eduardo Santos
Translation: Isabel de Reynal and Mario Mariscotti

Mariscotti, Mario A. J.
The Atomic Secret of Huemul Island. A history of the origins of atomic energy in Argentina/ by Mario A. J. Mariscotti
1.Atomic Energy in Argentina – History. 2. Argentine Physics Association. 3. Richter and Peron. 4. International impact. 5. Huemul Island. 6. Bariloche Atomic Center and Balseiro Institute of Physics. I. Title. II, Title: The Atomic Secret of Huemul Island.

ISBN-13: 978-1545569948
ISBN-10: 1545569940

First Edition in Spanish, Sudamericana Planeta 1984.
Second Edition in Spanish, Sudamericana Planeta, 1987
Third Edition in Spanish, Sigma, 1996
Fourth Edition in Spanish,Sigma, 2004
Fifth Edition in Spanish, Lenguaje Claro, 2016

To Amalia

CONTENTS

Prologue

What led me to undertake the investigation of Project Huemul? To make use of free time in a leisurely holiday? To satisfy my curiosity on a subject that had remained obscure for two decades? To learn how the current activity in nuclear energy in Argentina had come about, more precisely the origins of CNEA, the institution where I worked when I started this project? To fill in the vacuum before some foreign historian would take up the subject, and accomplish what our apathy or negligence has failed to do? To make Argentine society more conscious about this activity of great importance for the country nowadays?

I guess it was a combination of all these reasons which kept me on track when at one time or the other my enthusiasm faded. Beyond these motivations I recall three events which aroused my curiosity in a special way.

The first occurred in an afternoon of 1958 while I was browsing some books in an old family library which was especially appealing because it was in the backyard somewhat isolated. At siesta time on Sundays it was nice to go there and poke around old books at our leisure. There were many books and I never got to explore all of them. Most of them preserved stories which we, the younger generation, had not lived.

Opening one of those books was like shaking dust off a glass and discover on the other side the life of our grandparents. That afternoon I was leafing through a collection of the Bibliotheque de Philosofie Scientifique published in the 1930´s, which reproduced papers by Einstein, de Broglie and Poincaré. In 1958 I had decided to switch from Engineering to Physics. Being a recent convert, the titles and the authors caught my curiosity and opening the yellowish pages of one volume an old newspaper clip fell to the floor. It was an article that immediately rekindled recollections of my own of a few years earlier. I pictured again the large headlines of Buenos Aires newspapers announcing that Argentina had the Bomb and other similar claims.

I carefully unfolded the frail clipping. It was from 1951, when I was 11 years old. I had only a vague memory of the events that had taken place then. The article described a press conference by Dr. Ronald Richter the central figure of an important atomic development in Argentina. I came upon a dialogue. A journalist asked Richter:

- "Was there an explosion?" to which Richter had replied:

- "Yes. For example, in a uranium pile there is also a tendency to an explosion, though dwindled and controlled in intensity so as to establish a dynamic equilibrium."

I read again. Had there been an explosion or not? It was a good question followed by a curious answer.

- "But was there a big noise?" insisted the journalist justifiably unsatisfied.

- "Yes, there was a huge explosion."

Now the exchange seemed to make sense, stimulating the wish to know more. But the logical sequence was again broken.

The journalist wanted further details: "Could it have been heard beyond the island?"

- "That depends on whether there is a storm.", was Richter´s sharp answer.

This intriguing dialogue stayed in my mind for years nourishing an unsatisfied curiosity and I think it was, at least partially, responsible for the making of this book.

The second event that naturally inspired this work was the opportunity of sneaking into Huemul Island in several occasions during my youth.

Playa Bonita is one of the most beautiful places in the vicinity of Bariloche. The view of the Lake Nahuel Huapi and of the Andes from there is exceptional and since 1960 it has been the habitual site of our summer vacations. The lawn slopes down toward the beach. From this vantage point the most notorious geographic element is the Huemul Island, where at one time it stood a secret atomic laboratory…and only 1 mile away. It did not take long to get hold of a canoe and cross the lake to explore this island´s secrets.

To get on the island and roam every corner, like one would do with an abandoned castle, was a fascinating pastime. Gradually, we ventured deeper into the underbrush, finding new buildings and structures hidden behind thorns and thistles grown unrestrained for years

The climax was to reach the only laboratory that showed signs of having been used. The main door was not locked so we could get inside. It did not have windows nor electricity so it took a few minutes until we could adjust our eyes and see what was there. In our first visits, some exceptional instruments were still in place. We moved through a dark labyrinth of thick walls to reach the center of a weird chamber. After a couple of yearly visits, we took pride to bring friends there and show them these wonders that still bore the imprints of a mysterious past. There was a huge battery of large condensers and gigantic electronic tubes, the frames of a dash board, 4" holes drilled in the 3 ft. thick shielding walls neatly aiming at the center of a big magnet. Standing there we weaved all kinds of hypotheses, coveting at the same time that Richter could be by our side to tell us the true purpose of all this marvelous setting. So obviously these visits were a real incentive to take up this investigation.

Yet, there was a third motivation for this work, of a different nature but that eventually converged into the same objective of knowing more about the atomic story of Huemul.

When the idea of studying Huemul was born in 1976, I had one year as Chairman of the Department of Physics of CNEA and three as leader of a research group using a particle accelerator called Synchrocyclotron. This machine had been in operation since December 1954 and many new radionuclides were soon after produced thanks to its energetic particle beams. This instrument had been indeed a key element in the early development of nuclear physics in Argentina. Being now in charge of this laboratory I felt I should be acquainted with its past. The list of publications was a good starting point. But I also wanted to know how this big machine, the largest in Latin America, came to be purchased some 20 years earlier, who decided it, what criteria predominated to select this particular type of accelerator, how long the decision process had taken, how much it cost, etc. By that time, we were preparing a proposal for the acquisition of a new accelerator, an additional motive to learn how it had been done before. Hence I went to talk to my older colleagues who had worked in the laboratory but unfortunately they did not know much about its history. Then I went to see Mr. Ernesto Galloni, an able engineer turned physicist, now retired, who had been responsible for receiving the parts of the machine and assembling it. It seemed a sure bet but surprisingly he did not know who had decided to buy this machine. As a last resort I went to see retired Admiral Pedro Iraolagoitia, who was President of CNEA between 1952 and 1955. He did not know either. Naturally far from declining, my curiosity was increasingly aroused at every step. Ultimately, I found the elusive answer in the story of Huemul. This is why the Synchrocyclotron also played a part as an incentive for this work.

The history of the origins of nuclear energy in Argentina and of Project Huemul in particular, was little known when these worries were roaming in my head. The fragmentary nature of the available information had given rise to a number of conflicting opinions, generally tinted by political prejudices. Moreover, due to its mainly technical character, assumptions by lay people mostly lacked seriousness and rigor. Therefore, it is not surprising that many candidly thought that political reasons were behind the abrupt end of this project. "Was it a fiasco or Richter did indeed have a true secret?", was a common question voiced at the time.

Political polarization has indeed hindered our (Argentine's) capability of seeing historical facts in its true dimension without distortions or mutilations and this has added confusion and doubts about a subject on which there was no solid information.

I hope this work fills in the vacuum or, at least, inspires others to do it. Some may find this book unfriendly to Peron and to his government, others, the opposite. I trust it will not be so, but if the inevitable polarization of one or other side is about even, then my desire to achieve impartiality will be rewarded. I have made an effort to be objective but I know that, in absolute terms, this is impossible. I am convinced of the importance of seeing things as they are and I have tried to be faithful to this imperative. In any case, the historical data will be there available to everybody and saved from being lost forever since most of the people who offered essential testimonies have now passed away.

The case of the beginnings of atomic energy in Argentina deserve some analysis. Some stay put with the Huemul episode, tasting its more sensational aspects. Others prefer to forget it all together. But the history of atomic energy in Argentina starts before Huemul and continues successfully thereafter. Looking back, one cannot fail to think in the early and very important contribution of the La Plata Physics Institute right before WWI, due to Joaquín V. Gonzalez and German physicist Emil Bose, and after WWII the enlightened proposals of Enrique Gaviola, Domingo Savio and many others, dealing with the advancement of nuclear physics in Argentina.

After Huemul, the Dirección Nacional de Energía Atómica (DNEA), (later CNEA), became an institution of great importance for Argentina, not only in nuclear matters but also for its contribution to the development of science and technology in the country. The Bariloche Institute of Physics (now Balseiro Institute) is another fruit of the atomic activity in Argentina that cannot go unmentioned since it placed Argentina at the forefront of physics education.

The question that still persists when one ponders the Huemul story is if it was necessary to pass through this negative experience in order to materialize the idea of investing in nuclear research that sprouted with vigor in 1946. When in 1948 Richter arrived in Argentina and enthused Peron with a project that lacked scientific seriousness, this project overshadowed all the previous initiatives and appealed the Government as a tempting shortcut for acquiring cheap atomic energy. Argentina was not mature enough to avoid falling into a trap but it was nevertheless able to correct the course with its own resources.

The answer to that question which naturally springs negative, is not so obvious as it may seem because, would CNEA have existed without Huemul taking into account the historical circumstances of Argentina right after WWII? Would Argentina have reached the current level of atomic development if it had not gone through the Huemul adventure? There is no question that the resources were at hand to do things better, but human beings are inevitably subject to conflicts, ambitions and ideologies and the political disputes and disagreements among the Argentine ruling class could well have marred the development in this field as it happened in others.

The atomic activity in Argentina, after 1952, has been in the long run a successful experience. Its main contribution probably has been to show that it is possible to solve technological problems in spite of political and economic crises and even adverse international contexts.

Shortly before finishing this work, CNEA President Carlos Castro Madero made the announcement that Argentina had attained the capacity to enrich uranium. Because the enrichment of uranium is a sensitive technology, for necessity it had to be fully developed with own resources. In this way the atomic program proved that Argentina can tackle technological challenges and in doing so gain "autonomy as a sovereign nation" as expressed by Jorge Sabato, the initiator of Metallurgic Science at CNEA.

The conquest of the enrichment technology opened a new chapter in the history of atomic energy in Argentina and deserves a new book. It was achieved by a relatively small group of researchers most of them educated in the Bariloche Institute under the leadership of Conrado Franco Varotto, a physicist of boundless energy and indomitable faith. This achievement, however, would not have been possible without the continuous effort, guided by clearly defined goals, of many people along three decades. Sabato, one of the main advocates of this technological challenge, died only two days before Castro Madero´s announcement. He could not enjoy the best homage to his efforts. His premature death, as that of Jose Antonio Balseiro illustrate to what extent this activity has been a relay race.

The recent history of CNEA lies beyond the scope of this book. People say that it is advisable to wait some thirty years to write history. This is why our chronicle ends in 1955. But it is important to bear in mind where the events described in this book have led us to, so that we do not judge them lightly as if they were totally irrelevant to our reality of now and here.

Acknowledgments

I started gathering information about what had happened in Huemul Island one day during the summer holidays of 1976. It was "siesta" time and I was seating on the lawn of my in-laws feeling uncomfortable of being idle. Huemul Island was in front of me, a mile away. I decided to use my free time to go around and ask old neighbors what they knew, or remembered, about Richter and his scientific adventure. I got up, took the car and drove to Professor Gaviola's house, only a couple of miles down the road. He had retired a few years ago and I knew he lived there in relative solitude with his wife. I surmised that retired people liked being interviewed about their past and would not mind the intrusion. I was right.

This was the beginning. It started as a hobby and so it remained until the end, eight years later. Gradually the amount of commitment, that is time invested, increased. The experience of becoming a mix of historian and reporter was pleasant, though demanding as I only had nights and weekends to work on this project beside the summer holidays. One particular aspect which I enjoyed was that this activity of historical reconstruction was, to some extent, similar to my research in Nuclear Physics; only that instead of protons and neutrons the subject of study was human beings. Because this work was indeed a puzzle of dates, facts, motivations, human conflicts and scientific arguments, same as when one carries out an experiment for the first time and the recorded data comes full of uncertainties. Not without a touch of nostalgia, I recall the hours spent at libraries in Buenos Aires, New York, Grenoble and other cities; the process of gaining access to classified information from the U.S. Government; the tracking down of European witnesses in relation to events which had occurred four or five decades earlier; the cooperation I got from so many who helped all along and, primarily, the testimonies of the leading characters in this story who so generously shared their memories with me.

Indeed, I am indebted to so many. The most important testimonies were those of Enrique Gaviola, who greatly stimulated me to save that part of Argentine history of which he was a leading figure; of Enrique P. González, who generously shared his personal file, a major source of information for this book; of Medardo Gallardo Valdez who, not without reluctance, eventually agreed to talk of events he would much rather have forgotten; of Cesar Ojeda, who kindly granted me an evening of simply told, thrilling anecdotes, brimming with enthusiasm and humor; of Ronald Richter, singular and fascinating personality, who overcame his initial aversion to speak with a CNEA official and treated me as a friend; of Guerino Bertolo, knowledgeable guide of an awesome tour of Huemul Island and witness of the most bizarre events to take place there; of Heinz Jaffke and his wife, without whose assistance Huemul's major secret would not have been unraveled; of Heriberto Hellmann, to whom I am indebted for vital information on the equipment built for project Huemul.

Peter Alemann, Mario Bancora, Mario Della Janna, Pedro Iraolagoitia, Fernando Prieto, Oscar Quihillalt, Antonio Rodriguez, Ricardo Rossi and Jorge Sabato, kindly provided me with important information and material for this work.

I am also grateful to Fidel Alsina, María Cueto de Balseiro, Guido Beck, Daniel Bes, Jorge Cosentino, Ernesto Galloni, Francisco González, Juan Lobo, Alberto Maiztegui, Carlos Mallmann, Clara Mattei, Carlos Monti, Cecilia Mossin Kotin, Nicolás Nussis, Ilse Richter, Soledad Rivero, Walter Seelmann Eggebert and Ruth Spagat for very fruitful interviews.

My friends and colleagues Andres Kreiner and Peter Thieberger, helped me analyze various scientific hypotheses wielded at one time or another in support of project Huemul. From Europe, Walter Davidson provided me with a copy of Huemul's only scientific paper, published in an obscure German journal. A. J. Caraffi, from Birkbeck College, competently assisted me to locate Prof. R. Fürth, former Richter's thesis director in Prague. Prentice Dean, of the U.S. Department of Energy, obtained pertinent hitherto classified documents. Kurt Sitte sent me from Germany a detailed description of his early years in Prague. Mario Bancora and H. Campos provided valuable photographic material.

I have benefitted from information and assistance given by M. Alvarez, Carlos Balseiro, Omar Bernaola, Joan L. Bromberg. Norma Badino, Pedro Bicain, Edgardo Browne Moreno, Peter Bergmann, Jorge Coll, Martin Crespi, Ramon Cereijo, Jaime Clavell Borrás, Ricardo Deza, Eduardo Duek, P. Focke, Mario Foglio, Dante Gamba, Otto Gamba, Federico Lachica, Arturo Lopez Davalos, R. Maglione, Wolfgang Meckbach, Ernesto Maqueda, Cayetano Pomar, Lewis Peynson, Juan Roederer, Eduardo Santos, Héctor Soler, R. Suarez, Walter Scheuer, H. van Luke, Manfred von Ardenne and Spender Weart.

Several persons kindly took the time to read and comment the original manuscript (in Spanish), contributing thereby to improve it considerably. My special thanks to Susana Testoni whose encouraging appraisal at an early stage, prevented this work from ending up in the wastepaper basket.

I am grateful to Roberto Perazzo, a constant supporter of the idea that this work deserved to be undertaken. I am similarly indebted to Conrado Varotto, without whose assistance and encouragement this work would still be unfinished.

I am much obliged to Carlos Araoz, Alberto Boselli, Alberto Jech, Jacinto Luzzi, Jorge Martinez Favini, Miguel Sanguinetti and Edgardo Ventura for their valuable comments on the manuscript. My gratitude also for the views and opinions of Pedro Iraolagoitia, Edgardo Bisogni, Daniel Bes, Emma Perez Ferreira, Oscar Astudillo, as well as my wife and my parents.

Marta R. Gismondi contributed the indispensable unfailing round the clock secretarial support. During the summer of 1984, I was fortunate indeed to rely on the decisive collaboration of INVAP S.E. secretaries G. Rodriguez, Isabel Reynal, S. de Cuervo, M. E. Marteleur and M. de Bondel, who typed the final version of the manuscript. My thanks to María Eugenia Mariscotti and Teresita Frigerio, who enthusiastically helped me copy and bind the manuscript.

Despite the fact that this work did not interfere with my regular duties at CNEA, I could scarcely have completed it had I not enjoyed the support of some sectors and authorities of CNEA, particularly Carlos Castro Madero, Hugo Erramuspe and Emma Perez Ferreira.

Finally, my deep gratitude to my wife and children who had the patience of bearing with me while I was confined with my typewriter all through summer holidays and weekends, and who offered me their silent support during my crisis of discouragement.

Addition to the English edition

The first translation of the manuscript was accomplished by Isabel Reynal of INVAP S.E. I am very grateful for the difficult task that she undertook and for her unyielding commitment to it. Also to Conrado Varotto who provided the resources for making this translation work possible and for his encouragement.

My gratitude to Manuel Cardona, Juan Roederer, Peter Thieberger, Daniel Poneman and Gary Wynia for their advice and help regarding publication in the U.S., to Lewis Pyenson for introducing HUEMUL to the English speaking public, to Carlota Alascio for a very proficient review, to Daniel Ross who championed this cause with unparalleled enthusiasm and more recently to Harry Cooper who kindly offered a new revision of the manuscript, helped greatly to improve it and especially for the encouragement to publish the English version of this book.

Valuable comments and encouragement from Larry Cohen, Barbara Ellington, Thomas F. Glick, David Perry, Robert A. Potash, Thomas Skidmore, Edward Tenner and Joseph Tulchin are gratefully acknowledged

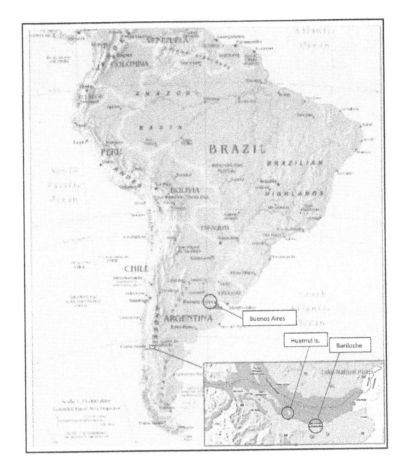

Map of South America showing the location of the city of Bariloche in the south-west of Argentina, next to the Andes. The insert shows Lake Nahuel Huapi, the city of Bariloche and Huemul Island some 5 miles west of Bariloche.

The map is from http://www.freemapviewer.com/es/

1 | The Announcement (March 1951)

Controlled Thermonuclear Reactions

-"Mr. President, the press is ready".

General Juan Domingo Perón nodded, gathered some papers and beckoned to Colonel Enrique P. Gonzalez and Dr. Ronald Richter to follow him. They crossed a small corridor and entered the reception room. A splendid autumn sun was shining brightly through the windows overlooking Paseo Colon and the vast estuary of the Rio de la Plata.

There were about twenty people, including journalists and government officials. Perón shook hands with the Speaker of the House, Héctor Cámpora and with Raúl Mende, Minister of Technical Affairs. He waved to the others. Expectations about this press conference ran high as it had been announced throughout the week and it was known that the President was to speak on Atomic Energy, an unusual subject, especially in Argentina. Though next to nothing had been publicly reported about the work in this field, stories of some secret laboratory on a distant island near the Andes had been circulating in recent months. Only Argentine pressmen were invited. Following Perón, they sat down around a large table.

The President broke the ice with his usual charm. "I apologize for having asked you to come so early, he said to the journalists without ignoring that it was 10 am, "I know that many of you work until late at night".[1]

The President explained that he wanted to keep the public informed on the latest developments in Atomic Energy in the country, but had waited until he had something absolutely certain before saying anything. "This sort of research - he told his attentive audience - is presently being conducted in many parts of the world. Some people believe in it, while others are skeptical, as usually happens with any new scientific breakthrough. Obviously we are no exception. It is quite natural in studies of this sort. But what is important is that when I say something, I know what I am saying. I say it earnestly and I have previously assured myself that the information I give is correct". He paused and with a slight change in his voice he added, somewhat clumsily: "At least up to now I have always tried not to tell the first lie - which I believe I have not done yet - and I would not like to do it now. Therefore, what I say is absolutely authentic and real".

Then he continued: "I wish to talk about the true author and maker of these experiments. This is Professor Richter, an Argentine citizen, who works quietly, doing and saying more than meets the eye." Richter was sitting to the President's left. Faces in the audience turned to him. He smiled briefly. "We owe him all this work - the President said while glancing at the scientist - "he will gladly answer any questions which you may wish to ask. I shall only read a communiqué which I have prepared with the professor's assistance and then add a few remarks. I repeat, the following statement was written on the basis of the information given to me by Professor Richter, and was reviewed by him so that this is real, scientifically valid and true to the facts."

A moment of silence followed. Only the sound of the President's fingers rustling his papers could be heard. Then he read: "On February 16, 1951, controlled thermonuclear reactions were achieved at a technical scale, at the Atomic

Energy Pilot Plant on Huemul Island, near San Carlos de Bariloche".

The concise, unadorned style of the statement betrayed its technical authorship. A minimum of expertise was required to fully grasp the connotations of what the President had announced. Most of those present were not likely to have that expertise. The text of the communiqué was not particularly startling to a layman. Nothing was said about bombs or atomic explosions. 'Controlled thermonuclear reactions' had an impressive ring, but an obscure meaning. 'Thermonuclear' was not a word widely understood in the 1950s, and only specialists could appreciate how crucial the word 'controlled' was in this context. Nonetheless these limitations did not diminish the impact of the President's words. Perhaps Perón's audience intuitively perceived the unusual importance of this press conference. As a matter of fact, it could be claimed to be the most sensational announcement ever to come out of Casa Rosada.

Perón's announcement took place on March 24, 1951. The response from the press was immediate. In particular, the unusual echo heard from beyond the Argentine borders in the following days provided the clearest indication for the man in the street that something important had occurred. In London, The Times informed its readers: "Cheaper Atomic Energy - President Perón claims original process". The New York Times published a full column on the front page of its Sunday edition with the heading "Perón announces new way to make atom yield power" and in smaller print: "He reports Argentina has devised a thermonuclear reaction which does not use uranium. Test held successful. Method likened to the Sun's. Skepticism shown by US officials and experts". In Buenos Aires, the late Saturday edition of Noticias Gráficas carried the headline "Argentina has the real secret of the H (bomb). The announcement that this country has the atomic (bomb) caused great excitement", while La Razón claimed "Argentina has succeeded in producing Atomic Energy".

It seemed incredible that Argentina could have achieved what virtually meant the ultimate answer to mankind's energy supply problem. Because nothing short of that was the implication of Perón's brief official statement: the discovery of a method to control thermonuclear - or fusion - reactions[2] at a technical scale opened the way to the prospect of an almost inexhaustible source of energy.[3]

In 1951 it was believed that this type of energy, based on the nuclear fusion process and fueled with light elements such as hydrogen, helium or lithium, could only be released in an explosion triggered by an atomic bomb. This mechanism later led to the development of the Hydrogen - or H - bomb. At that time, however, even such uncontrolled generation of energy was little more than a hypothesis. No H-bomb had been tested yet (the first detonation of this type took place in November 1952). Seemingly much more remote was the possibility of developing a controlled energy production device. In fact, very few people were even considering it and there was no officially funded research team in the world doing anything in this direction. Except for Richter's group which now, unexpectedly, appeared at the center of an empty stage. Could it be that Argentina had come across one of those rare scientific breakthroughs capable of changing the international scene overnight?

The first months of 1951 had, in any case, been laden with atomic news. A virtual race of testing devices loaded with enriched uranium and plutonium was in full course. By the end of January, and within a 96-hour span, the Nevada Desert was rocked by three atomic explosions. On February 3 a fourth test was carried out and another took place four days later. On Wednesday March 21 newspapers in Buenos Aires reported the atomic tests at the Eniwetok atoll in the Pacific next to the announcement of Perón's press conference scheduled for the following Saturday. On the next day, front-page headlines revealed that the USSR had gained access to the atomic bomb secret, and that the Julius and Ethel Rosenberg couple and David Greenglass were on trial for passing details of the Nagasaki bomb to the Soviets.

Now the world knew that Atomic Power had transcended the geographical borders of the United States and the United Kingdom. The secret was beginning to leak. And only three days after this political bombshell, a country totally removed from the usual chessboard of international affairs, Latin American, virtually unknown except for its cattle and wheat, had burst on the scene, creating a very disquieting third pole of attention. The news agency France Presse was quick to point out that beyond the scientific interest of the Argentine announcement, there was another aspect which would concern US policy makers; namely whether Argentina could eventually manipulate to her advantage the delicate balance of power between East and West should she be able to produce fissionable materials in a large scale.

The Politician and the Scientist

In the comfortable office of the Government House the journalists' attention was divided between listening to the President and scrutinizing the scientist who was behind this remarkable achievement. Until then he had not uttered a word, but it was known that he needed an interpreter to make himself understood. "Argentine citizen" Perón had said, and indeed he had become one a year before in a simple ceremony in Bariloche. A leaflet distributed just before the press conference indicated that Professor Richter was 42 years old and of Austrian origin. He was described as an internationally renowned scientist in experimental nuclear physics, whose "work is frequently quoted in the modern texts which deal with this kind of research". It was also pointed out that he had studied in the University of Prague under Professor Rausch von Traubemberg.

He looked older than 42, yet his appearance was quite healthy and strong. It matched the image a native of Buenos Aires has of a "typical German": upright, ceremonious, and slightly disdainful. He commanded obvious admiration and respect from those surrounding him.

Colonel Gonzalez, seated opposite to Richter, was another leading figure in the Argentine atomic success. He was Secretary General of the National Atomic Energy Commission and a close friend of Perón's. They had worked together -though competing for leadership - in the GOU (Group of United Officers) movement, a sort of fraternity which constituted the core of military officers behind a coup de etat in 1943. This organization had drawn much inspiration from the Nazi-fascist experience in Europe and its members did not hide their preference for the Axis. Their influence on the military Government that ruled the country until the elections of 1946 was dominant and the main reason for Argentina's much delayed declaration of war against Germany during World War II. The feelings of these men had not changed very much a decade later. Even though Germany had lost the war, Teutonic prestige survived largely unscathed within the Argentine military establishment. The old admiration was now rekindled by the enigmatic figure of the atomic genius. From the Argentine perspective, there was no great difference between being Austrian or German[4], and Ronald Richter evoked at that moment the century-old scientific prestige of the German nation.

Richter's aura did not reduce at all Perón's own glory. The President was obviously the political genius who had picked the right scientist. After all, others had had the chance and did not seize it.[5] Few knew how Richter had come to meet Perón and when, but the fact was that he was in Argentina owing to the President's foresight.

The atomic announcement and the excitement that naturally followed it were events not completely without precedent in the Argentina of that time. From its beginning in 1946, Perón's government had pushed forward a strong (as well as erratic) industrialization program. Almost any proposal, if it was deemed "modern" and "technologically advanced", was endorsed without much consideration for its economical plausibility. After five years this policy was beginning to bear fruit. In February, for instance, a fighter plane of advanced design named Pulqui II had been presented to the public. It had been built in Córdoba by a group of engineers led by German expert Kurt Tank. At about the same time an Argentine-made locomotive was also christened. New industries were sprouting up every day, especially in the greater Buenos Aires area. Official openings, installations, and inaugurations abounded. Citizens, especially those supporting the Government, were euphoric. A feeling of achievement and pride prevailed. Imports were replaced by domestic manufactures. Economic self-sufficiency seemed possible. Argentina had plenty of raw materials. If in addition, it was capable of developing its own industry, the country would be freed from unwanted foreign interference. In this climate, disquieting developments abroad seemed remote and unimportant.

On February 15 the USSR occupied Czechoslovakia. Shortly afterwards, on March 10, Tito denounced the increasing Russian military pressure on his country. On the same day that Perón broke the atomic news, General Mac Arthur ordered the controversial crossing of Parallel 38 in Korea, and his statements regarding the possibility of employing nuclear weapons against China were made public. But such news upset almost no one in Buenos Aires; they are dwarfed by local developments and by a fervent nationalism. "Argentine affairs are taken care of in Argentina", declared Ambassador Hipolito J. Paz to the American press in Washington on March 24.[6] The Peronist Party was running strong. Within a formally democratic framework - with a multiparty Congress in session - some disquieting demagogic distortions were already apparent. The exercise of power by the Executive was gradually becoming more arbitrary and more resistant to republican control. Perón and his wife Evita were gradually becoming voluntary prisoners in a web of idolatry. They were the dominant characters on the political stage. For some they were already legendary objects of devotion, especially for the poor who saw the President's wife as a saint who gave them the money confiscated from the upper classes. At the same time the slogan of 'the New Argentina' fell on fertile ground among people eager for national achievement. The leadership of Perón was the answer to age-old frustrations, to the country's dependency on the US and Europe and to the prevailing influence of the oligarchy. News of the technological successes only added strength to the Government, and further discredited a fading opposition.

The President continued reading. He explained that the United States, the United Kingdom and the Soviet Union had followed the path of nuclear fission using costly heavy elements such as Uranium 235 or Plutonium. "During the post-war period, Argentina put much effort into establishing whether it was better to copy the expensive route to nuclear fission, or to risk breaking new ground", he said. "The New Argentina decided to take the risk. Preliminary tests were successful. This encouraged us to build a pilot plant on Huemul Island. There, unlike projects carried out in other countries, Argentine personnel worked on thermonuclear reactions that are identical to those occurring in the Sun. To produce such reactions, it is necessary to reach temperatures of several million degrees. The fundamental problem is to obtain such temperatures. In order to avoid catastrophic explosions, it was necessary to find a method to control the thermonuclear chain reaction. This almost unattainable goal was reached."

Then he made a startling observation: "Foreign scientists will be interested to know that while working on the thermonuclear reactor, the problems associated with the so called Hydrogen bomb were studied in great detail. We have been shocked to find that results published by the most reputed experts are far removed from reality." He raised his eyes and concluded: "The Government intends to use this newly discovered process exclusively for peaceful purposes, in power plants, industrial furnaces and other applications including the production of radioisotopes. It was my wish to inform the people of Argentina, seriously and truthfully as I am accustomed to, about an event which will be of paramount importance for the future of the country and, no doubt, of the world. I urge you to participate in this great project."

He paused and then invited the reporters to interrogate Richter. Now standing below an enormous painting commemorating Loyalty Day,[7] the politician and the scientist were surrounded by members of the press. They both looked very much alike. A picture in Democracia next day shows them in the same pose, sharing the taste of success. It was apparent that they were equally committed to the atomic energy project and that they got along quite well. Colonel Gonzalez - as Secretary of the National Atomic Energy Commission - saw to it that the physicist got everything he needed but this role in no way hindered the direct channel between Richter and the President.

Perón and Richter had a great deal in common and during the following exchange with the journalists they replied as a team, complementing each other in perfect harmony: "This is a new system," - repeated the President - as Dr. Richter says, one which tries to light artificial suns on earth". The scientist added: "I would like to stress the fact that this is not a copy from abroad. It is a fully Argentine project. This is as new for foreigners as it is for us, and let me emphasize that it would have been impossible had not it been for the President's support". And Perón again: "But even more impossible if Professor Richter had not been with us."

"The project" - Richter continued – "was carried out by a group of people who daily faced serious danger, and danger that increases every day." Then in a sudden burst of excitement he added: "The situation is very extraordinary. As a scientist I am not used to creating such a state of affairs. With this project Argentina has challenged the very foundations of projects developed elsewhere. What the Americans get when they explode a Hydrogen bomb[8], we in Argentina achieve in the laboratory and under control. As of today, we know of a totally new way of obtaining atomic energy that does not use materials hitherto thought indispensable. This means that the others will eventually turn to our process".

Now he was not the formal, detached academic character of moments ago. The increased pace was beginning to bear on the interpreter, Captain Gonzalez (the Colonel's son). Richter stressed the absolute secrecy of the investigations. "Argentina has known the secret of the Hydrogen bomb for some time now," - he said – "but the President never asked for bombs. On the contrary, General Perón has always refused that sort of thing."

-"How is this explosion controlled?" inquired a journalist.

-"I control the explosion" - replied Richter – "I can increase it or diminish it at will. When an atomic bomb explodes without control there is terrible destruction. I have been able to control the explosion so that it develops slowly and gradually."

-"Which is the raw material used to produce the explosion?" asked another reporter.

-"You would be surprised if I told you what materials we use," - smiled the scientist – "but we have super secrets like others do. We must keep our friend's secrets so that they keep ours. We do not keep this matter secret for military reasons however, but simply for economical and industrial reasons. As you may know, in addition to military espionage, there is also economic espionage. Hence Argentina must protect its secret".

Reaction from Washington

By noon the atomic news began to spread over Buenos Aires and the rest of the country. Copies of the text read by the President were distributed to foreign news agencies and by the end of the day the information had reached most countries in the Northern Hemisphere including the Soviet Union. Details of the Argentine discovery were avidly read in the afternoon papers and the event became almost the exclusive topic of conversation in the fashionable cafes along Avenida de Mayo. Little attention was paid to otherwise popular subjects such as the lap time of Cabezón Froilán Gonzalez seating on Fangio's car in Rosario, or the stock car race scheduled for the following day in Mar del Plata. It also eclipsed other political news such as the remarks of former Chilean President Carlos Ibañez del Campo who voiced his confidence that Perón would be re-elected for a second term next year. Or the continued search for the director of La Prensa, the main opposition newspaper, fugitive since the paper had been closed by Government a month earlier. The atomic news was indeed a shocking piece in the headlines of the day. A foreign columnist described it as one of the most important scientific events in the history of mankind.[9]

The Argentine atomic development was also certain to have an impact on the Latin American Foreign Ministers Conference which was to begin in Washington the following Monday.

"Even though is not in the agenda, Argentina has appeared once more at the forefront of hemispheric events, precisely on the eve of the Conference. If there were any doubts that the La Prensa affair would place the Argentine problem on the table for discussion, the atomic announcement that originated yesterday in Buenos Aires merely reinforces this belief", wrote Milton Bracker, New York Times correspondent.[10]

The most sensitive subject on the agenda was a call for strengthening internal security in Latin American countries, which included the issue of perceived Soviet espionage and counter-espionage. For the United States, this was a genuinely sensitive question. Since the Conference's overall objective was to discuss continental unity against Communist infiltration, it was obvious that the United States had to play a key role, and had to offer logistic support for any operational efforts that might be agreed to. However - according to The New York Times - it was important for the US Government to refrain from giving tacit approval to regimes that sought to remain in power through the expedient of labeling as Communist anyone who opposed them. Within this context, it was reasonable to believe the La Prensa affair could be brought up for discussion. However, Bracker went on to ask, "which Latin American country would dare bell the Argentine cat?" The State Department was clearly divided as to what to do in the face of the recent steps taken by the Argentine Government, and lately crowned by Perón's announcement. American public opinion was particularly sensitive regarding the La Prensa affair. Statements by Ambassador Paz calling any American action "a meddling in Argentine domestic affairs" had far greater impact in Buenos Aires than in Washington. According to The New York Times US government specialists in Latin American affairs were exploring new ways of reaching an understanding with Perón, different from those used since Ambassador Spruille Braden's times in 1945. The unfortunate attitude of this US Ambassador in Buenos Aires who had virtually acted as Perón's political opponent during the presidential campaign which ended with Perón's triumphant election, was still fresh in the memory of some in the Department of State.

The impact of Perón's announcement on the conference was still uncertain. Some observers anticipated resentment from other Latin American nations if they felt faced with an implicit threat or warning "to be good to Argentina" during the Conference. The liberal wing in the US held this opinion and most likely it reflected their generally hostile attitude towards the Peronist Government. Others thought that the surprise factor of the atomic announcement could backfire on Argentina as the smaller Latin American nations - traditionally wary of Perón - might now react in a way opposite to what the Argentine Government expected. The truth of the matter was neither; in general, the reactions of the Latin American press in the following days were of goodwill towards the Argentine atomic development.

What did appear unambiguous, however, was the uneasiness of the US Government with respect to this last Argentine surprise - which could well interfere with their strategy for the Conference. The American reaction in non-political circles (particularly in the scientific community) towards Perón's announcement was rather skeptical and this was reflected in the tone of most of the US press comments. But within the Government the announcement produced some stir as revealed by the minutes of meetings and conversations held at the office of the US Atomic Energy Commission (AEC) Chairman Dr. Gordon Dean at that time:[11]

Early on Monday, March 26, 1951, Dean's deputy Dr. Walter F. Colby, went to see his boss to brief him on what President Perón of Argentina had said that previous Saturday about a new method of producing atomic energy. "They too have been able to develop a controlled atomic explosion" - he reported.

There was not enough information to assess the extent and implications of this striking news. The AEC chairman was worried. Should he hurry into doing something? Doing what? He was pondering these questions when another AEC official, M. W. Boyer, called from Los Alamos National Scientific Laboratory. Dean was anxious to hear the reaction from other centers.

- "Has there been any comment out that way about the Argentine story of a controlled nuclear explosion?" he asked Boyer.

- "No. There have been no comments. People haven't talked about it here. It is a little difficult to figure out what is going on. You would be surprised if the head of a state would come out and say it if it is not true, but there is some question of the stature of his advisors" Boyer answered.

- "Colby has been giving me the background on the fellow down there. We feel it is just possible that they may have something. I haven't read the material on him yet but I have had some rather interesting background that makes it just possible that something has happened" - the chairman said.

Boyer said he was a little skeptical.

- "OK, have a good trip and don't worry about things here"

The rest of the morning Gordon Dean spent scanning the daily newspapers to learn more about Perón's announcement and about the world reaction. Early in the afternoon he called his assistant John Hall.

- "John, I am disturbed by the statements made concerning this Argentine thing. In the first place, there has been some indication in the files that Perón is not the unfriendly soul to us as he might be in this field although it is true our people haven't been too alert in getting back reports on isotopes, etc."

Dr. Gordon Evans Dean had been recently appointed AEC chairman. He was a brilliant 45-year-old lawyer whose career included teaching positions at Duke University and Southern California, member of several bar associations and assistant to the Nuremberg trials. He was more of a politician than a scientist, but he was a good manager of scientists. The scientists were skeptical about Perón's announcement and had no qualms about letting the press know it, but their skepticism involved no risk. On the contrary, it was risk-safe. It was not so for Gordon Dean. His perspective, as a politician and government official, was exactly the opposite: it was safer to avoid being contemptuous towards the Argentine President just in case he had something.

- "Don't you think John, that he might even welcome a group coming down?" - Dean continued - "Would it be possible for us to get off some sort of official letter to him saying we have heard about this announcement with great interest and talk about our 'joint interest' and that perhaps we would like to send some people down?"

- "Yes, I think it could be done. Actually we had hoped to talk about the joint uranium thing also with Argentina.[12] Perhaps I can do something along this line" Hall answered.

- "Good. In the meantime, you might call Arneson [of the State Department] and talk to him about it. Perón is a little sensitive and has something like an inferiority complex. We might do ourselves a lot of good by being nice at this point. If he has something, we want to be there"

Hall agreed: "We have already discussed it a little and Arneson was also of the opinion that we should be a little reserved on this."

- "We here at AEC have certainly made no comment. I think that the comments that have been made [by individuals] have been unfortunate and don't represent the true feelings of the AEC. And this should be told to Perón. After you, John, talk to Arneson further on it, talk to Colby too, he has the CIA dope on it, you know, and he might be able to give a little turn that might be useful."

Next morning on March 27, Hall called Dean back to say he had talked to Arneson: "Arneson didn't know what the reaction of Miller would be. Miller is Assistant Secretary of State for this sort of thing, you know. I suggested to Arneson that perhaps we ought to develop a couple of paragraphs and then see if we can sell it to Miller."

- "The more I think about it, the more I feel that we shouldn't play with this thing too long, John. I think they do have this feeling of inferiority and a feeling of pride that often accompanies this inferiority feeling. Perón might tell Richter - his scientific advisor - to issue a big statement giving all details and we wouldn't like that."

- "All right, I'll do something right away and bring it down. Come to think of it, a letter that came to you a few months ago, a notification from Argentina that they had established an atomic energy commission of some sort, gives us a little stepping stone. Our statement should be confined to something like: we have noticed that you have been able to make developments in the field of atomic energy and we of the Atomic Energy Commission of the US, etc., etc., some statement which would not give credence to what has been done but that all scientists naturally welcome the solution of these problems, etc., etc."

- "Yes, that sounds good. By the way, do you know if our Ambassador is down there?" Dean asked.

- "No, he is up here now with the meeting of South Americans.[13] The top man down there now could probably orally deliver a message to Perón from you"

- "Couldn't our top man down there go and see Perón and tell him that we are sorry about the things that have been appearing in the American press and that we are most anxious to share in his discoveries, etc., etc.?"

- "I'll write something up in about 15 minutes"

"John, I don't think we should give the State Department boys many days on this thing"

- "Sure, I'll do my best to get hold of Miller this afternoon"

Hall was not successful but Dean was so anxious that he called him again late in the day. Hall explained that Miller was very busy with "these South Americans meeting here" The AEC chairman could only plead: "Please make them move. This thing is quite hot!"

March 24, 1951, front page of a popular afternoon Argentine newspaper the day of Perón´s press conference: The headline reads: "Great excitement due to the announcement that the country has the atomic (bomb)"

Above: View of the Perón's press conference. Richter is seated to the left of Perón who is at the table head.

Below: Ronald Richter and Juan Perón after the press conference.

Both pictures are from March 24, 1951.

March 26, 1951:

Dr. Colby came in to brief GD on report by Peron of Argentina that they too had been able to develop a controlled atomic explosion.

EXTRANEOUS MATERIAL DELETED

Mr. Boyer called from Los Alamos.

EXTRANEOUS MATERIAL DELETED

GD then asked if there had been any comment out that way about the Argentine story of a controlled nuclear explosion. Boyer said there had not been; they haven't talked about it. Thinks it is a little difficult to figure out what is going on -- you would be surprised if the head of a state would come out and say it if it is not true -- but there is some question of the stature of his advisors. GD said Colby had been in giving him the background on the fellow down there -- it is just possible that they may have something. GD said he hadn't read the material on him yet but he has had some rather interesting background that makes it just possible that something has happened. Boyer said he is a little sceptical. GD said for Boyer to have a good trip and not to worry about things here.

EXTRANEOUS MATERIAL DELETED

GD called John Hall and told him he was a bit disturbed by the statements made concerning this Argentine thing. GD said in the first place, there has been some indication in the files that Peron is not the unfriendly soul to us as he might be in this field although it is true they haven't been too alert in getting back reports on isotopes, etc. He might even welcome a group coming down. GD asked if it would be possible for us to get off some sort of official letter to him saying we have heard about this announcement with great interest and talk about our "joint interest" and perhaps we would like to send some people down. Hall said we had hoped to talked about the joint uranium thing also with Argentina and suggested he might try something along that line. GD said in the meantime Hall might call Arneson and talk to him about it. Peron's a little sensitive and has something like an inferiority complex. GD thinks we might do ourselves a lot of good by being nice at this point. If he has something, we want to be there. Hall said he would talk to Arneson. Hall mentioned that they had already discussed it a little and Arneson also said that we want to be a little reserved on this. GD said we (AEC) has made no comment and he thinks that the comments that have been made have been unfortunate and don't represent the true feelings of the AEC. GD thinks this should be told to Peron. GD said after Hall talks to Arneson further on it he might talk to Colby (he has the CIA dope on it) and he might be able to give a little turn that might be useful. Hall said he would do that.

Minutes of the March 26, 1951 meeting of the US Atomic Energy Commission. Declassified by the State Department for the author. *Courtesy of P. Dean*

NOTES TO CHAPTER 1

[1] Details on the press conference throughout the chapter have been obtained from the Buenos Aires newspapers El Líder, Clarín, La Nación, La Razón and Noticias Gráficas of March 25, 1951, afternoon editions, and morning editions of following day.

[2] Nuclear fusion must be distinguished from nuclear fission. The latter refers to the now ordinary process, which uses heavy elements such as uranium or plutonium, to obtain atomic energy. In this case atomic nuclei of these elements are made to split (fission) in roughly two halves by neutron bombardment. These fragments strongly repel each other so that they take off at high speeds. In an A-bomb this (kinetic) energy gives rise to an explosion and its consequences, while in a nuclear power plant it converts into heat as the fragments are slowed down in the medium in which they are immersed. In the case of fusion, atomic nuclei of light elements such as hydrogen (deuterium or tritium) or helium, are made to stick together (fuse) by thermal agitation. When a nucleus "touches" another, a strong attractive force comes into play, which neutralizes the intense mutual electrical repulsion, and a compound system may be formed for a very short time. To achieve this, very high temperatures are required. The following disintegration or decay of this very excited system is analogous to the fission process and, provided the first stage - that of fusing two nuclei together - is reached, energy can be obtained in the same way as outlined above for the case of fission. As this is written, fusion energy for industrial purposes (i.e. controlled fusion) has not been achieved.

[3] Nuclear fusion (see note 2) could become an energy source which "burns" light elements. One of the most likely fuels is the hydrogen isotope, deuterium. Hydrogen is by far, the most abundant element in nature and is found readily in water. In 1956, R. F. Post (Review of Modern Physics, 28, 1956, 338) estimated that the amount of deuterium in the oceans could yield energy equivalent to 1000 times the rate of world production (in 1956) for as long as one billion years.

[4] Richter was born in Falkenau, Egerland, on February 21, 1909. At the time, Falkenau was part of Austria. After World War I, it became part of Czechoslovakia and then of Hitler's Third Reich.

[5] After the war Richter wandered across Europe for three years seeking a job before obtaining the Argentine contract (see notes in CRISIS below).

[6] Democracia, March 25, 1951.

[7] The day, October 17 of 1945, on which Perón was brought from prison to the balcony of the Casa Rosada to the cheers of a delirious populace (more about the political circumstances of that time is given in the next chapter THE EARLY YEARS).

[8] None had been detonated yet, but the remark shows that Richter was aware of the H-bomb project then underway in the US led by Edward Teller.

[9] Quoted in Democracia, March 25, 1951, page 3.

[10] The New York Times, March 26, 1951, page 1, col. 5.

[11] The material, on which the following is based, was kindly provided to the author by the US Department of Energy after being declassified by the Department of State. The author is grateful to Prentice Dean and Jack M. Holl of the Historian's Office at the Department of Energy, and also to Joan Bromberg and Lewis Pyenson, for valuable assistance in this matter.

[12] As early as 1946 the Argentine Congress debated the convenience of including thorium and uranium (as well as chromium, which however was not related to Atomic Energy)

among first-class minerals in the Mining Code (that is, minerals under State control). The bill was passed only in 1954.

[13] Reference to the Foreign Ministers' Conference which was taking place in Washington at that time.

2 | The Early Years (1945-1947)

An Argentine Haven for Science?

Enrique Gaviola kept up his old habit of leafing through the latest scientific journals even after becoming Director of the Córdoba National Observatory. In May 1946, he came across an article in Science entitled "Science and Our Future" written by the Director of the National Bureau of Standards, Prof. E. U. Condon. This article, which reproduced Condon's address at the Fifth Annual Science Talent Search, in Washington D.C. on March 5, 1946, made quite an impact on Gaviola and gave rise to some historic developments in Argentina.

"What is going on?" – Condon asked – "Prominent scientists are denied the privilege of traveling abroad. Physicists are not allowed to discuss certain areas of their research with each other, even as individuals working on closely related phases of the same subject. They can communicate only through official channels involving censorship of their communications by army officers who are without knowledge and so without competence. Information essential to understanding is being denied to students in our universities, so that, if this situation were to continue, the young students we honor here tonight will get from their professors only a watered-down army-approved version of the laws of nature."[1]

Condon was just echoing the fears of a score of US scientists. To what extent their freedom to do science would be curtailed in the post war era? Gaviola was quick to grab the connection between Condon's¡**Error! Marcador no definido.** article and a long-standing crusade of his own. He turned to his desk and wrote[2]:

"As a consequence of its decisive importance during the war, science is going through a severe crisis which endangers its future. The scientific accomplishments of Western nations have been achieved by placing international science at the service of human progress. Countries that until recently were at the forefront of our civilization, have now nationalized science and have placed it at the service of war. This circumstance offers a unique opportunity - and makes it quite possible - for those countries not directly confronted by a Third World War to raise and keep alight the torch of free international science."

"Hundreds of scientists, and the best leading the way, will leave those countries where they feel oppressed if they find the opportunity to work elsewhere enjoying full scientific freedom. Argentina, if it wants to, can host many of them. Their coming may signify an industrial, scientific and cultural revolution for this country. To make this possible we need to offer them economic support, good working conditions and scientific freedom. And this can be done through a trustworthy institutional base. This could be a National Research Council run by the few active scientists in this country with an international reputation. They must be trusted with resources and authority. A proposed draft for a law creating such Council is annexed to this document."

Gaviola's style is direct and precise. He knew his subject and was able to describe a situation both without precedent and full of promise. He was the first and probably the only one to recognize the unique possibilities that the post-war situation presented for the scientific future of Argentina, if it was intelligently managed. This was indeed a novel circumstance. Never before had science - through the atom bomb - had such an effect on the outcome of history, and now that its power had been revealed, governments were actively intervening in scientific activity. Scarcely a year had gone by since Hiroshima and Nagasaki had been devastated. In the mind of many people, the very survival of the West was now tied up with the national ability to keep scientific secrets. Should scientists expect to enjoy scientific freedom under such circumstances? At least Condon in the North, and Gaviola in the South, thought so.

For Gaviola's Argentina, this new state of affairs represented a great opportunity. Since the decline of the Institute of Physics in La Plata after World War I, Argentina had been lagging in scientific development. There had been sporadic (some say exploratory) visits from renowned scientists such as Einstein, Fermi, Compton and Langevin, but none of them had stayed. Now there was a possibility of receiving a powerful impetus in the right direction. This was at least the way Gaviola saw it. After all it was the first time that scientists might wish to emigrate to escape censorship and restrictions on their work. There had been politically motivated emigrations of scientists in the past. To a large extent the US, now the most powerful post-war nation, owed its present status to the foreign scientists who had come in search of a sanctuary. It was a sanctuary of a different nature that Gaviola was envisioning now, but what better example was there to illustrate the enormous potential of his scheme?

"In times of freedom and security in Europe and the United States, it was practically impossible for Argentina to attract top scientists. Economic and political uncertainty in Europe and the imposition of secrecy and censorship both in the US and many European countries now make such immigration feasible. Such men would come to Argentina if given the means to teach and do research, and freedom to publish without interference. Such an opportunity may not come our way again for a hundred years" - Gaviola insisted. According to him, the number of physicists and chemists productively engaged in research in Argentina was "certainly fewer than twenty and none of them has yet proven first class. In England they think national subsistence requires approximately ninety thousand scientists; in Argentina there should be at least five thousand including one thousand physicists and chemists."

"If we had a thousand - he said - and among them three or four first-class men, large industrial concerns could open laboratories, universities could appoint full time researchers to teach, institutes and research centers could publish in the best international journals, and we could organize centers for technological development. However, we have only twenty such people. There is a very long, hard way ahead of us. Whoever believes that with our natural resources, our industry and our scientists we are in a position to have atomic bombs or build nuclear power plants in the next 5 to 10 years is suffering from hallucinations. Before even dreaming about it, we must train people and attract others from abroad to help us in our endeavor".

Gaviola wrote a memorandum developing these ideas which he entitled "Argentina and the Atomic Age". Revealing his strong inclination to put ideas and action together, he adds the proposal of a bill to create a National Research Institute. It was emphasized that the Institute should have full academic freedom and should encourage the immigration of leading foreign scientists.

What to do with this document? Whom did Gaviola have in mind when he sat down to write it? Probably his peers, but in June, when he finished, a change of administration in Government had just taken place and Gaviola decided to send it to the newly appointed Ministers of War and Navy. Perón had won the presidential election held in February and had taken oath on June 4, 1946.

The document reveals Gaviola´s style at its best: a vigorous statement keeping a delicate equilibrium between good sense and fantasy. Gaviola was one of a few in the country with enough foresight to know that at least in science, Argentina needed help and a lot of it. According to him, Argentina had no first rate scientists (a bit of an exaggeration if we note that Bernardo Houssay won the Nobel Prize in Medicine the following year), and they were an indispensable ingredient in his plan. He was at that time President of the Argentine Physics Association - which he had helped to create two years earlier - and had a pretty good idea of domestic limitations with respect to international scientific standards. But that did not intimidate him, on the contrary, it prompted his natural inclination to undertake new challenges. His program was out of the ordinary, but it was not impossible. Given support and enthusiasm it could be carried through.

As far as Gaviola was concerned, Condon's article fell on fertile ground. Condon's anxieties translated into opportunity for Gaviola. One man's fear became the other's hope.

A Dream is Born

This sort of initiatives was not unusual for Gaviola; it was rather part of a crusade that he had begun some sixteen years earlier. Since his return to Argentina, Gaviola had made a great effort to foster the creation of first-rate training centers and to encourage basic research. He yearned for the level of excellence that he had experienced, and admired, in Göttingen and Berlin, and later in Johns Hopkins, Carnegie and Caltech.

The gap between the state of science in Argentina and that in Europe and America was immense, but during most of his lifetime Gaviola thought that it was possible to bridge the chasm. Based on this conviction he knocked on countless doors, wrote articles, prepared legislation for the creation of scientific institutes and mobilized all sorts of people with his own enthusiasm.

Gaviola had returned to Argentina in 1930, when he was offered the Chair of Physical Chemistry at the University of Buenos Aires. The letter of invitation reached Gaviola when he was about to accept a permanent position in Wisconsin. The letter succeeded in tempting Gaviola. It was not usual to be offered a chair at the age of 30. He was also homesick[3] and we can speculate that his dormant political vocation was awakened by this invitation. Memories of his homeland and countrymen - that store of personal, secret treasures that is never abandoned even when one decides never to return - surfaced when he had to make the choice[4].

Soon after his arrival, Gaviola wrote his first political article, in which he decried the problems of the Argentine University system and pointed out the urgent need of educating dozens of young people abroad. He had been away for almost a decade and was coming back with a strong background, a lot of prestige and full of energy. He knew he could see much farther out than his countrymen and that it was his duty to change the status quo. He had been privileged to work with the giants of modern physics during the most fascinating years in the history of this field, the 1920's, and in the best places, Berlin and Göttingen. His university records bear the signature of professors such as Hilbert, Courant, Born, Planck, Franck, von Laue, Einstein and Meitner[5]. Those were the days when the Theory of the Relativity came of age, when Quantum Mechanics was put into a solid theoretical framework, and when the first transmutation of elements - that age old alchemists' dream - became a reality.

The second part of his sojourn abroad was in the United States, first at Johns Hopkins with Robert Wood[6] ("the best experimental physicist of his time"), and later at Carnegie Institute with Merle Tuve and Larry Hafstad[7]. In the US Gaviola continued to be in the midst of the elite of international physics. He took part in the sweet, exhilarating pleasure of venturing where no one else had ever trod, on the very frontiers of knowledge. He learned that this rare experience has a price. The giants of physics were extremely competitive and demanding. Only selected people were admitted to this small community. Work was unremitting and exacting. Each group of scientists strove to be first to report a discovery. But an error, or a conclusion arrived at a trifle too soon, might bring fatal discredit and scientific death. Those who make it are few, but they command almost unlimited prestige and authority.

This was the atmosphere in which Gaviola's personality was forged, and with this experience under his belt, combined with the natural arrogance of a brilliant young man who at 30 has become a citizen of this unique world, Gaviola returned to Argentina ready for an ambitious crusade.

Fifteen years later Gaviola was still committed to this same goal. The memorandum, which he sent to the War and Navy Ministers in June 1946, was another link in the chain. In the interval between 1931 and 1946 there were other projects - such as the creation of a private university, something unheard of in Argentina until then -, which would be modeled after his beloved Johns Hopkins. He also worked hard to convince the Navy that a new Radio Technical Institute should - and could - enroll world-renowned scientists. During the three-year period between 1945 and 1947, he was particularly active. He was Director of the Córdoba National Observatory and at the same time President of the Argentine Physics Association, and he managed to keep up his own research work as well[8], while attending to those other projects aimed at placing Argentina at the forefront of international physics. Plans, projects, memoranda, guidelines, letters (sometimes over a dozen a day) pile up in the files of those years as silent witnesses of one man's dream.

Political Turmoil Stifles Good Initiatives

A year before writing his memorandum inspired by Condon's article, in July 1945 Gaviola had tendered his resignation as Director of the Córdoba Observatory. The motive — the aim, rather - was to keep Dr. Guido Beck in Argentina.

Beck had come to Argentina in 1943 at Gaviola's invitation. Gaviola had learned that Beck was seeking ways of leaving Nazi Europe through his former professor James Franck (later Nobel laureate). Beck was an eminent physicist. Not only he had worked closely with Werner Heisenberg (father of the Uncertainty Principle) in Germany, he also made substantial contributions in nuclear physics, particularly in the theory of beta decay, the shell model and the energy released in fission. Gaviola's initiative in this case, so important for Argentine physics, was in stark contrast to that of his colleagues at the University of La Plata who, unable to appreciate Beck's stature, had turned down his application a few months earlier. Upon his arrival in Córdoba Beck began holding informal scientific seminars, which attracted many young talented students. This was the starting point of a small but intense activity in modern physics in Argentina. Gaviola knew how important Beck's contribution was to the development of physics in Argentina and was willing to support him to the utmost of his considerable ability. His resignation was just a gesture to obtain the money to give Beck a proper salary.

Gaviola's resignation was widely covered in the newspapers and had a conspicuous effect. Many years later he recalled: "They did everything just as I hoped. The purpose of the resignation was none other than to call attention to Dr. Beck, so that he would receive the treatment he deserved." Gaviola remained as Director of the Observatory. He had tried his hand at politics and had won. Not only with regard to Beck's situation, but also because his action elicited numerous gestures of sympathy from colleagues and friends.

One of the notes Gaviola received at this time was from industrialist Leon F. Rigolleau, owner of a large crystal factory: "I would like to see you. Kindly indicate whether you plan to come to Buenos Aires soon". Gaviola had reasons to assume that if he lost his job, Rigolleau would offer him the chance to organize a private research laboratory. Since he did not plan to go to Buenos Aires until late September to attend the Physics

Association meeting, he invited Rigolleau to come to Córdoba instead.

The meeting took place on September 7. Earlier that same day, Gaviola had read in La Prensa the text of a lecture delivered by Dr. Eduardo Braun Menendez in Buenos Aires. In it the renowned medical researcher proposed the creation of a private university. Such an idea aroused Gaviola's enthusiasm, and when he met Rigolleau later that day, he suggested funding a 'Rigolleau Physics and Chemistry Institute' as part of Braun Menendez´ initiative, with an annual budget of $150,000 pesos (then about US $37,500). Rigolleau accepted and even offered to contact some friends, including the powerful landowner Otto Bemberg.

Gaviola wasted no time. He sent Braun Menendez a telegram and on the following day a letter. With Rigolleau`s support and with Braun Menendez' Biology and Experimental Medicine Institute, there should be enough to start a private university at a high level of excellence. The Beck affair was now history. Gaviola was now "ready to leave the Observatory and dedicate his full attention to this cherished project". [2]

On September 17 the sixth Physics Association meeting began in Buenos Aires. Gaviola was so eager to talk to Braun Menendez and contact other industrialist friends about the private university project that he paid attention to nothing else. It was one month prior to the fateful 17th of October 1945. At the time the physicists meeting was taking place, important political developments were brewing in the country. General Farrell's military government was growing weaker as crucial support from General Avalos and the garrison of Campo the Mayo under his command, was fading. The issue was Colonel Perón's increasing influence in Government. Perón had been a leading figure behind the 1943 coup. Later, the new military administration appointed him Director of the hitherto obscure Labor Affairs Department. At the beginning, Perón's comrades were quite supportive. So much so that they were willing to overlook Perón's unconventional liaison with Eva Duarte, a former actress of uncertain reputation. But Perón's political genius, his outstanding trait, eventually backfired, as it brought him into the limelight. In two years since the coup de etat he had managed to build a powerful political base within the labor unions. Once Perón's own power became apparent, his military comrades, as well as other sectors of Argentine political life, began to feel uneasy. Suspicion and resentment towards Perón spread, and such labels as "Peronist" and "anti-Peronists" became part of the domestic political lexicon of those days. Polarization in Argentina´s political history was not new of course, but this was the first time in the century that it was going beyond partisan lines. The new element - a politically unaligned labor movement whose real dimension was difficult to gauge — spurred a strong reaction from many sectors. Thus an odd alliance, which spanned the entire spectrum from the extreme left to the most conservatives, was established among the old traditional parties against Perón. The figure of Perón became so threatening that, under the slogan 'Freedom and Constitution', this mélange of parties organized an immense civic rally on September 19 of that year of 1945 to protest against fascism, a clear indication of what was feared of Perón's incipient movement.

The Argentine Physics Association (AFA) did not remain aloof from these events, and in the evening session of September 18, the physicists debated whether they should take sides in the brewing political storm. For the first time the AFA's traditional neutrality in political matters was questioned. A member rose to propose suspension of the meeting in order to participate in the anti-Peronist march the next day, and "not to resume the sessions until the country regained normality". [10] Several other professional organizations had made similar decisions. Gaviola, and with him the majority of the members, voted against this proposal. Their position was that the Association dealt with Physics, not politics, and that should its members wish to engage in politics, they could do so as private citizens - either individually or within their respective political parties - but not as members of their professional organization. Amidst the general uproar, Gaviola declared that "if we should all have to go to a concentration camp, even there we will continue our research". And it was not that Gaviola did not care about politics.[111] His position was that physics and partisan politics should not mix. Indignant, one member rose to leave and invited others to do the same. Two out of fifty followed him.

All this turbulence did not stop Gaviola and Braun Menendez from meeting that same day at the aristocratic Jockey Club in downtown Buenos Aires. It was a fruitful encounter and they agreed that the new university would start with a School of Medicine organized by Braun Menendez, a School of Mathematics, Physics and Chemistry and Technology under Gaviola.[112] Braun Menendez agreed to compose a memorandum containing the plan of the university and to send it to Gaviola in Córdoba.

When Gaviola read Braun Menendez' paper he was disappointed. Braun Menendez emphasized the creation of research institutes, while Gaviola wanted university students - not graduate students - "since the latter are already malformed and there is nothing that can be done about it. You have to start early if you wish students to turn out well," was Gaviola's acerbic comment. His unwillingness to compromise is striking. Given the importance of the project and Braun's reputation it seems odd that he should take such a rigid stance. Further down his response was even stronger. "In order to avoid misunderstandings, I must say that your memorandum distresses me very much. Please indicate whether you still think along the lines we discussed at the Jockey Club, or if you would rather kill your spiritual son before it is born."[113]

Yet the project of a private or free university, as they began calling it presumably sharing a concern over a perceived threat of fascism in Argentina, did not end with that letter. Braun Menendez responded in a firm but gentle tone, and kept the discussion at a level commensurate with his intellectual probity. On the other hand, Gaviola was stubborn enough not to give up easily, especially now that Rigolleau, as well as Pratti of the powerful Fabril Financiera had pledged financial support.

Gaviola chooses his own trail despite the fact that no amount of support would be enough to face the gathering political storm. There was a renewed exchange of letters, yet no common understanding. "As you well put it, we agree regarding the ultimate objective. We differ, however, over the best way of achieving it. Our positions are so far apart, that I doubt a close collaboration between us would be feasible, at least as long as our differences remain. Therefore, for the time being, I think we should pursue our separate ways completely independent of each other. It is a pity to duplicate efforts when a concerted action would be so much more effective, but it would be bad politics to cover our differences with a sieve."

Looking back, one wonders about Gaviola's inflexibility and about the new frontiers that this project could have opened in Argentina. On the other hand, was Gaviola's intransigence the only obstacle, or was the project doomed anyway? Leaders are responsible for breaking new grounds and pulling society forward. But they cannot go too fast. Neither can they remain aloof from circumstances or ignore them. In this regard it is amazing that the letters which Braun Menendez and Gaviola exchanged during October 1945 carry no reference whatsoever to the undeniably relevant political developments which were then taking place. How could they possibly fail to take them into account? Indeed, strange and unsettling events were shaking the structure of the Argentine society.

Under severe pressure from the military in Campo de Mayo, on October 9, President Farrell forced Perón to resign all his posts in Government. Perón had by that time become also Minister of War and Vice President, in addition to the suddenly crucial post of Secretary of Labor. This unusual concentration of power partly explained the great anxiety of Perón's comrades. But mere resignation was not enough to calm his comrades and on October 12 Perón was confined to his home with the excuse that his health and safety were in danger. This triggered a reaction from the labor unions, coordinated by Perón's close friend Colonel Domingo Mercante, which led to the famous mass demonstration in Plaza de Mayo, on October 17. All that day, workers from the southern industrial districts, poured into the Plaza in front of Casa Rosada, demanding to see Perón. The gathering grew stronger as the hours went by before the astonished eyes of President Farrell and General Avalos (who in the meantime had been appointed Minister of War). Around 9:00 pm Perón was brought to Government House and two hours later he appeared on the balcony to face the greatest popular clamor ever in Argentine history. It was a glorious moment. Nobody could fully ascertain what was happening, not even those who had waited so many long hours to see Perón. Totally unexpectedly, the political situation had changed 180 degrees in a few hours. The taste of victory of Perón's opponents, those in the military barracks in Campo de Mayo and the many people who had recently marched down Buenos Aires streets chanting against Perón was now gone, replaced by a sentiment of utter defeat.

While this was going on in Buenos Aires, Gaviola himself was immersed in his own world, thinking on how to pursue his project with the backing of a few wealthy people. He did not want to acknowledge that the new circumstances would naturally cool the enthusiasm of his supporters for fund-raising programs involving something so unusual - for Argentina at that time - as a private university.

Gaviola tried in vain: "I quite understand that as things are now, you and other industrialists have plenty of problems," he wrote to Rigolleau. "In just such times, however, one perceives most clearly the errors of public education in Argentina and their consequences. As for politics, Argentina lacks first class statesmen. The duty of forming intellectually and morally worthy men is the most important and also the most urgent task the country should undertake. This is why I dare call your attention to the problem once more." His letter to Rigolleau was dated November 23 and in it he suggests opening classes at the university in March! Gaviola's eagerness was remarkable. He should have known that on top of everything else, the Argentine summer was like a deep-freeze for all kinds of projects, political, scientific or whatever. As a matter of fact, however, that summer turned out to be exceptional because the Government decided to call for elections in February, the first open and honest presidential elections in fifteen years. Undoubtedly a positive event for most everybody, it was not necessarily so for the members of the elite from whom Gaviola expected help. They were worried and welcomed no distractions. A double handicap: holiday months and election time. Gaviola was frustrated. The political campaign, like the weather, was hot. It was the Democratic Union, a coalition of all the traditional parties spanning from the extreme left to the extreme right, against Perón. The latter cleverly took advantage of the meddling of former US Ambassador Spruille Braden, who had openly - and tactlessly - opposed Perón before being summoned back to Washington. This gave Perón the opportunity to set the tone for his political campaign as a nationalistic rallying cry. During the summer the streets of Buenos Aires were placarded with posters reading: "Braden or Perón?" a direct and powerful message in a country weary of foreign - particularly American - interference in internal affairs. It was a close election, but heavy Peronist majorities in the working-class districts combined with enough support of middle class and nonaligned voters - intuitively aware of the hollow opportunism shown by the alliance of the traditional parties - tipped the scales. Perón won.

The Atomic Bomb

While swallowing defeat in early 1946, Gaviola came across an article in The Review of Modern Physics, which could not but catch the eye of a physicist, as well as anybody else interested in nuclear physics. It was a surprisingly complete description of the Manhattan Project and the development of the first atomic bomb. It was written mainly for specialists as it contained mostly technical data. But it also revealed a lot about the organization of the project, its evolution, the people involved, their contributions and some of the important scientific problems they faced while pursuing the release of atomic energy for the first time. Obviously it left some gaps, but it offered information on the most spectacular scientific feat of all times, which had been tightly classified during the war years.

Gaviola, like any physicist of his time, was utterly enthralled by this report. It was written by Henry D. Smyth and entitled Atomic Energy for Military Purposes.[14] Smyth was a member of the team working at Los Alamos Scientific Laboratory and soon after the conclusion of the project he was commissioned to prepare this report.

The theoretical possibility of obtaining energy from the atomic nucleus arises from the famous Einstein's mass-energy formula $E=mc^2$, which has become a popular symbol of contemporary science.[15] This formula is one of the results of the Theory of Relativity that Einstein proposed in 1905. The equivalence of mass and energy implied in Einstein's formula was observed in a nuclear reaction for the first time by Ernest Rutherford in 1916. He exposed nitrogen to alpha particles from a radioactive source and obtained oxygen, thereby achieving the secular alchemists' dream of transforming one element into another. In this nuclear reaction (and others as confirmed later) a small quantity of matter disappears and energy is released in the exact amount predicted by Einstein. A minute quantity of matter represents a strikingly large amount of energy: for example, the transformation of one gram of matter releases the energy equivalent of thirty billion watt-hours. How can this energy be obtained for domestic and industrial use? Until 1932 there was no answer to this question.

Two fundamental hurdles for obtaining energy out of nuclear reactions were apparent. First, finding a nuclear reaction where the decrease in total mass is large enough to compensate - or rather, exceed - the energy used to initiate the reaction. The difficulty here is that a lot of energy is necessary to overcome strong repulsive electrical forces between nuclei in order for them to come into contact with each other and produce a nuclear reaction. Secondly should there be a reaction with a positive balance of energy, it is necessary to find a process that multiplies itself and keeps the reaction going in identical successive steps (i.e., a chain reaction).

The discovery of the neutron in 1932 by James Chadwick, in England, made it possible to overcome these two obstacles. The neutron is an elusive particle owing to its peculiar property of being electrically neutral. This feature makes the neutron the microscopic equivalent to the cartoon character, the invisible man, who can move about without being noticed. The neutron can move through matter mostly unhindered. It is invisible to electrons and penetrates the electrical barrier of the atomic nucleus without losing energy. It only interacts with atomic nuclei when it comes very near them. If neutrons can induce nuclear reactions - as it was shown soon after - at no energy cost, then it is possible to achieve a positive balance of energy in nuclear reactions induced by neutrons.

The second hurdle, that of finding a chain reaction, was solved soon after during the scientific race the top laboratories in the world entered to investigate nuclear reactions with neutrons. Foremost were Enrico Fermi and his research group in Italy, who discovered that neutrons were much more effective triggering nuclear reactions when they were "thermalized".[16] Close behind in these studies were the Cambridge group with James Chadwick and Maurice Goldhaber and the French group of Frederick Joliot and Irene Curie. They were all first rate scientists. Joliot and Irene Curie (the daughter of Marie Skłodowska Curie and Pierre Curie, the discoverers of Radium) had been awarded the Nobel Prize for discovering artificial radioactivity in 1933, as Chadwick received a Nobel in 1932 for his discovery of the neutron.

In the midst of this intense scientific competition, Cecilia Mossin Kotin arrived in Paris to work with Irene Curie. She had first graduated as a teacher of physics, then went on to the School of Sciences.at the University of Buenos Aires There, she had good teachers: The Spanish mathematician Julio Rey Pastor, and the physicists Teófilo Isnardi, Ernesto Galloni and Gaviola, among others. In Buenos Aires, Physics did not have a formal curriculum at that time. Mossin Kotin made her way in the dark, taking courses here and there, as suggested by her teachers. In 1935, on Rey Pastor's advice, she went to Spain to study X-rays, just as Galloni had done earlier. Upon her return, she continued studying at the University. In 1938, she left for Paris.

Irene Curie entrusted Mossin Kotin with an intense source of radioactive radium that had been purified by her own mother - a scientific object of immeasurable value. Even then, four decades after the pioneer work of Marie Curie, research on radioactivity represented one of the most attractive fields of nuclear science. The work she had been asked to accomplish - the study of the radiation emitted by an isotope of actinium - paved the way for Mossin Kotin to obtain one of the first breakthroughs in nuclear spectroscopy.[117] During that time, she also helped Irene Curie in the study of the radiation produced when lead and uranium were bombarded with neutrons. There were significant differences in the results that puzzled them. Meanwhile Joliot, assisted by Lew Kowarsky, was doing research on the possibility of producing a chain reaction.

-"Irene was a good radiochemist", - Mossin Kotin recalled years later - "while studying the elements produced after bombarding uranium, she identified light elements but didn't know where they came from. And they (Joliot and Irene) lost the race: They didn't dare identify those elements with the fragments resulting from the fission of uranium when bombarded with neutrons. Otto Hahn and Lise Meitner got ahead of them in the correct interpretation of the new phenomenon" - and she added with a touch of sadness: "A few years earlier, they hadn't had the courage to recognize the neutron either."[118]

These events took place shortly before the beginning of World War II. On September 1, 1939, Adolf Hitler invaded Poland, and was to march into Paris a little over a year later. Mossin Kotin was forced to interrupt her studies and returned to Argentina in October 1939.

Ten months earlier, Otto Hahn had sent his colleague Lise Meitner, in Sweden, some amazing results. Meitner, an excellent researcher forced to emigrate by the Nazis, realized the enormous importance of the data she had received and immediately devoted herself to analyzing and discussing results with her nephew (also a physicist), Otto Frisch. Soon, they reached the inevitable conclusion that the light element detected by Hahn resulted from uranium fission. The effect of the neutron on the uranium nucleus was to split it up into lighter fragments releasing not only energy but also other neutrons. These neutrons could in turn react with other uranium nuclei. This discovery opened up the possibility of obtaining an energy producing and self-sustained reaction. Hahn, Fritz Strassmann (Hahn's assistant), Meitner and Frisch sent their results for publication right away. Meanwhile, Frisch confided their results to Niels Bohr - the patriarch of nuclear physicists - asking him to keep them for himself until they came out in print. Bohr was on the verge of leaving for America. Times were difficult and people were anxious about the looming war. America was looked upon again as the land of the future. The time was ripe for passing on the torch to the New World, and scientists probably perceived this with particular clarity.

Bohr and Leon Rosenfeld, a Belgian theoretical physicist, traveled together. During those long days on board, Niels Bohr could not stop thinking about the new phenomenon, and he shared his musings with Rosenfeld, but failed to ask him to be discreet. Upon their arrival in New York John A. Wheeler their host from Princeton met them. Fermi was also there; He had arrived in December after receiving the Nobel Prize in Stockholm. He too wished to greet Bohr, who had helped him leave Italy.

While Bohr and Fermi talked together, Rosenfeld inadvertently broke the news to Wheeler. When Bohr found out, it was already too late. The news ran like wildfire through US labs. Fermi learned the news rather indirectly, and was upset at Bohr for not having told him. He immediately set out to confirm this amazing discovery by himself, a discovery that had almost been his to make.

For reasons totally unrelated to this exciting scientific event, Gaviola traveled to the US in July of that year 1939. His mission was to bring back to the Córdoba Observatory the 60" mirror that was being polished in Pittsburgh. It was to be the largest mirror in the Southern Hemisphere. Upon arriving in the States, he found the scientific community intent on the study of the properties - and of the consequences - of nuclear fission. Many were already convinced - after the numerous experiments carried out since January - that the discovery of nuclear fission transcended science and that the US Government ought to coordinate research activities on this matter. Leo Szilard decided to ask for an appointment to see President Franklin Roosevelt. He visited Einstein at his summerhouse in Long Island, asking him for a letter of endorsement. This was the origin of the famous letter stressing the military importance of the discovery and the need for strong governmental action.

Gaviola participated somewhat in the excitement of the discovery of fission due to his old friendship with physicists Tuve and Hafstad. In Pittsburgh, he was told the mirror glass was not ready, so he decided to visit his friends at Carnegie. They were among the first to confirm Hahn and Meitner's results. "Ideas were exchanged about the atomic bomb - how it could be built and how big it would be. There was still no particular secret about it. That came later, because of Szilard" - Gaviola recalled years later.

Upon her return home, Cecilia Mossin Kotin did not find adequate conditions for the continuation of her research. This was partly due to Professor Teófilo Isnardi, then Director of the Buenos Aires Physics Institute, who was reluctant to purchase equipment for a nuclear physics laboratory. Discouraged, Mossin Kotin dedicated herself to other activities until Guido Beck's arrival in Argentina in mid-1943. Her meeting with this distinguished Austrian Physicist was a powerful incentive for her and as a result she wrote a detailed report on the current state-of-the-art in nuclear physics. This was indeed pioneer work in Argentina, and of interest to a wide audience since during the war all such research was shrouded in a mantle of secrecy.[19]

Along with the Smyth report, Gaviola also used Mossin Kotin´s work to attempt a reconstruction of the atomic bomb, in early 1946.[20] Gaviola's analysis is noteworthy. In the introduction, he writes: "Scientific publications on nuclear fission in general, and uranium fission in particular, stop in 1940. This was due to Leo Szilard's campaign, started in the US in February 1939, to prevent the potential enemy from learning about scientific findings, which according to E. Fermi (in his Washington lecture, on January 26, 1939) might have military importance. The censorship imposed in 1940 brought about the end of an era - that of international free science - and the beginning of another era - that of national science at the service of war."

"In order to have a relatively clear picture of the work and progress achieved between 1940 and 1945, one has to resort to what was public knowledge before the war and to reading reports between lines and guessing. This is what I shall do in this report. There is, of course, considerable risk of making mistakes. It is indeed one of the perils imposed upon us by this new era of secret national science. Anything that can be done to mitigate this evil will be beneficial to science."

In this paper Gaviola analyzes the available data on fission reactions induced by neutrons on uranium and plutonium. He describes the necessary conditions to obtain a chain reaction. Difficulties and possible solutions are discussed. He produces a sketch of the heterogeneous pile like that used by Fermi in 1942 to produce the first nuclear chain reaction. Then the possible industrial uses of such a pile are reviewed. The possible use of plutonium and the difficulties involved in the isotopic separation of uranium and deuterium are considered. He also discusses some possible scientific applications such as the study of physical systems at temperatures of several million degrees. The article concludes with a model - remarkable in 1946 - of the likely design of an atomic bomb. Based on today's knowledge,

Gaviola's analysis - arrived at groping in the dark - is essentially correct. He wanted to understand the phenomenon out of mere curiosity and went all the way through laborious calculations to reach his goal, all of which was in line with his characteristic pride and talent.

Attempts to attract first rate scientists

This work, which Gaviola entitled "Use of Atomic (Nuclear) Energy for Industrial and Military Purposes", was submitted to the seventh Argentine Physics Association meeting, in La Plata, in April 1946. The contact with his colleagues during this meeting perhaps rekindled his spirit of leadership, conscious as he was of his prestige. And the success of his report probably helped Gaviola regain his self-confidence and renewed his enthusiasm for his projects.

It was in those days that he found himself reading Condon's article in Science mentioned at the beginning of this chapter. As we have seen this article inspired him to think about a National Research Institute. Different as it was from a private university project, because this was a Government entity, the driving spirit behind it was the same: to bring Argentina up to international standards in Science.

So Gaviola involved himself in a new task, that of writing the memorandum "Argentina and the Atomic Age". After the frustrations suffered at the beginning of that year seeking in vain the support of industrialists to fund a private university, Gaviola was now fully resuming his old hectic pace in spite of the foreboding new political scenario. On June 4 of that historic 1946, Perón began his first six-year term as President. The general feeling (later proven correct) was that Argentina had entered a new political era. Some were hopeful, others feared the worst. A third group, probably the largest, remained neutral waiting to see how the situation developed. Gaviola, who later became a staunch anti-Peronist, remained politically indifferent during the first months of Perón's administration and was impatient with those who preferred to wait "until spirits calm down". For Gaviola, the Peronist phenomenon was irrelevant to his crusade. He was wrong, but this he learned later.

Gaviola spent the week of June 4 meditating on Condon's remarks on science and society and polishing his lucid memorandum. He saw no reason to wait and see how the new Government would act. On the contrary, getting them at their fresh start might be advantageous. Consequently, he sent copies of his paper "Argentina and the Atomic Age" to the top brass. He was convinced that no matter how busy they were in their first days in office, they could not possibly remain unexcited at the prospect of converting Argentina into a haven for world-leading scientists, and becoming thereby a world center for Science. As far as Gaviola was concerned the private university, the Argentine Physics Association and the National Research Institute he was now proposing to the Ministers, were different means to reach the same goal. While the rest of his countrymen became immersed in the startling political events of those days, Gaviola dreamed of an Argentina almost magically inhabited by a near-sacred caste of internationally renowned scientists.

According to Gaviola's later recollections the idea of approaching the War and Navy Ministers was to start his "civil science" crusade precisely where one could expect the strongest opposition. However, a more reasonable explanation seems to be that he sought the shortest route to the top of the decision-making process. He was not wrong in choosing the ministers with a uniform. They were the most valuable supporters President Perón had. Unlike the civilian ministers (who wielded little power in Perón's cabinet), the ministers of War and Navy were the link between the President and the highly sensitive Armed Forces. It is also possible that Gaviola grew tired of the industrialists' dispirited attitude ("we must wait until things calm down") and decided to act in a more effective way.

While he was waiting for a reaction to his memorandum, rather unexpected news reached him. The Navy itself was requesting Gaviola's advice for the creation of a Radio Technical Institute. Gaviola attended a first meeting on July 19. The noted mathematician Alberto González Domínguez was with him. The Navy's plans were unexpectedly progressive and made Gaviola tremble like sweet music. They wanted top-flight scientists and were willing to listen to proposals for hiring foreign minds. "A Nobel laureate perhaps?"- someone mused. The Navy was prepared to pay salaries of up to 10,000 US dollars a year. It fitted Gaviola's dream so well! Academic excellence. World-renowned scientists. Indeed, a remarkable perspective for Argentina. Was this initiative connected to Gaviola's memorandum? The time for this document to get from the ministry's desks to Naval Captain Rivero de Olazábal, Chief of Naval Communications, with whom Gaviola had the meeting, seems short but enough. Carried away by his enthusiasm, Gaviola returned to Córdoba and wrote to his old friends from Carnegie, Merle Tuve and Lawrence Hafstad.[21] The letter to Tuve, who was then Director of Terrestrial Magnetism, read: "Dear Merle: Congratulations on your spectacular success and new job. I look forward to seeing you soon as Carnegie's President. Our Navy is organizing a Radio Communication Institute (Radar & Co.). They have asked me to contact first class scientists who might be willing to come as professors and researchers. They are ready to offer good salaries (up to US$ 800 a month), with three to four year contracts. Would you be willing to lend us Larry (Lawrence Hafstad) for a couple of years? Or could you name one or two possible candidates for us, who might be willing to come? Kindest regards."

On August 9, Tuve answered: "Dear Gaviola: Many thanks for your letter of July 29. I can assure you that I am not too happy with the administrative duties associated with being Director. I expect them to diminish over the next few months and that we shall have a good time doing research again. I have sent a copy of your letter to Hafstad. He will send you a brochure of the laboratory of which he is now Director. Larry and I worked together during the war and the magnificent cooperation between the Government, industry and the university is a post-war result of our activities during that period. Hafstad resigned his position at Carnegie this last June and I am sure that you will have to use a lot of persuasion to induce him to go to Argentina. Physicists and radar men are nowadays scarce in America. I expect that you will have to fly a man up here for two or three weeks in order to persuade some competent scientist to go down there, even if it is only for one year or two. At present, scientists can be very choosy regarding positions they might be willing to consider. Cordially yours."

In turn, Hafstad, who was then Director of the Applied Physics Laboratory at Johns Hopkins University, replied: "Dear Gavi: I just received a copy of your letter to Dr. Tuve. Naturally I am delighted to hear about you again. There is a lot I would like to talk to you about but since I am in an administrative position now I have an enormous amount of letters to write and I just have not found the time for my personal correspondence. We have thought about you a lot and often wished we could have the opportunity to get together with you and chat about international relations, trends, etc. However, we will have to put that aside until we have the chance to get together around a giant beer (or should it be yerba mate?). One thing we can be sure though, is that science is becoming more important every day in social and political matters, and that the exchange of professors or students is one of the best ways to promote understanding and good relations. Regarding the specific point of your letter: there is nothing I would rather do than taking time off to teach in a foreign country. That is my immediate personal reaction to your invitation. However, once administrative responsibilities are taken, it is not easy to shove them off on somebody else. This is why I doubt I could accept the job offer. To get young scientists - which is what you should do - is difficult because there is a lot of competition for their service in this country, as Merle pointed out. I enclose a graph on the job market for physicists in America today. In view of this I suggest that you come yourself to visit your old friends and see how things really are here. I am sure that it would give you a good basis on which to plan your long-term goals more effectively. Looking forward to seeing you soon. P.S. By the way, now that we have the atomic bomb, what do you think we ought to do with it?"

Indeed, war and the atomic bomb had created a great demand for physicists in the United States. The secrecy factor did not affect everybody and those working in classified areas were appropriately rewarded. The answer Gaviola gets from his friends in the US suggests that Gaviola had been a bit unrealistic when he enthusiastically argued that the new military science - which Condon condemned - would dishearten most scientists.

Yet Gaviola's ideas were not totally utopian as shown by the result of his correspondence with colleagues in Europe. The situation for physicists in the Old Continent was altogether different. There was not enough work and many were under allied surveillance. Actually some lived as prisoners of war. Consequently, for these people Argentina could look like a possible oasis they could turn to for better working conditions. This was probably the case with Werner Heisenberg, the eminent physicist Gaviola wrote to next.

Gaviola was not such a close friend of Heisenberg as he was of Tuve's and Hafstad's. As a student, he had met Heisenberg in Göttingen 22 years before in the good old days when Heisenberg had just developed a new way of understanding quantum mechanics and had proposed the famous Uncertainty Principle that governs the microscopic world. Gaviola had not forgotten the Congress at Düsselford, in the summer of 1926, "during which Heisenberg - barely 25 then - outshone hundreds of the best scientists in Europe". It was unlikely, though, that Heisenberg would remember him. "Therefore I asked Guido Beck, former assistant and old friend of Heisenberg's, to help me with a letter of his own. I knew well enough that an invitation from Beck would be far more effective than an invitation from me, or any government official", Gaviola wrote sometime later. Gaviola's letter to Heisenberg read: "Dear Professor Heisenberg: Science in Argentina is beginning to tread firmly. The coming of Professor Beck in 1943 was a great help. We already have a Physics Association that will hold its 8th meeting next September. We are now in a position to invite two or three physicists from Europe. The Navy and the University of Buenos Aires are organizing a Radio Technical Institute. Their objective is to make it a leading scientific institution and they are prepared to offer good salaries and good working conditions under five-year contracts. Salaries are up to 800 dollars a month. That is about three times what I get as Director of the Córdoba Observatory. The Navy has asked me, as President of the Argentine Physics Association, to contact physicists and technicians in Europe. I have taken the liberty of mentioning your name. In your case the Navy is ready to accept your terms with regards to salary and duration of the contract. If you wish to return to Germany in two or three years, this can be arranged, or if you decide to stay longer that would also be possible. The Navy would pay for your salary and your travel expenses. You could also name an assistant. Your duties would be those of a professor of theoretical physics. The contract could state that your research and publications would not be subject to any form of censorship or secrecy. Your coming would open a new era in South American science. I am asking you to please consider coming even if it is just for a couple of years."

At first, Beck was reluctant to write to Heisenberg. He considered it unwise for Gaviola to make an offer without a written commitment from the Navy or from the University. However, confronted with Gaviola's insistence, he finally gave in and wrote to his old colleague. Beck had a solid and well deserved international prestige and Heisenberg himself in his book "Physics Principles of the Quantum Theory" had warmly acknowledged Beck's proofreading and valuable comments on the manuscript. Obviously, if there was someone in Argentina able to influence Heisenberg's decision, that person was Beck.

At the Senate

Meanwhile, Gaviola got an extra kick with a promising new development. "Science here is starting to tread firmly", he had written to Heisenberg. On the following August 9, 1946, General Domingo Savio sent an invitation to Gaviola to see him. He was CEO and founder of Fabricaciones Militares, the manufacturing complex setup by the Argentine military to overcome wartime shortages, and he enjoyed a good reputation for his consistent and successful efforts to provide Argentina with its own steel production.

He had read Gaviola's "Argentina and the Atomic Age" and immediately grabbed the idea of doing something about atomic policy. That was an area of development he had not thought of before but now he considered it as important as steel. He was a man of action, very much inclined to major undertakings. He was, therefore, easily carried out by Gaviola's proposals. As a matter of fact, when Gaviola visited him two weeks later in Buenos Aires, Savio already had before him a draft for the creation of a National Physics Research Institute, prepared by Teófilo Isnardi. His style was not Gaviola´s. Isnardi was much more circumspect. Even though they were very courteous to one another, it was extremely unlikely that the two scientists could work together. In addition to their different personalities, Isnardi, the senior active Argentine physicist was educated in the "classical" school while Gaviola, as well as Beck, were "born" to physics together with the development of Quantum Mechanics. After graduating from La Plata, four years before Gaviola, Isnardi had also gone abroad, but, unlike Gaviola, he just missed the glorious fury of the new physics. He studied thermodynamics with Professor Walther Nernst, and later in his life he became a respected member of the International Committee of Weights and Measures with headquarters in Paris.

ola's account of his discussions with Savio unveils a profile of these two people:[22]: "My letter to the Navy and ministers had landed on Savio´s desk and somehow he felt had to manage the whole show. He first called Teófilo Isnardi and asked him to outline for him a plan for an Atomic Energy Institute. Isnardi showed it to me and since I didn't want to collaborate with the military I gave him a good piece of my mind. I told him it was rubbish; that presenting such a project was like playing into their hands, like helping the military to dominate science; that what I intended with my notes to the ministers was to obtain their support for civilian physics, not to place civilian physics under their thumbs. A few days later Savio called me and asked me to organize a Nuclear Physics Laboratory, for which he guaranteed 40-million pesos - for those days, an outrageous amount of money (approximately 10 million US dollars of that time). Dr. Delfino, Savio's lawyer, was present at this meeting. I told him it was absurd: I would be forced to place a bunch of bureaucrats and good-for-nothing people in positions they didn't deserve. With far less money a lot more could be accomplished. I proposed 5 million. At that time, the Córdoba Observatory had a budget of one million and it worked fine. We argued. It was lots of fun arguing with Savio and Delfino. We bargained like merchants at a bazaar. Savio said, all right, 30 million. No, general - I said- 5 million. Well, 20 million. No, general, 5 million. Then, 15 million. This went on, and on. I stuck to 5 million. Reluctantly, he finally accepted."

While recollecting these events Gaviola seemed euphoric by his exchange with Savio. Although he tried to make it clear that he strongly disagreed with Savio it was obvious that he liked him. Gaviola found in this general a competent adversary, intelligent, strong willed, stubborn, highly motivated, idealistic and anxious to put his ideas into actions just as himself. This feeling may explain why Gaviola would get excited recalling his bargaining about the budget, and forget to mention what happened with the military-dependence issue. On this matter he was ambiguous: "The project, as I outlined it for them, had a certain autonomy. At the end of the second meeting, Dr.

Delfino and I agreed to prepare a new version of the agreement without military dependence."

However soon afterwards, on September 12, 1946, a bill on atomic energy was introduced in the Senate, bearing Perón's signature and those of his War and Navy Ministers. Savio had decided to ignore Gaviola's recommendations and persuaded the Ministers and Perón himself to submit his own project to Congress. He sent Gaviola a note saying, "I should like to point out that we have not gone into details to achieve a perfect project. I am sure that those who will be in charge of implementing the project will make things work and improve them as time and experience indicates." Savio wanted to go ahead. In this he resembled Gaviola, only they disagreed in the extent to which the military had to be involved.

Savio's letter reached Córdoba two days before the eighth meeting of the Physics Association. This meeting was being held in Córdoba to commemorate the 75th anniversary of the Astronomical Observatory and was attended by several invited foreign scientists. It was an important event where Gaviola was the commanding figure in his double role of President of the Association and Director of the Observatory. Physicists in Argentina could sense signs of upcoming good times, particularly their President. In this state of mind Gaviola replies to Savio in a clear, uncompromising way, adding some prophetic remarks in relation to events which were soon to tarnish science in Argentina[23]:

-"I must insist, however, that if the Institute depends upon the War Ministry, it is condemned to failure. The principal reasons are as follows; first, the basis of military training is discipline while the basis for scientific training is intellectual questioning. The scientist has an inquisitive attitude towards existing theories and methods, and rejects the `magister dixit' rule for imposing new ideas. Secondly, military actions are usually cloaked in secrecy, while science and technology thrive in an environment of open discussion and free publication of results. The secrecy that surrounds scientific activities very often merely serves to disguise incompetence and quackery. Even though the bill is not explicit on this, any dependence on the War Ministry will make it impossible to escape the cloak of secrecy. "Thirdly, foreign scholars and qualified technicians - essential for our progress- would back away from military oversight. Since a Ministry of Scientific Research does not seem plausible at the moment, I would like to propose that the Institute be dependent upon the Ministry of Industry and Commerce. Scientific activities are more akin to industrial endeavors than to military pursuits."

Despite treading on some important toes - precisely General Savio's - he also added: "Fabricaciones Militares itself will someday recognize the convenience of being subject to Industry and Commerce. Becoming an industrialist is not one of the War Ministry's assigned functions."

The letter was distributed among legislators and scientific colleagues. As could be expected, such a provoking piece produced a measurable impact. Its author was surely not disappointed, as most certainly this is what he had in mind when he wrote it. A few days later, Senator Sosa Loyola told Gaviola: "As a consequence of your letter, the project is dead. I have it in my drawer and there is where it will stay."

Savio's project, however, was not all that bad. Judged from a perspective of almost half a century later, the text submitted to the Upper House was under the circumstances fairly reasonable. One can only wonder at what would have happened, had it been approved. With regard to the highly sensitive issue of military control, the organization plan was that of a relatively independent institution. There was no reference to military involvement other than the presence of just one member of the Board of Directors representing the Defense Ministry while the other five were scientists. This does not seem inappropriate insofar the Institute was supposed to deal with all matters related to Atomic Energy. On the other hand, the project explicitly included such things as cooperation with universities and hiring foreign scientists, two cornerstones of Gaviola's original proposal. Savio also backed the idea of an Executive Director with true authority, chosen from a list submitted by the universities, the Academies of Buenos Aires and Córdoba and the officially recognized Professional Societies - i.e. the Physics Association-. The Executive Director was to be appointed for a ten-year period and could be re-appointed for a second term. A clear indication that stability was a concern.

After hibernating for several years, Congress had resumed its activity following the return to democracy marked by the elections in February and the installation of the new authorities in June. Naturally the new legislators were busy looking for good projects to endorse. After all, they had been in their benches for no more than a few weeks. There were a thousand things to do. It was like fertile soil waiting to be sown. For the newcomers, it was an opportunity to start a political career in a new chapter of Argentine history. Both Houses were churning up initiatives. And among many secondary topics - a grant for the Sacred Heart School, a new procedure to identify newly born babies, a subsidy for the Horses Association - there were valuable ideas and well prepared projects. Among them, a proposal to establish a national organization for scientific research enjoyed strong support in Congress, no doubt influenced by foreign models and by the role Science had played during the war.

In a few weeks the initiative got unanimous support in spite of the fact that there was no precedent for such an effort in Argentine science and that a project of this magnitude would require a respectable budget. It was not even a question of trimming budgets here or there, or beginning slowly to gain momentum as things developed. Nobody was questioning its priority. During the war years, Argentina had accumulated considerable amounts of hard currency from beef and grain exports. Therefore, there was no impediment to be ambitious.

This explains the fact that in a relatively short span of time other legislators produced alternative proposals on the same basic idea, trying to improve on each other. Two weeks after Savio's project reached the Senate, the representatives from Mendoza, senators Alejandro Mathus Hoyo and Lorenzo Soler, submitted their own version of a similar idea. It was far longer and more detailed. It had 41 articles compared with Savio's 21 and only 5 in Gaviola's original draft (annexed to his Memorandum on Atomic Energy). It reduced the authority of the Executive Director considerably. In fact, an Administrative Board of seven members replaced the Director. The chairman would stay for only two years and could not be re-appointed. Clearly, in seeking to design a finished product, the authors of this project bogged down in stilted and bureaucratic prose as some articles dwelt in details not proper of a Congress Law. Mathus Hoyo and Soler unfortunately overlooked this and their undoubtedly good intentions became muddled when put down on paper. The original sound and forceful idea was being dangerously affected by cosmetic changes. At the same time, the proposal was very generous insofar as salaries for scientists and operating budget were concerned, a sign of the importance of the project. The level of financial support for science was well beyond the historical average. But the sensitive military element was, in a sense, aggravated, because this project included a Defense Division as part of the Institute. On October 15, Gaviola wrote to Mathus Hoyo and Soler, calling their attention to "the unreasonable dimension of their proposal". Some of Gaviola's colleagues, excited with the possibility of enjoying a completely new employment situation became a bit restive with his inflexible opposition to any military involvement. Another letter went to González Domínguez, whom Gaviola had seen recently in connection with the Radio Technical Institute that the Navy was trying to organize. Gaviola enclosed a copy of his letter to the Senators, and asked González Domínguez to contact them and organize a meeting with General Savio. It was an indication of Gaviola's willingness to negotiate and seek a common ground, now that his original idea had snowballed so unexpectedly in the Senate. This peacemaking initiative was rather unusual in Gaviola, and perhaps pressure from his colleagues who were apprehensive about missing this unique professional opportunity played a role. After all, his memorandum had had its impact. Gaviola could feel deeply gratified. There was a new awareness about Science in Argentina and he could not have planned a more effective strategy to get a good part of Congress and the Executive on the move, genuinely interested in seeing the project realized. A dramatic change had taken place in a very short time: Beck coming to Córdoba, the first Physics conferences there, the foundation of the Physics Association, the now active research groups of brilliant young students, the favorable winds in Congress, "science is now treading firmly". He could indeed feel proud. He was only 46 and in his letter to González Domínguez on October 15 he also acknowledged his recent nomination as Professor Emeritus of the University of Buenos Aires, which he declined: "I prefer to wait another ten years", he tells González Domínguez. Now it was the time for action. Almost exactly one year had passed since Perón was carried from prison to the balcony of Casa Rosada. Gaviola could feel he had been right in admonishing the industrialists then for their pusillanimity, now that he could show the results of his efforts on this other shoulder (government rather than private funding) of the same road.

Good News

That day, October 15, 1946, Gaviola sent a third letter to a friend. The private university project was still in his mind -and heart- and now his optimism was aroused: "I believe time is ripe to call a meeting of University founders. Would you be willing to send out invitations for a meeting towards the end of this month or beginning of November? I would like to ask you, in spite of your own possible misgivings, to include Minister Miguel Miranda among the participants. I had him talk with General Savio, and he seemed forthcoming."

Miranda was Perón's powerful Economy Minister. He was regarded by many as the "inventor" of inflation in Argentina, namely, the magic of making budgets stretch by printing money without proper backing. Gaviola was well aware of the Minister's influence and knew that if he could win him over to his cause, the reluctant industrialists would soon follow.

In November Beck got news from Heisenberg. Unlikely as it seemed Heisenberg was willing to come to Argentina. He said he only needed a special permission from the Occupation authorities. Gaviola's account on this matter is as follow[24]: "As a result of such excellent news for the progress of Argentine science, I wrote a letter to the Navy Minister on November 21, informing him about the situation. Then I traveled to Buenos Aires to help activate the creation of the Radio Technical Institute. The situation was clear: it was almost impossible to bring scientists from the United States, as shown by Tuve's and Hafstad's letters and by the letter of Professor Guillemin of MIT to the Navy Chief of Communication. But Heisenberg's acceptance was enough to be optimistic. We had to look for candidates in England, France, Italy and Germany, especially among top scientists who had been displaced from their work places as a consequence of war. And it was necessary to act promptly because several countries, particularly the United States and Russia, were persuading them with tempting offers. What we had to offer -and they did not- was scientific freedom in addition to personal and economic security. It was urgent, therefore, to send out invitations to as many scientists and technicians as might be required, as soon as the Executive signed the agreement between the Navy Ministry and the University of Buenos Aires. After much discussion, the list of people to be invited (apart from Heisenberg) was prepared by the Navy Chief of Communications, the Dean of the School of Engineering, and myself. The list included Professor Leon Brillouin, from France, Professor Giancarlo Vallauri from Italy, and Dr. Kurt Sitte, an Austrian then resident in England. On November 27 the Navy informed me that the agreement with the University had been approved by the President. That same day, I had a meeting with the Navy Chief of Communication and we discussed the names of Dr. González Domínguez and Mr. Galloni as possible candidates to head the Institute. I said both had the appropriate qualifications. González Domínguez was a distinguished applied mathematician with a long list of first rate scientific publications. I pointed out that the study of the radar required Mathematics as well as Physics, since the calculus of electrodes, resonance and amplification cavities, wave conducting tubes, etc., required a lot of differential equations. Later we went to see the Navy Commander. We had a pleasant conversation. We discussed Heisenberg's acceptance of the invitation to come and how to arrange his leave from Europe. When I suggested that our diplomatic service could help, the Navy Commander said he preferred to let Heisenberg do all he could himself first, in order to forestall unfriendly suspicions. I agreed. Then we mentioned the names of the other scientists we had thought of inviting as well. The Navy Commander expressed his full support for what had been done. Next day, November 28, we had another meeting, now with the acting President of the University, architect Otaola. We again discussed the invitations, the names of González Domínguez and Galloni as possible directors and the salaries that we would offer to our foreign guests. We were all in agreement. The official letters of invitation were sent off a few days later. The Executive now had to appoint the Director based on the joint proposal of the Navy and the University. Things could not have looked better. Shortly, Argentina was to have a first class scientific Institute. It was to be a leading Research Center not only for Argentina but for all Spanish speaking countries."

Heisenberg's favorable answer was a demonstration that Gaviola's ambitious and perhaps a bit extravagant idea of getting first rate scientists to come to Argentina could be implemented. Argentina now had the chance of becoming a reputable place for Science.

In the meantime, congressional interest in a National Research Institute was at its peak. A third, perhaps better proposal was submitted by Senators Gilberto Sosa Loyola and Francisco Luco from the province of San Luis, early in December. It bore Gaviola's trademark. Top salary levels were reasonable. Its annual budget was -as Gaviola had original envisaged- 5 million (about U$S 1.25 million). An Executive Council would be responsible for establishing the Institute's internal structure, salaries, hiring and promoting personnel, distributing scholarships, sending people abroad, giving grants, etc. And most important it had no relation with the Military.

Now things seemed to be running smoothly. The projects in the Senate were passed on to the special committees, as was the rule before returning to the Chamber for final approval. The invitations to top European scientists were on their way. Physicists could be satisfied. They could have not dreamed of reaching this status in the Argentine society a year earlier. New Year was near and with it the summer and the holidays. It was time for a rest.

Stranded Within Sight of the Harbor

While all this promising activity was taking place, an American journalist interviewed Guido Beck. William R. Mizelle came to learn the news of all this excitement around physicists in Argentina. Beck received him kindly and candidly. They talked about the invitation to Heisenberg and other distinguished men of science, about the projected National Laboratory which was being discussed in the Senate, about the new uranium deposits recently discovered near the Andes in the western province of Mendoza, and also about the Argentine Physics Association and its growing membership.

Mizelle took notes, interviewed astronomer Teófilo Tabanera, and wrote an article for New Republic, which he entitled "Perón's Atomic Plans".[25] The first paragraph, under the heading "Exclusive", gave an effective summary of its content: "With world famous German atom-splitter Werner Heisenberg invited to come to Argentina, this Nation is launching a military nuclear research program to crack Pandora's box of Atomic Energy wide open."

New Republic enjoyed an excellent reputation and a large readership in the US, and emphasized coverage of American foreign policy. The Editor, former Vice President Henry Agard Wallace, was a strong minded and progressive member of a Corn Belt family. Wallace had for years been at the center of political tempests, and his combative spirit infused his widely read publication.

Perón was still largely unknown in the Northern Hemisphere, and Argentina was a distant country thought of primarily as a grain provider, for Great Britain in particular. Consequently, the news that Argentina could be launching a military atomic program, at a time when even the Soviet Union had not yet had its baptism as an atomic power, was obviously destined to have considerable impact.

No doubt Mizelle was aware of this when he continued: "Argentina's determined atomic adventure and its frankly military purposes cannot be dismissed as the impractical dream of a small nation. She has the materials and the money, and she has made provisions to get the men with the necessary scientific and technical know-how to carry through with the job."

Mizelle pointed out that Argentina had uranium and thorium, and that the Argentine government had invited Heisenberg to come "and work for the government on a hush-hush basis," and indicated that "Heisenberg knew more about nuclear fission than any living man, except for the handful of scientific pioneers who developed the atomic bomb in the United States." Guido Beck was described as a first rate atomic expert, a former assistant of Heisenberg's, who "for the last three years had been quietly at work in the Córdoba hills." As for the young Physics Association Mizelle said "it is composed of 110 of the country's most promising and imported scientific minds."

The author also added that the three projects which were being discussed in Congress "have recently been re-classified as `secret military legislation' (and) even though Heisenberg was invited to work at a Navy Radio Technical Institute, scientific circles in Buenos Aires believed the expert would have more to contribute to the atomic program than to teaching electronics."

The article left no doubt as to the potential threat posed by a distant and small country. The report was tendentious; the story line was direct, straightforward, with characters acting and speaking in accordance with the script. Mizelle hovered over this scenario, manipulating data and facts until they fit the preset frame. There was little risk. Only a few people in faraway Argentina could denounce his inaccuracies even if they put their hands on his work, an unlikely possibility since New Republic was not normally distributed in South America. Moreover, if they complained, what chances did they have to obtain a sympathetic hearing from the New Republic's readers? Mizelle's dramatic description of the leaders of a not-so-friendly government trying to secure help from unscrupulous foreign scientists (mainly Germans) to perpetuate their power, fitted well with a widely-held, if unsophisticated, view of South American realities.

From his interview with Tabanera, Mizelle elaborates a suggestive analogy: "The Argentine pampa provides ideal terrain for the Institute since its wide open spaces are similar to those in Los Alamos, New Mexico (where the first atomic weapon was built). Argentina has all the materials she needs for building atomic reactors within her own borders."

"It would still take Argentina at least two years - as it would for any other Nation - to produce practical quantities of fissionable materials and turn them into atomic weapons. Argentina does, nevertheless, have as good a chance (of success) as any other Nation that has launched an atomic project since the United States produced the atomic bomb." Mizelle concluded.

At the time only the United States and the United Kingdom were in possession of the technology of this revolutionary new weapon (the U.K. having acquired it from the US). The perspective that Argentina might emerge overnight as an independent power sharing the secret, was a matter of concern.

Consequently, Mizelle's article had an immediate and strong effect. It had been carefully worded for that and the journalist's expertise as well as the magazine's reputation helped to increase its repercussions. One may wonder to what extent Mizelle was actually aware of the efforts of Gaviola and Beck and the spirit which moved them, and whether he anticipated that the tone of his article could strike a heavy blow against the sane initiatives of these men. Given Beck's naiveté and unsophisticated manner, it seems unlikely that Mizelle could have misread Beck's good intentions when he interviewed him. Perhaps the quest for professional success played a dominant role, as it is clear that Mizelle's story would have been devoid of interest if he merely described Gaviola's and his colleagues' struggle to organize Physics in Argentina on a serious and competitive basis. In any case the publication of Mizelle's article, in February 1947, coincided roughly with the beginning of the end of Gaviola's long progressive crusade just as the first promising signs of success had appeared.

Beck was one of the few physicists to read the article south of the Equator. He was also one of the most affected by it. After all he had been the main source of information and rightfully felt betrayed by Mizelle. Also, having been a victim of the Nazis, it was galling for him to be depicted as a collaborator of Perón in a secret program to develop atomic bombs. Clearly disturbed by this circumstance, he overcame his usual reluctance to engage in non-scientific disputes, and wrote to New Republic editor, Henry Wallace:[26] "Dear Sir: "I have read the article which appeared in New Republic on February 24, under the title "Perón's Atomic Plans" and I regret sincerely both its spirit and its content. 1. I do not remember to have said, when I met in November last Mr. W. R. Mizelle on his request, anything that could make him believe that my activity in this country, as astrophysicist of the Córdoba Observatory, had any relation with government plan or research on atomic energy. It has none. 2. I pointed out to Mr. Mizelle, that our problem was to form a group of young physicists for university teaching and research, a task which would keep us busy for many years. 3.

The Asociacion Fisica Argentina (AFA) – Argentine Physics Association - had been founded in 1944, without my initiative, by a small group of Argentine physicists. I have contributed to it as a secretary of its smallest local group (Córdoba). If any personal merit exists, it belongs to Dr. Enrique Gaviola who lent it his support and his great personal prestige and who became unanimously elected its president. 4. The AFA is a private society of physicists: it does not have any connections with government plans or any government support. If we thought it to be our duty to criticize two published law projects on research institutes, it was because we felt that any failure in this respect might seriously affect and discourage the young and weak scientific movement in this country, a movement which is still insufficient even to provide trained personnel to modern physics teaching in the six universities. 5. The initiative to invite Professor W. Heisenberg to the University of Buenos Aires was not due to the government, but to Dr. E. Gaviola. The collaboration of Professor W. Heisenberg with respect to the problem of forming physicists will, at any moment, be very welcome here. Very sincerely yours,"

In spite of its straightforwardness, it seems that the letter had little effect on Wallace. He answered promptly but firmly supporting Mizelle's claims:[27] "In your letter. I did not find any mention of what I consider to be the most important facts reported by William Mizelle..Three Argentine congressional measures designed to provide funds, equipment and experts for the Argentine atomic research program were recently reclassified as `secret military legislation'. As a result of the `secret-military' classification, the Argentine five-year plan clause making all national-defense expenditures unlimited and secret also applies. The first paragraph of the bill to create the Argentine War Ministry atomic center provides for the `collaboration' of all laboratories conducting scientific research relating to atomic energy in Argentina."

It is paradoxical that Wallace's main concern was also Gaviola's and Beck's, as they had fought -and succeeded with the last proposal of Sosa Loyola and Luco- to make this research activity independent of the military. Only in Wallace's mind any research activity in this field was a threat, while for Gaviola and Beck supporting the development of science was of paramount importance for the future of the country.

-"I have constantly fought" -continued Wallace- "for international civilian control of atomic energy in the interest of world peace and the raising of living standards everywhere in the world. I object strongly to the continued manufacture and development of atomic weapons in my country, in your country, in all countries of the world. I have constantly advocated freedom for scientists and scientific research to proceed without being monopolized by the military."

It could have been a paragraph taken from Gaviola's own Memorandum. Wallace's admonition was praiseworthy, but it was addressed to the wrong people as Gaviola and Beck were just as committed to the same ideals.

Wallace concluded his letter with the following warning: "The reports by Mizelle seem to me to show dangerous directions and dangerous steps being taken in Argentina at a time when the international peaceful control of atomic energy is the world's No. 1 problem. It distresses me deeply, Dr. Beck, that scientists like yourself, perhaps innocently, are being edged or forced into actions which may easily result in world catastrophe at some future time. Sincerely. Henry Wallace."

It must have been frustrating for Dr. Beck. He did not protest further. The physicists in the Physics Association were doing their best to avoid the shroud of secrecy over scientific research, as well as military supervision of these activities. It had been just that point that had inspired Gaviola after reading Condon's article almost a year earlier, to initiate the campaign which was now unmercifully attacked by the New Republic.

Neither Wallace nor Mizelle had read the three projects under study in the Congress. Their main point was the reclassification of these projects as "military secrets", justifiably the most worrisome, had it been true, but it was not. It is possible that Wallace did not know this and that would explain his forceful stance, but Mizelle should have fully checked this information if indeed he had been initially misled by hearsay. Sosa Loyola himself protested forcibly against this accusation in an article published in La Prensa in which he not only denied the secret nature of the projects but also stressed the fact that they were openly discussed in Congress.[28]

Mizelle's article had worldwide repercussions and produced harmful consequences. It gave rise to all sorts of far-fetched reports. For example, Brazil's Folha da Noite claimed that "two thousand German experts were actively building an atomic bomb in Argentina." Other papers in Brazil, Chile, Bolivia, Uruguay and Paraguay also echoed the story. O Globo of Rio de Janeiro had a front page headline announcing "Military Atomic Plan in Argentina".

In Argentina the matter was mishandled by the press making things worse. The accusations were not adequately answered. Instead of pointing out errors, the Peronist newspaper Democracia launched a childish and xenophobic attack on Mizelle calling him "blond and superficial reporter who seeks the applause of his readers and the dollars of his bosses."

The government's Information Bureau released a communiqué on March 8 calling the New Republic's claim of a connection between Heisenberg's invitation with a military program of nuclear research, totally unfounded.

It did not shake Mizelle a bit. On the contrary he used the reaction as a springboard to write a new article.[29] By then he had also learned about the Argentine invitations to the distinguished European physicists Richard Gans, Kurt Sitte, Giancarlo Vallauri and Leon Brillouin. Gans was already well known in Argentina. He had succeeded Emil Bose as Director of the famous La Plata Institute of Physics after Bose untimely death in 1911. He had been Gaviola's inspiring teacher, who in 1920 had recommended Gaviola to his colleagues at Göttingen University. By mid-1920's Gans had left Argentina, to return twenty years later.

Mizelle's new article was entitled "More About Perón's Atom Plans" and came out in the March 31, 1947 issue of the New Republic. After repeating his earlier allegations -secret military legislation, discovery of new uranium deposits, Heisenberg's invitation- Mizelle claimed that the main obstacle to the Argentine government's atomic plans was its lack of expert human resources. According to "reliable sources", there was no one in Argentina capable of building a cyclotron, he said, because "the heart of a cyclotron is a pair of semi-circular opposed electromagnets matched and minutely adjusted. The job of building and adjusting them requires an electrical expert of the highest quality." This assertion was intended to explain the invitation to Professor Gans, an expert on electromagnetism, a field related to, but distinct from the technological requirements of building a cyclotron. Mizelle stressed the fact that the plans for the creation of a Physics Research Institute included a clause requiring the collaboration of all scientists working in the different laboratories and universities. Therefore, in answer to the government's disclaimer of March 8, Mizelle pointed to this clause to refute the official communiqué.

In concluding, Mizelle stated: "The galvanic Argentine government reaction to the New Republic's article and news story is the best measure of the importance of Perón's atomic plans and of the determination that lies behind them."

The "galvanic reaction" was a reference to Democracia's irrational answer to Mizelle's story. It was unfortunate that the Argentine press knew little about the whole matter and could not answer Mizelle more effectively, but it is even more surprising that the physicists -except for Beck- kept so silent. They did nothing, in spite of the fact that they had implicitly been accused of secret (as well as an unethical and unprofessional) involvement in military plans precisely the kind of action they had cautioned against. The reporter's allegations, moreover, represented a serious menace to their plans and projects, which had seemed so promising. The fact is that other than Beck's reply, and a letter from Dr. Sitte who protested

Mizelle's inaccurate comments on his Jewish ancestry, no one else added a word.[30]

The story was a success and other journalists tried to capitalize on it by further elaboration. It was definitely a hot issue. Almost any bit of information a reporter could pick up or manage to extract could be made into news. Virginia Prewett was a case in point. Somehow, she had learned about Cecilia Mossin Kotin's work, under Beck's supervision, on the atomic factor of beryllium and her report on nuclear fission. On April 5, New York newspaper PM, contained an article of hers with the headline "Argentina Works on Atom Despite Denials", which said: "Dr. Guido Beck, world famous atomic physicist, once interned by the Free French, who in a letter to the magazine New Republic last week denied that he and associated scientists are engaged in atomic investigations in Argentina, began directing his most brilliant disciple in experiments in atomic physics in the period between 1943 and 1945, according to records of the Córdoba Observatory. Beck personally suggested and directed an investigation called `A Detailed Report on Nuclear Fission' by Russian woman scientist Cecilia Mossin Kotin, who was connected with the Physics Department of the University of Buenos Aires, these records reveal. "Although Beck flatly denied that the group of Argentine scientists of which he and Kotin are prime movers are studying atomic physics, the scientific journal Revista Astronomica (revealed) in its September-October of 1946 issue that the Argentine Physics Association on September 22, at its meeting in Córdoba heard a Kotin report called `Experimental Determination of the Atom Factor in Beryllium'. Beryllium 8 under bombardment by alpha rays produces a slow neutron that physicists consider the ideal projectile for atom splitting, I was told by a well-known physicist here."

This time Beck did not bother attempting to straighten the record. There were plenty of reasons to try, but he must have thought it was useless. In the first place it was not true that he had denied that he was working in atomic physics. It was his field; why should he be reticent about it? It is odd that Prewett should choose to imply that this was something worth hiding. Secondly, Cecilia Mossin Kotin (a native Argentine, not a Russian) had worked on Beryllium during the 30's (before fission was discovered) and this work had nothing to do with the nuclear properties of Beryllium 8 associated with the production of neutrons. Her work had to do with the properties of this element in connection with the diffraction of X-rays. However, for the non-specialist, the article was loaded with suggestive connotations. This level of superficiality was unfortunately to become the rule, not the exception, in the many other stories published throughout the world as a result of Mizelle's dispatches.

As soon as this news became public knowledge in the Northern Hemisphere, the situation in Argentina altered drastically. The Navy changed its mind regarding the Radio Technical Institute. Rear Admiral Carranza informed Gaviola that the candidates for the Institute's directorship - González Domínguez and Galloni- were no longer suitable, and that it was decided to advertise publicly to fill the post. Moreover, the Navy had lost interest in Heisenberg. They argued that English Occupation authorities in Germany were opposed to his leaving; but as Gaviola pointed out: "It is strange that some officials in Argentina seem to be happy with the English attitude. Is it perhaps that Argentina continues to be a British `honorary dominion', as in the times of the Ottawa Conference? Or is there someone here afraid of Heisenberg's scientific stature? If there is no opposition to Heisenberg's coming, how come nothing has been done to secure the British authorization? The diplomatic service must be able to do something about it. Surely, England would not be against Argentina's scientific and technical progress."

Gaviola had good reasons to be upset. His prestige (as well as that of Beck's and the Physics Association's) was involved in the invitation to Heisenberg and the other three European physicists.

"If such commitments are broken, it will mean a severe blow to Argentina's international image. From now on, no reputable scientist will take seriously an invitation to come to this country. We trust the Navy will honor its commitments, just as the Physics Association honors its own."

Thus Gaviola ended a disheartened letter to the Navy authorities. But this chapter of his crusade was finished.

The End of the Dream

Congressional committees continued to study the projects dealing with the creation of a National Research Institute. On April 10, the Argentine Physics Association issued a communiqué in support of the Sosa Loyola and Luco proposal. The influence of this small group of scientists was still remarkable.

The communiqué was entered in the Congressional Records and the La Prensa published a long editorial on it the following day.

However, as the projects were examined in committees, there was a noticeable change of pace. The original momentum seemed to have vanished. It is difficult to assess precisely what affected the will and enthusiasm in Congress.[31] Perhaps, after the initial burst of enthusiasm, the physicists tended to relax convinced that the conclusion was merely a matter of routine. Surprisingly, neither they assigned much importance to Mizelle's articles and their effect not only abroad, but also, and most immediately, within local government circles. The fact is that the initial excitement was gone and the Navy's change of heart regarding Heisenberg was not irrelevant to this new situation.

Gaviola had little left of his dreams except for his old project of a private university. Whatever had seemed promising with the government's participation, had evaporated. Only a private effort, free of political interference and international pressures, could bear a long lasting result. At least this is what Gaviola thought. But he was wrong to believe that a private effort would be free of political influence. On the contrary, although he had not wanted to heed their misgivings, wealthy people in Argentina were quite apprehensive about the political situation and had little enthusiasm for undertaking ambitious projects.

Gaviola's fighting spirit was nevertheless still alive and on May 9 he delivered a very strong speech on the state of public universities. As had happened on other occasions the outspoken physicist got an enthusiastic response from his colleagues and acquaintances. There were congratulatory letters, meetings and interviews. At one of those meetings a wealthy ranch owner offered him 400 acres of land fifty miles from downtown Buenos Aires as a site for the University. Quite a boost to restart the campaign. He then decided that the time had come to devote his full attention to this undertaking.[32]

He resigned his post at the Observatory in Córdoba on July 15, 1947. There had been some frictions but no serious conflicts or ill feelings. He simply felt committed to accomplishing his lifelong dream: the founding of the first and finest private center for scientific study and research in Latin America.

He then prepared a list of the country's most prominent industrialists and bankers.[33] The list included Minister Manuel Miranda. In August he distributed 250 copies of a document outlining his ideas about the new university. It was modeled after the much revered Johns Hopkins University where he had worked twenty years earlier with Robert Wood:[34] "The Argentine universities have never been good. They lack the very essence of any good university anywhere in the world: original research, and teaching by full time researchers. Rare exceptions due to individual merits are not significant. The (Argentine) universities are presently victims of networks of multiple vested interests, which thwart any effort for basic progress that comes from within. Our country's moral, scientific and technical level need be greatly improved. We must try to place the nation in a position compatible with present day requirements. Men of science are more important than buildings; first we have to find the scientist, then build the laboratory for him."

It is interesting that he should also be concerned with the transfer of science to industry: "The Physical-Chemistry School should aim at the development of basic and applied research and at the preparation of able professionals to cope adequately with the problems of industry. The School needs industry for two reasons. For the financial support industry will provide and for the natural absorption of graduates by industry."

This document dealt with all sorts of details about the university campus, curriculum, personnel, and even included recommendations about the social environment and family life of those associated to the university. Some were a bit extravagant and bore the elitist convictions of the author ("a place where students and professors' families may interact closely; where faculty children may marry each other, instead of marrying others with no scientific, cultural or moral tradition."). The last paragraph was a moving call for those whose collaboration was sought: "The creation of the private university will represent a major undertaking both for Argentina and for South America. Its founders and supporters will have accomplished a task of historical importance and will have served their best interests and those of their children."

He then sent out invitations for a crucial meeting in the University Club on September 15. Many refused to attend. Dr. Houssay wrote saying that he hoped the idea of a private university would someday materialize since "it will be of the utmost importance for our country. However, he added, I do not wish to become involved until there is absolute certainty that it will have the financial backing to operate for at least five or ten years. Until such time, I do not consider appropriate for me to sponsor several scientific organizations, especially taking into account that there is now so little money available for these activities."

Houssay, who received the Nobel Prize later that year, had already had serious difficulties with the Peronist government. Records show that in a first draft of that letter he had written a paragraph which he later chose to delete. It read: "Another important reason for not wishing to appear on the invitation list is that my name may prove distasteful to many people in government circles. I have recently realized that industrialists are very sensitive to this sort of thing."[35]

Naveira, who had offered the 400 acres, excused himself because of family problems, but made it clear that he maintained his offer, although he was of the opinion that it might be better to wait a bit longer since "new developments have now taken place. Each day we hear of new government policies which oppose private initiatives."

Out of 140 people invited, 17 attended the meeting.[36] Gaviola stressed that the university was not going to be "for or against the government", and in order to remain fully independent, it would not accept a penny from any official agency. He added, probably in reference to the recent dismissal of many professors from official universities because of their political views, that "the university was not being organized to absorb otherwise unemployed professors simply because they had lost their jobs. Only excellence will be taken into account."

The attendees discussed at length how to get the necessary funds. Some thought the minimum amount required would be 70 or 80 million (approximately 20 million dollars). Others said that 5 million could be enough. In the end it was decided that in order to get going, a committee would work to secure the first million. The meeting was adjourned, but not before those present saluted Gaviola with warm applause for his initiative. It was a small step, but a positive one.

A few days later, Gaviola's worst fears became reality. Francisco Pratti, director of Fabril Financiera, had access to Perón and went to see him. After the meeting he phoned Gaviola and told him: "Perón has just told me that he is not going to tolerate this private university business, and if he has said so, there is no point in investing our money in it".[37] Deeply distressed Gaviola called Torcuato Di Tella for help to no avail: "If Pratti is out and Perón is against it, there is nothing more we can do about it", Di Tella answered. As a last resort Gaviola decided to seek the help of Miranda, the powerful Minister of

Economy. He then wrote a letter he would regret for many years to come. A copy in his file bears a sad handwritten note: "humiliation without reply". Less than a year earlier, Gaviola had taken the trouble of visiting Miranda at his factory in the suburbs of Buenos Aires. The meeting had not been pleasant. Miranda treated him contemptuously, saying he had much more important business to attend to than worrying over a private university. Gaviola would never forget the experience.[38] And yet, his devotion and commitment to the cause was such that he overcame his feelings, swallowed his pride, and wrote: "Dear Sir, I have silently admired your economic policies in defense of national interests and your courage and integrity in carrying out, for the first time in the history of our country, a policy which is not dictated by foreign embassies. I have tried to continue my campaign for the creation of a university which complemented the role of the official university, without distracting you from the most important matters that you must attend to. I have received both moral and financial support from various gentlemen from the banking, industrial, commercial, scientific and cultural sectors of our society. But I have reached a point where I cannot go on any further without disturbing you again. Those who are willing to contribute to the project are afraid that their action might be interpreted as an act of political opposition to the government. I can assure you that nothing of that kind is in our minds. Your moral and material support, Señor Miranda, would be the best way to show that our purposes are constructive, patriotic and non-political. Your material support will serve to stimulate others who are willing to help, and would allow me to start in the best situation, with the collaboration of all the progressive industries in the country. My apologies again for taking your time but without your support, the cause to which I want to devote the rest of my life, is doomed. With your support, it will be a success."

It must have taken a lot of inner strength to write this letter. Gaviola was not seeking official favors such as a declaration of interest for the project, or money from the Government. He was only asking one man to support his crusade. In this letter he asked for 200,000 pesos (about U$S 50,000) from Miranda's private fortune. Miranda's support would be as unofficial as Gaviola hoped, but politically decisive nevertheless. All mixed feelings in the industrial sector would immediately vanished if Miranda joined in. The last paragraph of the letter is particularly moving. Here is a man behind a project that he visualizes as permitting important progress for his country. For Gaviola there was no question of material personal benefit involved. Taken at its face value no countryman could disagree in calling the plan constructive and important. Gaviola was desperately reaching for a helping hand, but the hand did not come. As a corollary to this story, the last chapter of Gaviola's crusade, which came to nothing, but could have been of transcendental importance for Argentina, it is interesting to read one informal note found in an old folder - written by the frustrated warrior fourteen years later when half the country waved banners in the streets for or against a similar project championed by the Frondizi's government:[39] "The private university concept has germinated. In this respect, our meeting of 1947 was fruitful. Until now, no university satisfies the objectives that motivated us in 1947. The (Peronist) dictatorship did not allow it. Our hopes and expectations after the change of government in 1955 have come to nothing in the midst of general dishonesty, demagoguery, economic frustration and symptoms of institutional dissipation. Fourteen years have gone by since the meeting at the Buenos Aires University Club. Some of the most enthusiastic participants -Torcuato Di Tella, Enrique Gil, R. D. Spradling- have died; the rest of us have matured or have simply grown old."

Another year was coming to a close. The projects in Congress were still under study. But the spirit was quite different from that of a year before. The excitement swirling around the physicists had vanished. Finally, in September 1948, the Sosa Loyola - Luco proposal came back to the Chamber. It had very few changes but one was significant: The Institute was to be attached to the War Ministry. The scientific community raised no objections. Senator Pablo A. Ramella explained the modification as convenient because "it would make it more viable for approval by the Executive". It was approved unanimously by the Senate on September 15, 1948. It went essentially unnoticed. Physicists and government were by then far apart. The scientific community, now an anti-Peronist stronghold, continued their meetings and activities with a minimum of publicity. The government continued on its way. New winds were blowing and a period in the history of Argentine science, quite different from that envisaged by Gaviola and his colleagues, was about to begin.

The required sanction for the creation of the National Research Institute by the Executive never came. In August 1948 a scientist arrived in Argentina who was to lead the President to lose all interest in it.

Copy of one page of Enrique Gaviola´s records as student in Berlin in 1924-1925. In the third line is Albert Einstein´s signature, professor of "Relativitatstheorie". Below are the signatures of Walter Nernst, Max von Laue and Lise Meitner. *Courtesy of E. Gaviola*

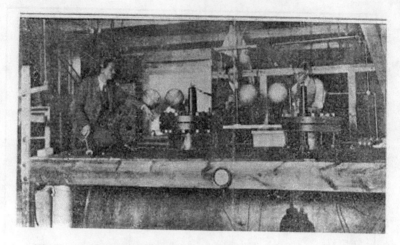

Picture published in The Sunday Star, Washington D.C., November 11, 1928 under the headline "Atoms Shattered with Current of High Voltage". From left to right is Larry Hafstad, Enrique Gaviola and Merle Tuve. This machine was the first to reach five million volts and it is the first known attempt to build a particle accelerator. Because of its historical value this picture was exhibited in the Smithsonian Museum of Science and Technology in Washington D.C. for many years.

Picture published in the first page of The Baltimore News, March 10, 1928. The picture caption reads: "Dr. Robert W. Wood, professor of experimental physics and Dr. E. Gaviola of Argentina, a fellow of the International Educational Board, working on the spectrum of Mercury

Dr. Guido Beck (1902-1988, born in Reichenberg, Austria), left and Dr. Enrique R. Gaviola (1900-1989, born in Mendoza), right, at the time when they founded the Argentine Physics Association in 1944. Knowing that the Jewish-born Beck wanted to escape Europe, Gaviola, possibly the only one in Argentina capable of fully grasping the importance of having Beck in this country, invited him to join the Córdoba observatory in 1943. Beck had been assistant to Werner Heisenberg and was the "academic father" of a new generation of Argentine "modern" physicists including Balseiro, Giambiagi, Bollini, Bes and others.

Fifth Meeting of the Argentine Physics Association. Actually the first one held after the creation of the Association, but the founders wanted to pay recognition to the fact that there had been four previous meetings. The picture was taken on March 31, 1945 at the Córdoba Observatory. From left to right, front row: E. Galloni, Prof. Würschmidt, C. Mossin Kotin, Mrs. Würschmidt, H. Isnardi, E. Gaviola, S. Gerschanick. Second row: J.A. Balseiro, J. Bobone; F. Alsina, A. Cicchini, A. Volsch, G. Beck. Back row: A. Rodriguez, R. Platzeck, M. Dartayet, Porto, D. Papp, J. Goldschwartz. *Courtesy of C. Mossin Kotin*

First page of Gaviola´s Memorandum of 1946 published by Unión Matemática Argentina (front-center), that gave rise to a strong international reaction initiated by American journalist William R. Mizelle. Mizelle wrote two articles published in the February and March 1947 issues of New Republic (left- and right-hand side of figure) that shattered Gaviola´s and Beck´s efforts to bring first rate, post-war physicists to Argentina by falsely accusing them to be working for Peron´s atomic plan. Mizelle´s denunciation was accompanied soon after by Virignia Prewett who wrote an article published by PM New York on April 6, 1947 (top-center).

NOTES TO CHAPTER 2

[1] Edward U. Condon, Science, 103(1946) 415.

[2] Enrique Gaviola, Revista de la Union Matemática Argentina, 11(1946) 213

[3] In an interview with the author on January 30, 1979, Gaviola said: "...the best offer was probably that of (Professor) van Vleck from Wisconsin. I was offered a chair on theoretical physics, in addition to teaching electromagnetism eight hours a week. In the meantime, however, a letter arrived from the University of Buenos Aires. They invited me to take up the Physical-Chemistry chair. Well, I accepted. I wanted to do something in Argentina. How very wrong I was. It would have been much better for me, as well as for science, if I had gone to Wisconsin instead. But be it as it may, I returned." Gaviola was born in the city of Mendoza at the foot of the Andes, in 1900. In 1917 he went to the University of La Plata to study engineering. There he met Professor Richard Gans, a German expert in magnetism. It was Gans who awakened in Gaviola his love for Physics. Before World War I, La Plata had reached and extraordinary level of excellence under the guidance of Professor Emil Bose, another German who had been invited by Joaquín V. Gonzalez, founder of the University. When Gaviola went to La Plata the University had lost much of its initial quality. Gans suggested that Gaviola go to Germany, and wrote letters of recommendations on his behalf. "In those days, it did not occur to me to apply for a scholarship or anything of that

sort. There was no such type of assistance available then" - Gaviola later explained to the author. "So, I thought the best thing I could do would be to finish my Surveyor studies, since I had just one more year to go, and work as one only as long as necessary to get enough funds to pay for my travel expenses."

[4] An abortive attempt to secure a place in the University of La Plata the previous year had left a scar, but not serious enough to deter him from accepting the invitation from the University Buenos Aires.

[5] David Hilbert and Richard are two pillars of Modern Mathematics; Max provided the now currently accepted interpretation of the wave function in Quantum Mechanics; Max Planck is considered to be the father of Quantum Mechanics; Max became famous for his work with X-rays; James Franck was awarded the Nobel Prize, with Heinrich Hertz, for his experimental confirmation of the existence of quantum states in the atom; Einstein, the father of Relativity Theory; Meitner, with Hahn, discovered nuclear fission.

[6] Concerning Robert Wood, Gaviola wrote the following (to the author, October 10, 1981): "Wood was known to be difficult to work with. I soon learned why: Wood was an extraordinary experimenter and an indefatigable worker. He worked with four or five experiments at the same time, in three large rooms, mounted according to his particular method with matchboxes, soft wax, wood matches, string and sealing wax. Soon I realized that in order to earn his respect, I had to work like a madman just as he did. One of his experiments gave me an opportunity. (Gaviola tells how he managed to improve it, in Wood's absence). When Wood returned and saw the results, he did not say a word. Yet I knew that having shown him that I was good at improving experiments, and was just as crazy as he, I had earned his trust and respect." During the year Gaviola spent with Wood, he published six papers, half of them in collaboration with Wood, the rest by himself. They were published in Phil. Mag. and Nature, and dealt with atomic spectroscopy, particularly of mercury.

[7] "I had been invited to go to the Carnegie Institute by (Gregory) Breit. They had a huge apparatus there; an enormous condenser made of glass plates and aluminum sheets, which was discharged by means of a solenoid. They also had a sort of Tesla transformer that was capable of producing several million volts. The object was to produce high-energy particles. I tried to design a sort of discharge tube, but it didn't work." (author's interview with Gaviola February 11, 1980). Today this apparatus is considered the first forerunner of a particle accelerator. It achieved 5 million volts. A photograph of the large Tesla transformer and Hafstad, Gaviola and Tuve standing on it, was published by the Washington Sunday Star, on November 11 1928.

[8] In those days Gaviola worked on: vertical currents, hail and ice formation on airplanes (Journal of Meteorology, August 1947, in collaboration with Fidel Alsina), star images (Astronomy Journal, June 1949); determination of solar eclipse instants (Nature, 163 (1949) in collaboration with Ricardo Platzeck and Alberto Maiztegui) and the Eta Carinae Nebula (Astronomy Journal, March 1950).

[9] Letter of Gaviola to Braun Menendez, September 8, 1945 (Gaviola's files, Library of the Bariloche Atomic Center, Comisión Nacional de Energía Atómica, San Carlos de Bariloche). Further material quoted in this chapter on the Private University project comes from the same source.

[10] Biannual Report by the President of the Argentine Physics Association, Spring 1952-54 by E. Gaviola (unpublished). Library of the Bariloche Atomic Center, Comisión Nacional de Energía Atómica, San Carlos de Bariloche.

[11] It is interesting to hear Gaviola telling about his affiliation with the Socialist Party in the early 1930's: "I had known (Nicolás) Repetto (one of the leaders of early Argentine Socialist Party) since our days as teachers at the Colegio Libre de Estudios Superiores. Quite often, Repetto insisted that I join the party. I finally gave in because I thought it might be

interesting to learn how political parties functioned. I kept my membership for two years; that was long enough to realize that the Socialist Party, like all the others, was demagogic and corrupt. Then, I resigned. As you know, I have always liked to do exactly the opposite of what people expected me to do. While in the party, I enjoyed fighting Repetto and his entire group. I prepared a proposal to modify the Socialist Party charter. It was discussed in a meeting in Santa Fe, which I did not attend because my asthma was getting worse. Anyway, there they decided to divide the party, and the Socialist Workers Party was created based on my proposal." (Talks with Gaviola, February 11, 1980)

[112] Interestingly enough, taking into account that both Gaviola and Braun Menendez were "basic" researchers, they also considered a School of Technology. Funding for the project would come from industry and the private sector, and Dr. Bernardo Houssay (who two years later received the Nobel Prize for Medicine) was to be offered the presidency of the university. The foundation of a private and secular university was a completely unprecedented effort in Argentina, and was not to be attempted again until more than a decade later, and when it did it was not as ambitious or quality-conscious an effort as that contemplated by these two men. The idea was so ambitious and pioneering in the local context that it appeared a bit unreal. Gaviola and Braun Menendez also were counting on a number of generous offers of financial support.

[113] Gaviola's files, Library of the Bariloche Atomic Center, Comisión Nacional de Energía Atómica, San Carlos de Bariloche.

[114] Henry D. Smyth, Atomic Energy for Military Purposes, Rev. of Mod. Phys., 17 (1945) 351.

[115] Here E denotes energy, m is mass and c is the speed of light (equal to 300,000 km/sec, or 184,000 miles/sec).

[16] "Thermalized" neutrons are those which by multiple scattering with atomic nuclei in a medium, slow down to reach the average kinetic energy of the latter. This "average kinetic energy" of the atoms in a given material is a measure of the "thermal" state or simply the temperature of this material. Paraffin or any other material abundant in hydrogen is an efficient "thermalizer" of neutrons. "Thermalized" neutrons move at the speed of a few thousand feet a second as compared to the speed of several tens of million feet a second, typical of neutrons when they are released in nuclear reactions.

[17] Mossin Kotin's work was the identification of a 50 keV gamma line of actinium, by the absorption method.

[18] Interview with C. Mossin Kotin on May 21, 1980. She referred to the fact that the French group had been very close to identifying the neutron when Chadwick, from England, reported its existence.

[19] C. Mossin Kotin, Revista de la Union Matematica Argentina, 10(1945)130. Also, this material was adapted for the general public and published in a series of articles Mossin Kotin wrote for the newspaper Crítica in August 1945, a few days after the Hiroshima explosion.

[20] E. Gaviola, Revista de la Union Matematica Argentina, 11(1946)220.

[21] E. Gaviola, On the Invitation to professor W. Heisenberg and the Radio Technical Institute, unpublished (1947). Archives of the Bariloche Atomic Center library, Comisión Nacional de Energía Atómica, San Carlos de Bariloche.

[22] Interview with E. Gaviola, February 11, 1980.

[23] E. Gaviola, La Asociacion Fisica Argentina, su Historia hasta 1965, unpublished (1965). Archives of the Bariloche Atomic Center library, Comisión Nacional de Energía Atómica, San Carlos de Bariloche

[24] Ibid, 23.

[25] William R. Mizelle, <u>New Republic</u>, February 24 1947, pag. 22.

[26] Guido Beck, <u>New Republic</u>, March 31 1947, pag. 21.

[27] Henry A. Wallace, <u>New Republic</u>, March 31 1947, pag. 21.

[28] Senator Sosa Loyola, <u>La Prensa</u>, April 11 1947.

[29] William R. Mizelle, <u>New Republic</u>, March 31 1947, pag. 20.

[30] The case of Gaviola is remarkable. In a letter to the author dated April 10, 1983, he says: "In connection with Mizelle's article in <u>New Republic</u>, your reference is the first news I have of it. I had heard about it but I never had definite knowledge of it. Could you get a copy for me?" In a new letter dated August 17, 1983, after acknowledging receipt of the article, he added: "The Radiocommunications Institute, as a joint venture with the University of Buenos Aires, failed because of the change of the Navy Commander. I had talked to one who was in favor of inviting Heisenberg. Once Heisenberg accepted coming for two years, another Commander showed up, who wasn't interested in either the Institute or Heisenberg. I wrote a letter to this new Commander which concluded: `The Argentine Physics Association expects the Navy Command to meet its commitments as the Association has met its own', or something like that. Someone in the Navy asked that I be fired. González Domínguez knows the story. Heisenberg was invited by Beck and myself and the invitation had nothing to do with Perón. What Mizelle writes in his second, third and fourth paragraphs is partially or totally wrong. The rest of the article as well as Wallace's letter contains so many falsehoods that it would take too long to answer. It is strange that Mizelle didn't try to get in touch with me. I would have helped him to clarify a lot of misconceptions." (paragraphs #2, 3 and 4 of Mizelle's first article deal with the invitation of Heisenberg "by the government on a hush-hush basis"; the "quiet" work of Dr. Beck in the Córdoba hills; and the re-classification of the three projects in Congress as military secrets.)

[31] On April 10, 1983, answering the author's query as to the possible reasons for the downfall of all the promising projects underway in 1947, Gaviola remembers that "Westerkamp and Galloni were the two physicists who had closer contacts with the Senate (Westerkamp was a part time stenographer in Congress). As for my part, after resigning from the Observatory and having had the terms of my resignation officially rejected (which earned me the reputation of a political foe of Perón's), and having finished my term as President of the Physics Association, I was totally without any official capacity. My marriage took place after the resignation was accepted. Acting on Houssay's suggestion, Luis Fourvel Rigolleau helped me out by appointing me to a `decorative' position in his plant at Berazategui (outskirts of Buenos Aires). My time was completely taken up in shuttling between Berazategui and Córdoba, where I continued attending seminars and working with my project on vacuum pumps. Therefore, my marriage had nothing to do with my staying away from the Senate. Regarding Mizelle's articles, this is the first time. (see ref. 30). Probably Mizelle's version originated in my article on the bomb, and in Don Guido's (Beck) summer seminars at the Achala (in Córdoba), where reportedly there were some uranium deposits." It must be pointed out that in his letter to Gaviola the author suggested the following three possible reasons for the failure of the projects then under way, and asked Gaviola to comment on them: 1) the coming of Richter (see following chapters); 2) Mizelle's distorted reporting and, 3) Gaviola's marriage (in 1947). A similar inquiry was forwarded to Dr. Westerkamp and Professor Galloni. Neither of them could offer a definite opinion on this matter.

[32] E. Gaviola, El Problema Moral Argentino, unpublished (1947). Archives of the Bariloche Atomic Center library, Comisión Nacional de Energía Atómica, San Carlos de Bariloche.

[33] The list included: Francisco Pratti (Fabril Financiera Co.), J. Martin (Crédito Industrial y Comercial, member of the Otto Bemberg group), an unnamed representative of Bunge y Born, R. Lamuraglia, Mr. Maiza (Rigolleau crystals), E. Herbin, T. Di Tella, H. Roberts, M. Herlitzka, L. Serrate, A. Salamanca, G. Buzon, M. Alemann, O. Sassoli, L. King, P. Gambino and Minister M. Miranda. (Gaviola's notes, Bariloche Atomic Center library, Comisión Nacional de Energía Atómica, San Carlos de Bariloche).

[34] E. Gaviola, Archives of the Bariloche Atomic Center library, Comisión Nacional de Energía Atómica, San Carlos de Bariloche.

[35] Ibid, 34.

[36] Attending were: J. Allende Posse, E. Artaza, F. Alsina, R. Busch, A. Garcia Olano, E. Galloni, E. Gil, C. Ruiz, T. Di Tella, Buenano, J. Martin, Sanchez Elia, O. Sassoli, A. Salamanca, Torralba and two unidentified ladies. (Ibid, 35).

[37] About Perón's strong reaction against the Private University project, Gaviola told the author, on February 21, 1980, that he believed Perón did not want to hear anything about it because one of the main contributors was Otto Bemberg (who was represented by Martin), an enemy of Perón. Bemberg had a virtual monopoly on beer sales and, according to Gaviola, Martin had once whispered in his ears `ask for twice as much (from Bemberg)' alluding to this man´s wealth. Hard feelings with the Government were due to suspicions that the Bembergs has evaded taxes on their large inheritance. At that time, this accusation had come out in print in a widely - read booklet entitled A Hundred Ways to Rob the Country.

[38] Gaviola had harsh words for Minister Miranda. "He was the one who taught Perón to steal, by means of inflation. Perón referred to it as `Miranda's magic wand'. He taught him how to mint inflationary currency... I not only wrote to Miranda, but also went to see him. The impression it made on me was

horrible. He told me: `Don't come here and waste my time, there are fifteen ambassadors waiting to see me at the Government House, and you come to bother me with that project of a private university', and then he showed me the door". Interview with Gaviola, February 11, 1980

[39] Perón's first six-year term as President ended in 1952. Perón was re-elected a second term which would have finished in 1958 but he was forced into exile in 1955. After an interim military government Dr. Arturo Frondizi became President in 1958, and during his first years as President he pushed for a law allowing private universities in the country. Gaviola's notes may be a little too gloomy, considering that a National Research Council was created in 1958 under the chairmanship of Houssay and became instrumental in Argentine scientific development. Also the universities improved in those years, after many good scientists returned to their chairs on full-time appointments and research got support.

3 | Project Huemul (December 1947 – March 1951)

Mission in Norway

Major Medardo Gallardo Valdez opened the telegram. "Await instructions" was its concise and disappointing message. Sweden was supposed to be only a stopover in his way to the Argentine Embassy in Moscow. He had been asked to wait in Sweden a few days. Not only this telegram prolonged his quandary and meant further delays; it had the worrisome taste of an implicit change of plans.

The Major felt frustrated and deceived; he had withdrawn his request for early retirement only in exchange of this trip to Moscow. Such was the agreement reached with his boss, Commodore Bartolomé De la Colina. Though he could not think of De la Colina as a man who would not keep his word, it looked like his word was in peril. Then he thought nostalgically of his farm in San Juan where he had planned to retire.

Sad and confused, he tried to guess at what would lie behind this message. He was well aware of the discrepancies between De la Colina, the man who wanted him to stay in the Force, and Major César Ojeda, second in command but closer to Perón. He also knew that Ojeda - his classmate - disliked his liberal ideas. Were they going to ask him to return, or send him somewhere else?

A few days later he got a second telegram announcing he had been appointed attaché at the Embassy in Sweden. It was now clear that the agreement had been broken; his studies of meteorology in Moscow would not take place and he was not given the chance to quit either. The new appointment looked like the worst, of all alternatives; a standoff between his bosses translated into locking him up in a geographic midpoint. Could his bosses' conflict have reached such an aimless climax?

As he was pondering these questions and attempting to foresee his uncertain future, he got a third telegram. He could not fully grasp its implications, but the new message left no room for speculations. An attractive proposition had unexpectedly reached the Foreign Affairs Ministry in Buenos Aires a few weeks earlier, and the dynamic Ojeda tried to seize the opportunity as soon as he heard about it. But while he worked at it, Ojeda efficiently anticipated his next moves and identified Gallardo Valdez as a useful pawn on his chessboard. This explains the ambivalent, `stand by' nature of the first two telegrams. The last one was, by comparison, very clear and straightforward, once declassified: It commanded Gallardo Valdez to fly a secret mission to Norway, pick up three Germans in custody of the Argentine consulate there, and bring them down to Buenos Aires under false passports.

In recent years Gallardo Valdez had gradually become more of a scholar. He had taken up Meteorology at Caltech in California in the early 1940's. Before travelling abroad, he had met Dr. Enrique Gaviola and attended several of the periodic seminars Gaviola used to conduct at the Córdoba Observatory. Being a military officer this contact with physicists served him well during his stay at Caltech where he met several distinguished scientists. "I always kept Gaviola in high esteem" - he recalled many years later – "and (Robert) Millikan and (Carl David) Anderson (both Nobel laureates at Caltech) remembered Gaviola well". [1]

Back in Argentina he worked on a draft of a National Law of Meteorology. It called for the creation of a National Meteorology Service and the organization of a school at the University of Buenos Aires. When he handed the proposal to his superiors later in 1945, it met unexpected resistance. "It was filed away merely because it was mine. When I came back in early 1943 some colleagues approached me with something like the declaration of principles of an officer's society. I read it and told them `Look this is Nazi stuff, I am not a Nazi and I don't want to have anything to do with it'".

This `society', later known as GOU (Group of United Officers in Spanish), was responsible for the June 1943 revolution and had quite a following among the military in those days. Valdez' blunt rebuttal displeased his enthusiastic comrades and marked the beginning of the end of his military career. In 1945, when his project was `frozen', he decided to apply for retirement but was persuaded to stay by De la Colina's insistent offer to go to Moscow. De la Colina knew that Gallardo Valdez' work had elicited favorable comments at a Conference on Meteorology in London. His work had been compared to its equivalent from Russia. It was tempting for Gallardo Valdez to have the opportunity to go to the Soviet Union. thus he accepted his boss' proposition and in late 1947 he found himself in Sweden on his way to Moscow.

It was in the spring of 1947 that the Spanish Embassy in Buenos Aires informed the Government that expert Kurt Tank and a group of aeronautical engineers wished to escape to South America. Tank and his group were former employees of the Focke-Wulf Aircraft Company and reportedly had with them the blue prints of the latest designs. De la Colina and Ojeda appreciated the opportunity of fostering Argentina's incipient aeronautical industry, and they masterminded the secret mission of which Valdez was to play unwittingly a leading role. It was necessary to get the experts out of Germany. They were being tracked to face war trials. "The Russians did the same thing. They whisked away blue prints and experts and they eventually got their Mig 15 at about the same time we got the Pulqui II", explained Brigadier Ojeda [2].

Importing brains, that for which Gaviola had struggled so hard a year earlier - to bring Heisenberg to Argentina -, for Ojeda was much simpler as he enjoyed plenty of official support. It took him little more than a couple of telegrams, to initiate a substantial flux of Germans experts into the country.

Ojeda was young, enthusiastic and plucky. During the early days of the military government installed after the 1943 revolution, he and a few colleagues had gone to see Perón with a project to create an Air Force. At the time Perón was formally Under Secretary of War but he had far more influence than an ordinary Under Secretary. Perón was taken by the idea of having a National Air Force. In those days the aviation was only a dependency of the Army. It was time to do something more about it. In the meeting, where Colonel Enrique Gonzalez was also present, Perón remarked that airplanes took off continually from Brazil's Santos Dumont Airport while "we look up the sky every time we hear a plane go by". He asked the group whether they had any proposals to offer. "Major Ojeda has got a draft", someone in the group said. Perón leafed through it and asked Ojeda to come to work with him on it.

Within forty-eight hours Ojeda was fully devoted to this new task. In order to avoid frictions with the Army he started with the creation of an Air Command within the Army. Perón and Ojeda, both bent to action, got along very well from the start. Soon Perón ended up calling "Ojedita" (dear little Ojeda) to his new assistant.

The project was successful thanks to Ojeda, who struggled hard against the usual odds and missed no opportunity to further its development. With Ojeda's enthusiasm plus hard work, and Perón's backing, they succeeded in obtaining President Pedro Pablo Ramirez' signature just on the eve of his departure from office, in February 1944. Years later, with a touch of pride, Ojeda remembered: "I believe it was the last thing the President signed". The approval of this bill was the first and most important step in the way towards the Air Force. President Edelmiro Farrell followed Ramirez. In 1945 he signed a decree creating the Aeronautic Secretary and in 1946, the Air Force was born.

Though an obvious candidate for the job, Ojeda -being only a Major - could not aspire to becoming Secretary. Perón then appointed Commodore De la Colina, a loyal man but with some handicap of a domestic nature: his wife refused to attend any official ceremony where Perón's wife Evita was to be present. Thus De la Colina was seldom seen at official ceremonies and even at his own office. In practice Ojeda had command of most every day matters.

It was near Christmas of 1947 when Gallardo Valdez got orders to go to Oslo. The Argentine Consul Muret handed him the three men. They spoke nothing but German. For forty hours - the time it took them to fly to Buenos Aires - Gallardo Valdez lived in confinement with these three men without practically exchanging a word. The embarrassed Major complied with his duty reluctantly. He was utterly in the dark regarding his mission's ultimate objective, yet he knew the men entrusted to his care carried false passports and regretted doing what he suspected: provide protection to Nazi refugees on the run from the Allied Occupation authorities. He tried hard to detach himself as much as possible from his unwanted role and made no effort to know more. Years later he could only barely remember the name of one of these men: "It was something like Matias or Mathies".

Gallardo Valdez kept for himself the details of this mission as much as he could, and unaware of the important consequences that such mission had for the development of atomic matters in Argentina, he intensely wished it had never involved him [3].

This mission was all he had to do with the coming of German experts to Argentina. He spent a lonely Christmas as his family remained in Sweden. A few months later he was notified his services were no longer required. He was relieved.

But the ghost of that mission was going to come back a few years later. Gallardo Valdez was a declared anti-Peronist and he participated in a failed attempt to overthrow Perón in 1951. In 1955, after Perón was ousted, President Pedro Eugenio Aramburu promoted Gallardo Valdez to the rank of brigadier and persuaded him to become Acting Governor in the Province of Córdoba. While in office a rather odd circumstance developed to the dismay of the circumspect brigadier.

In those days, anti-Peronist feelings ran high and a vicious campaign against the former regime was in full swing. Most everything was labeled good or bad depending on its political tint; if the Peronists had done it was automatically discredited. Some officials of the new government spent more time searching for wrongdoings in the files of the past government rather than planning their own programs. It was tempting, and rewarding, to dig out new evidence of misconduct.

Such was the prevailing atmosphere when the new Córdoba Chief of Police decided to investigate the case of the German experts who had come to Córdoba to work in the design of modern aircraft. He knew (or was told) that most of these people were holding false passports. Their quarters, near the aircraft factory, were a few kilometers away from downtown in a small village called Villa del Lago. It was a magnificent opportunity to gain reputation without too much sweating. All the right elements were at hand. A secret, spy-like story, involving the highest offices of the last Government provided an attractive background. At the same time, it was pretty straightforward: even the children of Villa del Lago knew that the real name of Mr. Pedro Matthies, the head of the group, was Kurt Tank!

The situation developed into a comedy. The Governor did his best to disguise his anxiety and avoided any interference with the inquiry, while the Chief of Police, full of zeal, strived ahead to fulfill his duty and... collect credits. He was far from suspecting that his own boss had been the one who had brought Tank to the country!

Eventually the case was dropped and Gallardo Valdez was spared of the embarrassment of having to explain publicly an episode which he regretted so much. But it illustrates the degree to which that secret mission was kept under the rug. Not even in private he wanted to talk about it. With one exception.

It happened one evening of 1956, after dinner, while Gallardo Valdez was still acting Governor.

After his ostracism from public life following the downfall of his ambitious crusade of a decade ago, Enrique Gaviola had come back to Córdoba again as Director of the National Observatory. In those days he still had his home in Buenos Aires so he used to stop at the Bristol Hotel. There he met Gallardo Valdez, his old acquaintance and disciple, several times. "I was often invited to lunch or have dinner at his table", Gaviola remembered years later [4]. In such encounters, the events of the past years were frequent topic of conversation. Memories of these two men's unfulfilled dreams merged together with their hopes for the future. They recalled the physics seminars at the Observatory, Gaviola's efforts to gain Perón's acceptance of a private university, the thwarted trip of Heisenberg to Argentina and many other frustrated projects which could now perhaps be revamped. In an atmosphere of friendly recollections and political affinity, one evening Gallardo Valdez broke his silence and confided to Gaviola the details of the mission to Norway.

"During one of those leisurely talks he told me the story of his secret activities when an engineer appeared with a suitcase full of microfilms with the latest Messerschmidt designs that they hadn't had time to build in Germany." [5] For many years Gaviola was probably the only one to hear the story straight from Valdez. The mission had been so distasteful for him that, even though Gallardo Valdez was a professional pilot, it took him thirty years to acknowledge that Tank was one of the men he flew with, and that he, Mr. Tank, had been responsible for the most modern aircraft ever built in Argentina, the Pulqui II.

Likewise, it took him that time to learn that his mission precipitated a spectacular atomic adventure in Argentina. [6]

A Decisive Interview

Almost a year before coming to Argentina, Kurt Tank had been in London and there he met Ronald Richter. The encounter produced a lasting impression on Tank. Richter told Tank about his ideas on nuclear propulsion for airplanes. Being an expert on the most advanced aircraft at that time - and not knowing much about atomic energy - Tank was immediately taken up by the perspective of a spectacular innovation such as that proposed by Richter. The physicist seemed to know very well what he was talking about and very convincingly put his ideas forward.

When Tank arrived in Argentina in December 1947, he had not forgotten Richter, and encouraged by the welcoming attitude of the Government towards German specialists who were willing to come to work at the Córdoba Aeronautical Institute, he strongly recommended Richter.

The first contact of Argentine officials with Richter was established in May 1948. At the time he was in Paris. A second, more formal offer was made through Air Force Captain Peters. By then, Richter was in touch with US army officers, looking forward to emigrating to the States, so he took some time to answer the Argentineans.

When the possibility of going to the States did not materialize, Richter decided to embark for Argentina somewhat abruptly without having signed a contract. But there was no need. Tank's recommendations had been excellent. Richter was received by Perón himself, on August 24, 1948, scarcely a week after his arrival.

Perón and Richter got along well with each other from the very first moment. Their characters and attitudes were alike. They both appreciated the advantages of a mutual friendship. Ojeda and Tank were also present at the first meeting which took place in Perón's executive office.

Richter, poised and self-assured, explained his ideas about the uses of atomic energy. He had a special ability to make himself understood by using illustrative analogies. He told Perón: "What I have in mind is the creation of a tiny sun. The immense energy of the Sun results from thermonuclear reactions fueled by hydrogen, the most abundant element in Nature". In order to illustrate the difficulties involved in confining a tiny sun and all its energy within a laboratory, he used the figure of the old movie projectors which were equipped with an intense voltaic arc to project light through the film. "If the film stops, the voltaic arc burns it", he explained. Richter's problem was to find an adequate container for such a staggering amount of energy.[7]

He described the principles of atomic energy and the differences between nuclear fission, involving uranium or plutonium, and nuclear fusion, which required hydrogen and other considerably less expensive light elements. The subject was entirely new for those present at the meeting and it indeed sounded as of paramount importance for the whole of mankind. The excitement grew as Richter proceeded with his inspiring explanations. The range of possibilities was tremendous. Richter insisted time and again that thermonuclear reactions by fusion would produce virtually unlimited energy in a very inexpensive way. The group listened with awe. Were they being recipients of a unique secret which could place Argentina at the forefront of the international stage?

Perón recalled the interview at a press conference three years later: "Richter told me we could start work on atomic energy using the North American method. To do that, however, we would need around six billion dollars. 'Is it possible?', he asked me. I didn't even bother to reply. So Richter continued: 'If you give me six billion dollars, I am absolutely certain we'll produce atomic energy with this method. There's no question about it.

The other alternative is nuclear fusion', and he explained it to me so well that now I am knowledgeable in nuclear matters. Then he added: `I can't assure you that we'll make it with the latter method. We would need to make two or three discoveries and then we may, or may not, succeed. But whatever the results, the money invested in the project would still be peanuts. Do you want to go ahead?' and I replied: `Do you?'. Richter said he was ready so I told him to go ahead. We gave him the means and he started to work. He rejected the other methods because they were expensive and inefficient. This is the way to do it cheap." [8]

For Perón, this was a challenge he could not let go. For Richter, it was a unique opportunity, a dream coveted for years. It seemed like a fairy tale. Richter was to benefit from privileges any scientist in the world would envy. And, if what Richter had said was true, Perón would possess the key to a fabulous treasure. Indeed, both men teamed up well to each other's ambitions.

Richter also kept a clear recollection of that first meeting. When in June, 1951 he was interviewed on Huemul Island, he told reporters: "On that first occasion, I was greatly impressed by the President of Argentina for his determined spirit, his understanding and his creative drive. It's unusual for chiefs of State to be so well informed on all kinds of scientific problems. When I told General Perón about my plans, he listened carefully and then he offered me his full support. He understood immediately the tremendous importance of my scientific project. In short, if Perón hadn't had the courage and drive, characteristic of him, Argentina would not have atomic energy."

On another occasion, he did not hide the impression Perón had made on him after that first meeting: "When I first came to Argentina - after living through countless difficulties which even increased in the wake of the war - I brought with me my past experiences and my faith, but also, my doubts. I had been warned that Perón was a fearful dictator. Now I know where this evil campaign against Argentina was coming from. It took me less than a week to talk with the President. I was amazed.

Where was the dictator? Where was the atmosphere of oppression in Argentina? Naturally, my doubts stemmed from dramatic reasons which you can easily understand: I was coming from an agitated and hysterical world and I had lived many years in Germany under a real dictatorship. It took me just a few days to realize that Perón was no dictator, but a progressive, democratic President. He is a simple, direct, upright man, unlike most rulers. He immediately understood the problem, and he encouraged and helped me. His enthusiasm comes from knowing that the work we have undertaken will be used for constructive, peaceful purposes." [9]

After his first meeting with Perón, Richter went to Córdoba to work with Kurt Tank. Ojeda had arranged for an exclusive laboratory for him. The formality of his appointment was taken care of later, in November. The first article of his contract stated that Richter "hereby agrees to offer his professional services to the Córdoba Aeronautical Institute, as scientific adviser in Atomic Energy matters, in any of its centers, factories or other installations in the Argentine Republic". The Government was to immediately provide Dr. Richter with laboratory facilities according to his specifications, as well as any other needs such as workshops, equipment, machines, tools, testing materials, office space, etc., in sufficient quantity and in time so that his work would not be delayed. The document cited research, studies, projects, building and testing as example of the broad range of activities foreseen for Richter. On the other hand, Richter was "to carry out the project with the maximum economy and to program his work so that disbursement of funds will take place gradually and according to the progressive attainment of practical results". His monthly salary was set at $ 5000 (approximately US$ 1.250 at the time). [10]

Richter's atomic research was beginning auspiciously. It was apparent from the text of the contract that he had ample resources at his disposal. The Argentine Government had pledged full support. The unconventional and daring atomic project had everything a project leader could dream of.

The men responsible for this initiative were extremely effective. Two weeks after his arrival Richter was already at work! Bureaucratic hurdles were absent. But so was Congress and the scientific community. The effectiveness with which this atomic project was started is remarkable, especially when compared to those of Gaviola, Savio and others. The beginning of Richter's undertaking actually coincided with the end of the project for the creation of a National Scientific Institution which, after two years wandering about in the Senate, had recently been passed away.

Eighteen years later, a journalist tried to persuade Richter to write his memoirs. When Richter prepared a list of chronological events for his hypothetical biography [11], his August 24, 1948 meeting with Perón deserved this entry: "A Decisive Interview". Indeed, it was so.

The Choice of Huemul

In Córdoba, Richter worked peacefully for a few months. The population of Villa del Lago, a picturesque little town in the Córdoba hills, grew gradually as new German technicians and some Italians, most of them associated with aeronautics, arrived. The famous pilots Behrens and Hans Ulrich Rudel were among them. The Government continued its policy of attracting foreigners and set up offices in Europe with that purpose.

Richter maintained himself in contact with Tank, though not with the others. He was not a genuine member of the aeronautic group. Richter kept certain degree of independence. He and Tank prepared separate lists of people they wanted the Government to bring to Argentina. At the Buenos Aires office, newcomers were identified as "engineers for the R. Project" or "engineers for the Córdoba Aeronautic Institute" indicating the reserved character already granted to Richter's work. [12] Yet

Richter was formally part of Tank's group. They went together to Buenos Aires every week to hold technical discussions with Major Ojeda and others. Years later Ojeda could not conceal his admiration for the scientific exchange with these two men. [13]

One night in early 1949, a fire broke out in Richter's laboratory and the guards burst in. According to the police report, the fire had been caused by an electrical short-circuit. Yet Richter interpreted it as an act of sabotage, or possibly an attempt to breach the previously agreed barrier of secrecy. The incident acquired unjustified proportions. Even the Federal Police got involved and there were accusations of espionage. The outcome was that Richter refused to continue working under such conditions, and the local security chief was mad for having had the "Feds" intruding.

As soon as Perón heard about the incident, he concluded that the line of command had to be modified, if Richter was to continue his work. There had been such a scandal that it was impossible to reinstate harmony. Richter would have to be moved out of the Institute, but it was necessary to avoid hurting his feelings. Perón did not lack skill for handling these sorts of conflicts and he had no intention of backing away from Richter's atomic challenge. He decided an outsider should take over the whole affair. With that purpose he turned to his old comrade, Colonel Enrique González.

They had been together in the Group of United Officers organizing the revolution of 1943. Later Gonzalez had assisted Perón as Secretary General in Government House. Their friendship actually dated from 1917, when both men were stationed at the same regiment in the Northeast province of Entre Rios. In interviews with the author years later González still remembered his comrade of those early days as a twenty-year old fun-loving dandy, who liked to go out with girls and took time off to show "westerns" to the neighborhood kids. Only their political activities during the late 1940's, had somewhat strained their relationship because of rivalry for leadership among the military. González had taken some distance from the government, and there had been rumors that he had lined up some connections against Perón. González was widely respected in the Army and Perón could not afford to let him go. Early in 1948, Perón called him and asked him frankly to resume their old friendship. Perón wanted him back in Government House. At that time, Perón was worried about the lack of population in the Patagonia region. He told González: "That region is empty. I want you to study how we can populate the Patagonia effectively." No doubt it was an interesting challenge and González accepted. He became Director of the Migrations Bureau. [14].

A few months later, Perón called his friend again and asked him to help solve the conflict with Richter. "Look, you have some funds at the Migrations Bureau, which you could use to assist this fellow. I am very interested in this project", he said. Then he quoted Tank's high opinion of Richter, and explained the possibility of conducting research on nuclear fusion instead of fission. "Do me a favor. This fellow made a scandal in Córdoba and he wants to leave for the States. I want him to stay. I have faith in him. You could use part of your funds to do whatever is needed to calm him down". Perón was genuinely interested. Once again, González accepted.

Actually, Colonel González was quite up to date on the latest developments at the Córdoba Institute. His son Enrique González Jr., an Air Force lieutenant, was fluent in English and German, and had been sent to the Aeronautical Institute to assist as an interpreter for the newcomers. He had been there for a few months and had, therefore, acquired a pretty good idea of what was going on at the Institute when Richter's case broke out. The case was bizarre enough to make for a good story and it is not surprising that González Jr. would mention it while visiting his parents in Buenos Aires.

Colonel González went to Villa del Lago, visited Tank and took a tour of the facilities. Richter had virtually discontinued his activities. It did not take long for the Colonel to realize that the man he was supposed to assist had a demanding and autocratic character, and that the task ahead might be not as easy as he first had contemplated.

While González was visiting the Institute there was another incident. Richter had ordered a dozen imported oscilloscopes and the parcel had arrived in those days without the addressee's name on it. Manlio Abele, an able Italian physicist in charge of supplies, not knowing any better left the oscilloscopes sitting in a corner. When Richter learnt that his equipment had been delayed in Abele's stock room, he used extremely harsh language and accused Abele of sabotage.

This kind of attitude made Richter persona non grata among his countrymen and other foreigners in Villa del Lago. When Heinz Jaffke - an old friend of Richter - arrived in Argentina (he was one of the two technicians Richter asked the Government to bring over), Richter and his wife's social life was practically limited to visiting with the Jaffkes. [15] Jaffke was an expert horseman; he spent long hours in the Córdoba hills teaching Richter how to ride. They also used to go on shopping expeditions together to Carlos Paz or to Córdoba City. [16]

Back in Buenos Aires, Colonel González asked General Joaquin Sauri to help him find a suitable place for Richter to work. Perón's orders were that Richter should work fully independently, with all means at his disposal, and that nobody should bother him. Tank, Richter, Ojeda and Lieutenant González Jr. also participated in the search for an appropriate place. They flew over a considerable portion of the country and crossed Patagonia several times. Ojeda was inclined to choose some place in the deserts in the Province of San Juan in the West at the foot of the Andes. The others thought of the desert areas in the Northwest. The implicit assumption was that the laboratory had to be located in a desert, possibly inspired in the legendary atomic facility at Los Alamos where the first atomic bomb was developed.

Since Perón was interested in developing Patagonia, he favored the provinces of Rio Negro or Neuquén. Flying over this region the group came right up to the foothills of the Andes, where the landscape suddenly turns to deep forests, blue lakes and snow-covered mountains. A sharp contrast with the region they had just left behind. The view immediately captivated Richter.

The group flew over Lake Nahuel Huapi, some 250 miles southwest of Neuquén city. Its half-moon shaped surface of 300 square miles extends from the tip of the desert almost to the line of the highest peaks. Brazo Tristeza, one of its branches, points towards the Tronador, an imposing mountain covered with eternal snows on the Chilean border. "I have never seen Nature looking as majestic anywhere. When people learn about this place, they'll flock from all parts of the world to admire it" - wrote an American geologist at the turn of the century shortly before President Theodore Roosevelt visited the place. [17]

Dr. Francisco Moreno was the first white man to arrive at the Nahuel Huapi area from the Atlantic side, on January 22, 1855. San Carlos de Bariloche was founded by the lake side in 1902, some 20 miles from the mouth of the Limay River, where the freezing waters of Lake Nahuel Huapi start their long journey down east to the Atlantic Ocean. Throughout the years, all kinds of prominent men have come to admire the breathtaking beauty of this region. Theodore Roosevelt's visit took place in 1912, and half a century later Dwight Eisenhower came to fish in Lake Nahuel Huapi and neighboring lakes.

Only nine years after the first airplane landed in Bariloche, Colonel Gonzalez and his group enjoyed the view of the small, Swiss-looking town from the sky, while searching for a suitable place to install an atomic research laboratory. Flying west they followed the lake shore for a few miles. A small island only half a mile from the shore line, captured Richter's attention. As he later noted, it seemed to comply with all requirements: abundance of water for cooling; absence of dust, a good feature for instruments and equipment; and an ideal geography for classified work. The island's name was Huemul. [18]

The Chief of the Bariloche garrison, located right opposite Huemul Island, was Major Carlos Monti. In June 1949 he was instructed by the Ministry of War to fly to Buenos Aires. There the Minister summoned him to a meeting in the President's office. When Monti realized that he would be meeting Perón face-to-face, he trembled. Bitter memories of the past came back. In 1945 when General Avalos was demanding Perón's withdrawal from the Government, military officers of the Warfare School had held several meetings to discuss ways of getting rid of Perón. One of the meetings, perhaps the most turbulent and aggressive, took place in the Officer's Club in downtown Buenos Aires. Several men had climbed on a table to cry out against Perón. "What we should do is to put a bullet through his head!" -shouted one. Monti was among them. A year and a half later, Monti got the bill for conspiring against Perón. A few historical events had overturned the political situation in the meantime and Perón was now President of Argentina. When Monti completed his studies in the Warfare School in November 1946 he was deprived of his degree and sent, instead, to a remote regiment.

Despite this, Monti nursed no ill-feelings. He actually doubted whether Perón had personally care to take his revenge; moreover, he suspected the Defense Minister, General José Humberto Sosa Molina, had put in a kind word for him. It was probably due to Sosa Molina that he finally received his diploma in 1947. Nevertheless, facing Perón was not going to be easy, or pleasant.

If Huemul Island was to become a secret laboratory for nuclear research, a reliable security system had to be established and the garrison in Bariloche was the natural base of operations for this purpose. However, when Perón was told that Monti was the man in charge of the garrison, he said `no'. But reportedly Sosa Molina interceded: "This man might be whatever you wish to call him, but he is a soldier above anything else. If you entrust him with a mission, you won't regret it." Perón gave in. And thus Monti came to meet the man who had been the target of his political hatred. [19]

The meeting started at 7 am sharp, and it was attended by Perón, Defense Minister Sosa Molina, Richter, Tank, Lieutenant-Colonel Plantamura, Mr. Siebrecht -a close friend of

Perón-, Ojeda, Colonel Gonzalez, General Lucero- Minister of War- and Monti.

Perón explained the atomic project while Siebrecht translated into German. He spoke about non-military, industrial applications. He also said "Tank is going to build an engine for a nuclear submarine" [20]. Gonzalez would be responsible for looking after Richter's needs. The project was classified secret. Then Richter said a few words in German which nobody cared to translate. Lucero issued strict orders that no one was to set foot on the island except Perón, Lucero, Gonzalez, Plantamura and Lieutenant Gonzalez Jr., in addition to Richter and his people. Monti became a direct subordinate of the Minister of Defense, General Sosa Molina. Construction plans, blueprints, etc., would be prepared by the Army Engineers Division, under General Sauri's command according to Richter's specifications. The Second Engineers Company, based in Neuquen and headed by Captain Pasolli, would be in charge of all construction works.

Richter and his wife were assigned the garrison's commander traditional residence. Monti was ordered to move over to the neighboring house. They had a superb view: The Andes sitting on the horizon a hundred miles away behind the sky-colored, crystal-clean surface of the huge lake. Only a mile away stood Huemul Island, the chosen site for the first officially supported controlled fusion research laboratory in the Western Hemisphere.

Bricks and Sparks

The first bulldozers arrived at Huemul Island on July 21, 1949. Soon the pace reached full momentum. The Second Company of Engineers disembarked people, machinery and materials. The quiet Huemul environment changed overnight. Large army barges were used to carry bricks, cement, concrete mixers, and other equipment, across the lake from Playa Bonita to the southeastern coastline of the island whose half-moon shape makes an ideal natural harbor. The island itself shelters the bay from the wind which usually blows hard from the Pacific over the Andes. The main dock was built right in the center of the half-moon bay.

Huemul is quite rugged. There is little levelled ground. Over an extension of half a square mile its highest point stands at about 400 feet above the lake. The army soldiers opened a winding trail to the first plateau.[21] Sentry boxes were distributed around the island and the guards´ headquarters was built near the dock.

On the first plateau three large concrete slabs provided the foundations for the soldiers' barracks. There were about 300 soldiers working on the island. Also, a canteen, a kitchen, an "Omega" warehouse and, later on, a small two-bedroom house and a shed to store instruments (the latter was known as Lab # 3) were built in that place. Two large laboratories were also started in that sector of the island a few years later.

The larger facilities were built some 600 feet further up, on a second plateau. The first building to be constructed (later known as Lab # 2), was where Richter conducted his experiments. The power plant, Lab # 4, and later, Lab # 1, were built nearby.

Construction work was under the responsibility of Captain Pasolli, who was assisted by Second Lieutenant Fernando Manuel Prieto who became associated with the atomic program after his military service as a conscript, under Pasolli, in Neuquén. Years later Prieto became a high-ranking official at the National Atomic Energy Commission. When he finished his service and the company was sent to Huemul, Pasolli persuaded him to come along.

According to Prieto, there was plenty of work in the first months. "We worked very hard. There was a lot of enthusiasm. As soon as there was electricity, work proceeded throughout the nights also. Everyone shared the conviction that the project was of crucial national importance". [22]

Soldiers and construction workers under Prieto dubbed him a dedicated, compassionate and intelligent man. Guerino Bertolo, an Italian immigrant and one of the ablest masons on the island, had the following story to tell: [23] "In a miserable, makeshift shed, Prieto had installed the technical office. He worked, ate and slept there. He never seemed to leave the island. During the war, I had been prisoner in Russia for three years. There, prisoners had to work hard. Since Prieto was an intelligent man and had people under his command, it occurred to me that he had been punished and was serving his sentence. Yes, that's what I thought. One day, an inspector came to control our passports and that sort of papers: he must have been looking for spies. The inspector had a daughter, but he didn't bring her over to the island; he left her at the other side. This police inspector was wearing a colonial helmet; I'll never forget that. He told Prieto: `Since you know Bariloche well, let's go to town this weekend and have a good time'. So they left on Sunday. Prieto took the inspector and his daughter for a walk to Cerro Otto. Of course...she's now his wife! He was a free man; yet he stayed on the island day and night, fully devoted to his work."

While work continued at a feverish pace, Dr. Richter busily collected instruments and equipment in Córdoba and Buenos Aires. After the important meeting in which Perón decided the creation of the Huemul laboratory, Richter took the opportunity to visit the San Miguel Observatory, a Jesuit institution in the outskirts of Buenos Aires, and met its director, Father Juan A. Bussolini. The Observatory dealt mainly with Solar physics, but it also manufactured Geiger-Muller radiation detectors. Richter was favorably impressed when he saw them and ordered some for the experiments he was conducting in Córdoba. There are no written records about these experiments. However, in 1963, Richter wrote a letter to Scientific American in New York, reporting a discovery he allegedly made in Córdoba, on October 3, 1949. The letter was never published.

Yet, its content is interesting because it throws light on Dr. Richter's scientific ideas [24].

The origin of the letter was an article published by H. W. Lewis in Scientific American [25] dealing with ball lightning phenomena.

Ball lightning, or balls of fire, are rather unusual atmospheric events which occur during heavy storms. "The evil light" in popular jargon, consists of ionized matter, or matter in which electrons get loose from the atoms, giving rise to uncompensated electrical charges. Thus, a ball of fire is a highly-electrified object, which, for reasons still unknown, lives for a few seconds and, occasionally, even minutes. The few registered observations have been described as a glowing suspended ball approximately a foot in diameter. The ball is reportedly capable of passing through windows and going down chimneys. In the common sense of the word, a real phenomenon!

In his article, Lewis stated: "If some day it should be discovered that ball lightning consists of a stable plasma configuration, such a discovery will be instrumental for a thermonuclear energy-production program."

Undoubtedly, this statement must have prompted Richter to write to the journal's editor: "Since I am not only one but, to the best of my knowledge, the first one who put forward the concept of a ball-lightning-controlled fusion reactor and even got some interesting experimental results (in 1948/52), I should like to contribute to the basic problem of ball-lightning by putting forward an even more exciting (so I hope) concept".

In the following paragraphs of his letter to Scientific American Richter describes what he thinks is a promising laboratory approach for studying this phenomenon and further on he makes reference to his experiments of October 3, 1949: "...when testing a self-confining plasma system, a tremendous but quite unexpected flash of visible and ultraviolet radiation for the first time revealed the existence of a suddenly collapsing, energy-storing plasma configuration."

Richter claimed that this observation proved the phenomenon's "electrodynamic" origin.

Therefore, according to this document, while Richter was still at his Córdoba laboratory before leaving for Huemul, he experimented with man-made balls of fire in order to explore the possibility of obtaining confined and controllable plasmas.

These and other thoughts which at the time commanded his attention were recorded in a long report [26] which his colleague and former assistant, physicist Wolfgang Ehrenberg, wrote upon his return to Munich in 1958.

The acquaintance with Ehrenberg dated back to the 1930's. In 1939 they had discussed the existence of confined plasma and the cross-like configuration of a pair of electrodes perpendicular to a pair of magnetic poles. According to Ehrenberg's paper, Richter had already experimented with this configuration and had shown him a photograph of the results.

Years later, in 1942 and `43, they worked together at the private laboratory of Baron Manfred von Ardenne in Berlin. There, they studied the stability of detonating materials. Occasionally, they also made experiments by bombarding pellets of lead and mercury with fast protons. For this, they used a small van de Graaff accelerator in von Ardenne's laboratory.

In August, 1949, Richter asked the Argentine Government to contact his friend Ehrenberg, and a year later both met again in Bariloche. [27]

Upon Ehrenberg's arrival, Richter showed him a film he had taken some months earlier where "the compacted energy at the center of the cross" was clearly visible, that is, where the lines of force of a magnetic field crossed the line between the two electrodes of a spark gap. This same scheme was later used at Huemul. It had apparently been mounted and experimented earlier in Córdoba.

Thus while construction tasks progressed speedily on Huemul, Richter made experiments, gathered equipment and personnel. Regarding the latter, Richter requested only two assistants from Europe: Jaffke and Ehrenberg. Dr. Greinel was also incorporated for a while, but he did not last long [28], and Dr. Pinardi, also at Huemul for a short time, was accused by Richter of indiscretion and was dismissed from the project in August, 1950.

The Big Reactor

Ronald Richter and his wife Ilse arrived in Bariloche in March, 1950. A few days later, on March 22, the local Justice of Peace presented Richter with his Argentine citizenship papers. It was more a government initiative than a request from Richter. Perón liked to introduce him as an Argentine citizen. Nevertheless, a confidential report [29] indicates that Richter also wanted his ID card to bear his Argentine citizenship. The required two-year residency clause was waived in his case.

Following the citizenship ceremony in Bariloche, Richter attended an important meeting in Buenos Aires. Perón wanted General Henneckens, who had succeeded General Savio as head of Fabricaciones Militares, to be informed of the government's atomic plans because this important industrial establishment was going to supply a good part of the heavy equipment needed in Huemul. On that occasion, Perón introduced Richter saying: "Now he's one of us. He has received his citizenship papers."

With Richter in Huemul, the program accorded with Perón in August 1948 was beginning its decisive stage. Virtually all needs had been satisfied. No one could have asked for more means, more support or a more attractive place to work. Huemul Island looked like a motion-picture setting: almost 400 men - soldiers, masons, electricians, carpenters, all working like ants, day and night; heavy machinery; large barges crossing the lake forth and back with trucks full of bricks, lime and cement, often under rough weather which turned the transport through the lake into a risky adventure.

National resources were placed at the project's disposal. Fabricaciones Militares and the Army had been ordered to assign first priority to any request from Huemul. The same applied to brick and cement factories. The Air Force had planes on standby to attend the needs of the project. Air Commander Blason - Colonel Gonzalez's first pilot - flew innumerable times between the southern lake region and Buenos Aires, with occasional stopovers in Córdoba and other cities. There were, in addition, flights to foreign countries to smuggle in strategic materials, particularly from England and the United States. "Under the excuse that our planes had to fly to the Antarctic, we brought lithium from England and the States. Probably half the required materials and equipment was smuggled from abroad." [30]

Also Richter enjoyed, at least at the beginning, ample financial support. Until the creation of the National Atomic Energy Commission in May that year, Colonel Gonzalez had funds from the Migrations Bureau under his responsibility and he was able to use them without much bureaucratic hurdles. As an example, among Colonel Gonzalez' files one finds that in the third week of November 1949, he authorized expenditures for 276 thousand pesos (about 70 thousand dollars of that time), a respectable sum if we note that in today's dollars the figure is more than ten times greater and take into account that civil work expenses were taken care of by General Sauri. Approximately half that amount went to engineer Heriberto Hellmann for construction of electro-mechanical equipment, and the rest was spent by Blason in miscellaneous purchases (optical equipment, drugs, electricity bill, books, etc.)

To complete the profile of a privileged project, there were the top level meetings which allowed Richter to keep a continuous and fluid contact with the President. Though Colonel Gonzalez' role was to look after Richter's needs there was no important meeting with Richter that Perón himself did not attend. And there were many of these meetings. [31]

Evidently, Perón considered the project top-priority. It is not surprising then that soon after Richter left for Bariloche, Perón and Evita planned a visit to the island.

The visit took place on April 8, 1950. During the few hours they spent in Bariloche, Perón, Evita, Richter and his wife socialized much among themselves. Ilse Richter, who spoke Spanish and other languages as well, acted as interpreter. "They held secret conversations" Gonzalez remembered later without hiding his discomfort for having been left out.

Soldiers and workers were dazzled by the presidential visit. For a short while Perón and Evita were the privileged possession of those working on the island. Some details remain vivid to this day: "They gave Pedrocca, the bulldozer driver from Córdoba, a watch. It was a just reward. He worked like mad day and night. He never stopped. They also gave a pair of pistols to Captain Pasolli." [32]

On the island, Perón and Evita saw the molding of the main reactor finished. The visitors were impressed. Its dimensions were staggering: 36 feet high and 36 feet in diameter, sitting on a 60 by 60 ft. concrete slab. Men working on this structure seemed like Lilliputians in Gulliver's country. Evita was moved, and she ordered Pasolli to increase the soldiers' wage to match that of a civilian mason. [33]

A month later, in May, concrete was poured. The reactor was a huge solid cylinder of cement, pebble and sand except for a central hollow space. Roughly 14 thousand cubic feet of cement, equivalent to almost 20 thousand cement bags, were used. According to Richter's specific instructions, no iron was used for the structure. The task took some 72 hours of continued work. Bertolo, the able Italian immigrant remembered: "We worked for 3 days, in three shifts, sixty people each shift, and 2 concrete mixers, non-stop to avoid any cracks. If work stops for an hour or so, the concrete is no good. One night, while I was on shift, it started raining cats and dogs. The concrete slid down from elevated towers into buckets and from the buckets into chutes. There were two or three of us inside making sure the mix settled without leaving holes. It was raining so hard that concrete turned gooey and slipped inside my boots. It made a nasty wound on my ankle. I still bear the scars, the cement burned my skin. A month later, we ripped off the plank molding and walked inside. There was still a tremendous amount of heat from concrete setting. Just imagine, a cement block 36 by 36 ft. and we had used fast-setting cement!"

While this work was in progress, brick walls 3 ft. thick and 50 ft. high were built around the reactor, and a wooden structure to hold a gable roof was placed on top. The monumental reactor structure was un-planked in June. It must have seemed like unveiling a gigantic statue. There was nothing like it on the island nor elsewhere. Those who took part in this spectacular undertaking deserved feeling proud. In Prieto's words, "everyone shared the conviction that the project was of a crucial national importance". When the big reactor was `unveiled', surely it was a moment of joy.

That moment did not last long, however. With the reactor in full view, Richter directed his attention to the 2" radial tubes pointing towards the inner chamber axis. The tubes were made of iron and embedded in concrete. Richter had seen, elsewhere on the island, some fiber-cement tubes 8" in diameter. Curtly and without bothering to explain, he ordered the iron tubes to be replaced by the latter. [34]

People around him were flabbergasted. Nobody knew him too well yet. Sometimes Richter adopted enigmatic attitudes so that his assistants had grown used to some eccentricities after four months. Prieto remembered that "occasionally Richter turned his gaze inward, as if he was staring into a vacuum, completely oblivious of everything around him." Hellmann in turn recalled: "He was a mixture of child and sage; an infant with scientific notions. I always thought he was a case of split personality." [35]

Hellmann was not the only one to mention the split personality syndrome. Richter was simultaneously good-natured and authoritarian, carefree and exacting. While he seemed oblivious of everything around him, he was also extremely scrupulous and severe. Again, in Prieto's words: "Before Richter came to Bariloche, he had no say in construction details and work progressed rapidly. When he arrived, work began to lag. He inspected every single detail and introduced all kinds of modifications. He was extremely meticulous... you know, German perfection."

Astonishment turned to dismay. The head of Huemul Project was not joking. He had apparently carried out studies which indicated the need to have larger openings. "The task of removing concrete-embedded tubes was virtually impossible. Somebody even thought of bringing special equipment from the United States to do the job", Prieto recalled. When Richter was told of the difficulties this modification entailed, he replied that in that case the whole cylinder would have to be demolished. Capt. Pasolli tried desperately to find a sensible solution. He was practically at his wit's end, when Richter added an argument in favor of demolishing the whole piece and do it again as he pointed out that a chimney would have to be built on top of the reactor but in the present configuration the chimney would interfere with the roof girders. To support his idea, Richter said it might even be better to build the reactor underground, excavating the rock. The girders-chimney argument by itself was obviously insufficient as demolishing the whole structure instead of simply changing the location of the girders did not make sense. He also mentioned that recent experiments conducted in lab #2 indicated the convenience of a rocky environment.

Changes of this nature would have been totally unacceptable in a conventional engineering project, but what of an atomic project, where new ground had to be broken at every turn? Or was this a case of outrageous lack of planning? Pasolli and Prieto were bewildered.

At this stage, Richter was informed of a crack in the concrete wall near the inner-chamber access. Prieto recalled: "We saw the crack first; Richter had not yet seen it when he said the tubes had to be removed. Imagine... the work was already completed, in accordance with his specifications...!" Richter declared the crack unacceptable and he said there was no doubt now that the reactor had to be demolished. Prieto and Pasolli considered that the crack could easily be repaired. Though they knew next to nothing about nuclear physics, they correctly guessed that if the wall was to shield the neutrons and other radiations, a well-repaired crack offered no problems. If, on the other hand, the structural balance of the wall was at issue, a small crack 1 and a half foot high and few inches wide and deep was negligible in a wall 12 feet thick. And along this line they argued against the scientist, to no avail.

Richter maintained his stance: he did not admit that the crack be repaired and insisted that the reactor be torn down. A long, heated discussion followed between he and Capt. Pasolli. The latter found very hard to understand Richter's arguments and accept that the huge structure had to be shattered.

This was the first major conflict that Gonzalez was called upon to settle, after the previous events in Córdoba. Colonel Gonzalez set off for Huemul, took pictures, heard arguments on both sides, and returned to Buenos Aires not knowing what to do. [36] Technically he wasn't knowledgeable enough and therefore he could only analyze the problem from a political point of view. Should he acquiesce to Pasolli's arguments and risk a confrontation with Richter? That would be the same as facing Perón himself. He surmised that if they did not know what Richter wanted to do with the reactor, they could not deny him the last word. To demolish the reactor seemed absurd...but how to be sure?

Richter remained inflexible, though not passive. In June, he and Blason flew to Córdoba. There, he watched the first test of the new plane Pulqui II, which, by the way, nearly killed Behrens, the famous German pilot. [37] Richter, aware of Tank's influence on Perón, wished to secure his support in case Colonel Gonzalez decided to back Pasolli. What could he do aside from discussing the matter with his friend? It is most likely that a report dated June 20, 1950 [38] sent by Tank to Brigadier Heriberto Ahrens, head of the Aviation Warfare School, was aimed at emphasizing Richter's scientific credibility and his achievements on Huemul. This was also a convenient, uncommitted, way for Richter to let the Government know about the progress of the Project. The report mainly describes Richter's ideas and in fact constitutes one of the few written records on his ideas. The technical details in it leave little doubt that Richter actively participated in its preparation.

Among other technical matters, Tank includes a very significant statement: "Up to the present, Dr. Richter's efforts have been focused mainly on developing the control process and, as anticipated, they have been successful." If Richter had, in effect, solved the nuclear-fusion control problem, he should also have obtained the fusion reaction itself, or be very close to it. Otherwise, the term "success" could not apply. This statement, however, was made by Tank, not by Richter, although this and other paragraphs leave no doubt as to the true authorship of the memorandum. Producing this report and arranging his final destination - Perón himself - in an indirect way, seems to have been the real purpose of Richter's trip to Córdoba. If indeed results of this magnitude had been achieved, demolishing a reactor was unimportant.

One day after the report's date (June 21), Richter flew to Buenos Aires to meet Perón. [39] Obviously, the topic of discussion with Perón was the crack in the wall and the need to pull down the reactor. As Colonel Gonzalez later explained [40]: "The work was carried out under intense rain and snow during three days and two nights and the setting did not work out properly and we got these miserable cracks."

The final decision was up to Perón. The arguments of his two main advisors - Richter and Gonzalez - coincided. Since the project was reportedly a success, what else was there to do?

The President decided the reactor to be demolished.

CNEA and DNIT

On May 31, 1950 Perón signed Decree # 10936, which gave birth to the Argentine National Atomic Energy Commission (CNEA). The need to provide a proper administrative framework for the activities on Huemul was by that time clear. The project could not continue at its current rate of investment under the umbrella of the Migrations Bureau.

The decree, signed by all ministers and secretaries, declared that the State could not ignore Atomic Energy developments on account of its "multiple derivations... insofar as practical uses and applications are concerned." It stressed the need for safety measures against radiation effects and its practical applications to medicine. It dwelt on energy production and its effect on industry and transportation. Finally, it stated the convenience of making a coordinated effort in all atomic matters, so that "the Argentine Republic, detached of any offensive purpose, may engage in these activities with the highest regard for peace and for the benefit of mankind."

The draft of this bill was prepared by Colonel Gonzalez. Albeit a bit stilted, it was at least brief and much to the point. It seems that Gonzalez did not think of a top level entity - as it turned out to be - when he conceived the idea. His main goal was probably counting with an instrument of public administration somewhat more likely than that provided by the budget of the Migrations Bureau. The Ministry of Technical Affairs was to provide the administrative backing and funding and the Commission members would be chosen among ministers and in accordance with the "specific regulations to be issued" (at a later time). This suggests that the constitution of the Commission in itself was not particularly relevant in Gonzalez' mind. On the other hand, the creation of a Secretary General position - which he envisaged for himself - is the specific object of one of the articles of the decree. The functions of the Commission were to coordinate, stimulate and control atomic research in the country, and to propose policies related to radiation safety and defense and better use and application of atomic energy in medicine, industry, transportation, etc. Another article (which had the curious effect of bringing Gaviola briefly back to the fore) established that any individual or entity performing research in this field should report to the Commission.

Probably exceeding Gonzalez' original idea, the Atomic Energy Commission was, up to 1952, presided by Perón himself and the other members were Gonzalez, acting as Secretary General, Raúl Mende, the Minister of Technical Affairs and Dr. Richter. [41]

The creation of the Atomic Energy Commission left no room for doubt regarding the interest of the government in such matters. Up to that time - May 1950 - there had been only rumors regarding the works on Atomic Energy, kindled by the most unusual movements of building materials around Bariloche and the extraordinary illumination seen every night on Huemul Island. Knowledge of what was going on was scarce and rather limited to gossip. Confidentiality was imposed on every man on the Island and to a large extent obeyed.

The decree now made this activity official and the press reacted in various ways, in some cases briefly - as The New York Times which allotted a couple of paragraphs to the subject, back on page 7 -, in some others more extensively as for example the International News Service [42] which informed that "political analysts in Buenos Aires are speculating on the extent of activities supposedly undertaken by German scientists in connection with nuclear physics in Argentina". It also reminded readers about certain rumors "heard of late, particularly during these last three years". The level of information was decidedly low. Surprisingly, the author of the dispatch knew nothing about Huemul. He mentions large uranium deposits discovered in the province of Catamarca the previous year, and identifies Dr. Guido Beck as the head of a "nuclear physics laboratory in

Córdoba, where Argentine uranium is processed", a double mistake. It is clear that the reporter had read Mizelle's articles of 1947 and little more as he goes on pointing out that American occupation authorities in Germany had denied Heisenberg permission to travel to Argentina. "According to US diplomats in Buenos Aires, there are several German atomic experts working in Argentina, though the US and Great Britain got hold of the best in the wake of the war." It was a long article, but outdated. It shows, though, that Bariloche and Huemul were too remote a place for journalists and that little was known on the subject at the time. Huemul activities had scarcely transcended beyond the shores of the island.

Agustin Rodriguez Araya, a vehement anti-Peronist political exile in Uruguay, seemed to be somewhat better informed. He used the atomic subject to lash out his fury against Perón and the Argentine military. His accusations were published in the Folha da Manha de Sao Paulo. [43] He said the Argentine Government wanted the bomb and the pacifist sentences of decree 10936 could not hide the military's real intentions of dominating Latin America and the world. Beyond these exaggerations, Rodriguez Araya does mention Huemul Island with the remark, "the Argentine military are so presumptuous as to occupy a zone which by all means should be reserved for tourism exclusively."

The creation of CNEA not only gave official status to atomic research in the country; it strengthened Gonzalez' unofficial but growing role as funding agent of most diverse initiatives. Indeed, while Gonzalez served as financial provider of Richter, he gradually started to assist other odd projects as well. These other projects were somewhat related to science and technology and Gonzalez, even though he was formally only Director of Migrations, felt it was his duty to oblige.

In a lengthy report [44] written years later, Gonzalez listed some of the programs he helped to fund in those days besides Huemul: a campaign against goiter and leukemia; General Pujato's first expedition to the Antarctic; a study of deuterium content in the Copahue Volcano region; a study and development of a remote-control submarine torpedo, and others.

The creation of an Atomic Energy Commission was the first step to tidy things up a bit. But something more was needed if this Commission was going to be faithful to his name and purpose (atomic energy), and other proposals were going to be funded at the same time. This explains why Gonzalez himself submitted a new draft a few months later aimed at the creation of a new institution, the National Department for Technical Research (DNIT). Perón signed this new decree without reservation. It did help to fill a vacuum. Gonzalez was sensitive enough to perceive the need of it and sensible enough to recognize the convenience of turning to experts to decide which project deserved funding, that is, people who could tell quackery from sane technological projects. The DNIT could do just that.

Viewed with a historical perspective, this development, in itself a positive move, is however paradoxical as well as sad. This new Institution was born almost exactly two years after the project of Gaviola and others had been buried. To the extent that both had common goals it is apparent that two years had been wasted. But actually it was worse than that because the projects discussed in the Senate were far more ambitious and, particularly that proposed by the senators Sosa Loyola and Luco, enjoyed the full support of the scientific community, a very important ingredient. Colonel Gonzalez' DNIT was marred by the absence of able physicists.

Gonzalez was aware of this limitations and he sought help. Little contact he had with scientists. His first contact was Dr. Cruz, the Cuyo University rector, who in turn recommended Mr. Otto Gamba, an able Chemical Engineer. Later on, Father Juan Bussolini and Navy Captain Engineer Manuel Beninson also acted as his advisors. It wasn't much. He had failed to relate to upper echelons of scientific circles and was hesitant even to try to approach them. He knew scientists were a difficult lot, yet he needed advisors.

Gonzalez was in the midst of this dilemma when a most welcomed surprise solved the problem for him. Gaviola himself offered to give him a hand.

Gaviola had read the decree establishing CNEA where it was stated that any atomic-related subject ought to be reported to the Commission. His famous memorandum on nuclear activities which years earlier had seemed so promising, had been forgotten by everyone except its author. It is apparent that Gaviola still wished to participate and on the basis of this clause he sent Gonzalez a copy of his work. In the accompanying letter he said that he was ready to help and would be pleased to supply any further information which might be deemed necessary.

Was Gaviola really willing to collaborate with CNEA? Did he wish to act as advisor to the atomic program and the many other projects that piled up on the Secretary General's desk? Gonzalez could not help being pleasantly surprised at what seemed like a friendly gesture from the most respected physicist in the country. The Colonel had heard all kinds of stories about Gaviola's unconventional personality. His political views were known to be clearly against the government. Yet Gonzalez had never met him personally. So, he chose to assume that the stories about Gaviola were exaggerated, and responded in the most amiable terms: "I wish to convey to you our warmest desire of counting with your valuable scientific collaboration, aware as we are of the great prestige you enjoy among the scientific community in the country".

Ever since Gaviola had tendered his resignation to the Córdoba Observatory in July 1947, he had worked as physics advisor for the Rigolleau Crystal Factory. Actually it amounted to a sort of ostracism imposed by the prevailing political circumstances. However, his own political vocation had remained intact; dormant until conditions changed. Perhaps the creation of CNEA awakened his restless spirit and tempted him to participate in the organization of CNEA and DNIT.

A bit intriguing in view of his unyielding temperament, this attitude of Gaviola suggests that his anti-Peronism was not as strong as it later appeared to be, and that a three year "leave of absence" from the political arena was hard for him to bear. Whatever the motive, he immediately replied to Gonzalez: "I am greatly honored by your invitation to collaborate with these institutions. I am willing to offer my modest scientific assistance at any time if it can be useful to the country. I should like to suggest that such assistance could be materialized - saving your better judgment - by an appointment as scientific advisor to those institutions, or to the Secretary General." The note was dated August 14, 1950. [45]

Dr. Luca Muro, Minister Mende's advisor, went to Córdoba a month later to discuss the terms of the contract with Gaviola. Shortly thereafter, Gaviola travelled to Buenos Aires and signed the contract at the Ministry of Technical Affairs. He was appointed advisor of CNEA and DNIT. Everything seemed ready for Gaviola to start his new job.

However, neither Gonzalez nor Mende ever affixed the final seal to Gaviola's contract. Their good intentions were hampered at the last minute. On the basis of later events, Gaviola assumed that Richter and Gonzalez had quarreled and therefore his services were no longer necessary. [46] But this was not the case.

What really happened was that after signing the contract Gaviola met Mende and the Minister was appalled by Gaviola's comments about the works being carried out at Huemul. According to Gaviola [47] the Minister refused to hear his opinion on the matter claiming that this was Colonel Gonzalez' business. But the truth of the matter is that Gaviola left Mende trembling in his chair greatly disturbed. No doubt Gaviola warring style had not changed. Mende immediately went to Gonzalez. The tone of the conversation was lively remembered by Gonzalez many years later when he confided to the author [48]: "I asked Gaviola to join us to collaborate but he was so pedantic that I could not take it... the least he demanded was that we should become his subordinates."

Family Life, Spies and Other Worries

By late July 1950, a happy event helped soften the hard feelings caused by the demolition of the big reactor. In the very heart of Patagonian territory, Mónica Richter was born. Epsilon - the Siamese cat which according to Richter had been responsible for his coming to Argentina - was no longer the sole recipient of family love. In a personal letter to an old friend in Europe [49], Richter reports that "...the whole family, including Epsilon, is in good health, at an altitude of 2400 ft., by a lake 1000 ft. deep. Monica is growing stronger every day and Epsilon is weighing 10 lb. My wife could not be happier." The Richter family had settled down to a comfortable life in Bariloche and they started to socialize an entertain people at their home. Mónica's birth was celebrated with a big party. Major Monti was one of the guests that night and from his recollections one gets a picture of a very lively party: "Jaffke gained great prestige as barman and many of us had difficulties walking back home that night".

Perón's endorsement of Richter's wish to demolish the big reactor was a strong shot in the arm for the scientist. He had won another battle and his authority and freedom were enhanced by it. The chief of Huemul Project had enough motives to be happy. In the spring of that year Richter wrote letters to some friends which reveal his enthusiasm for his work and his great hopes in the future.

One of these letters was addressed to "Professor Dr. P. Matthies" - that is to say, Kurt Tank. Among other things Richter wrote: "...After much snow, rain and bad weather, the Bariloche area has become beautiful. The lake has turned to an enticing blue and even though this is such a remote place, we are happy here."[50]

He wrote to another friend in England: "For the last eight months I have been living in a place 1200 miles further south (from his previous home in Córdoba), 25 miles away from the Chilean border, surrounded by mountains and lakes. Here in Argentina, particularly this far south, one does not hear much about the war roar in Europe. The Argentineans lack the Europeans' unwholesome experiences; that is why only a muffled rumbling reaches these latitudes. If there was a war, I would much prefer to be in England than in Argentina, because it is there where the western values will be in jeopardy. But who knows what will happen. I apologize for my prolonged silence. The reason will be clear some day; the more interesting life becomes the more silent one has to be." [51]

The same ideas are found in another family letter to a friend in Sweden: "I myself could not have chosen a more interesting life, in spite of the fact that we live in a very remote place and we should feel isolated, but this is not the case though and some day you will learn why." [52]

In another revealing paragraph of this same letter Richter says he is looking for a secretary, and asks his friend whether he knows of someone willing to come, perhaps among his own family: "I would like to avoid a German because I have had bad experiences with imported German people. She should speak English (German is not really necessary), must be intelligent, have a clear mind and a strong will, be ready and able to work with classified material, and be prepared to work around the clock on an irregular schedule. The pay is good with a five-year contract to work in one of the most interesting projects in the world. It sounds impressive, I know, but in time it will be shown to be so." And he closes: "Argentina has no restrictions, life is inexpensive and extremely pleasant; the candidate may enjoy extended trips by airplane, and tax exemptions. Things are done in grand style here."

Richter enjoyed being at the center of a spectacular scientific adventure, and liked to induce people to appreciate that. This is the impression one gets from reading these letters. Moreover, some of his actions suggest that he wanted to make sure his own people also got the message. Such may have been the motivation for taking all members of his group to the movies one evening. The picture, Nubes Negras (Black Clouds), dealt with espionage and the US atomic program, and presumably Richter wanted his people to learn from it what kind of risks they faced themselves. On another occasion he sent everybody to Monti's Regiment shooting range to practice and get prepared to repel potential enemies. One evening in his house he shocked his guests by announcing that radioactivity would cause loss of virility in the men working in laboratory 2. He also added that if one of the experiments went wrong the island could become a mass of glass and it could be necessary to evacuate the population of Bariloche, "although, he said, this was only a remote possibility". [53]

Beyond these anecdotes, life around the atomic laboratory was not free of frictions and problems among workers. There were problems originated in Richter's continuous changes of plans. The case of the big reactor had been the first signal of things to come. As construction work progressed the number of modifications and afterthoughts increased, usually when structures were already well underway.

There were also labor problems with individuals falling victims of Richter's authoritarian character. Sergeant Rodriguez was one of the first to be cast off. He was so hurt that he wrote to his friends: "...at least I will never go back to that hell. I was damned. I shall overcome this terrible experience." [54]. Rodriguez was not the last; others were also mercilessly fired.

In those days there were also rumors of espionage. Colonel Gonzalez had an informer in Bariloche (a noncommissioned officer) who periodically sent him intelligence reports. In one of these, he informed that a Chilean citizen had applied to work as brick layer on the island upon arrival from his country. Soon he was found to hold a University degree and to have already been suspect of espionage in another incident further south a few years earlier. [55]

Italian born Giovanni Pinardi, professor at the Cuyo University in the Mendoza Province for many years, was another case, probably overblown by Richter himself. He had been hired by Colonel Gonzalez after returning from a stay in the US, and had reportedly had access to classified information. He was charged with giving away some of this information abroad and fired, although the charges were never substantiated.

The Pinardi affair would have been really minor - little he had to report anyway - had not been used by both Gonzalez and Richter for their own personal purposes. The relationship between these two men was already showing signs of strain. Gonzalez had backed Richter in the case of the reactor to please Perón rather than Richter and was not really convinced that the scientist was right in his claim that the demolition of the reactor was necessary beyond doubt. But the initial impression left after the first battle had only been enhanced by a multitude of small bits of information that the Colonel collected from his men in Bariloche, during the following months. The physicist was eccentric and that had most everybody confused. It was difficult to evaluate his judgement and to be certain about the sanity -or insanity- of more than one of his decisions. Progress was slow and people started to wonder whether better planning was indeed so foreign to atomic laboratories. Was it really impossible to plan ahead and avoid so many changes? Was the apparent waste of effort actually inevitable? The recipient of all these worries was, of course, Colonel Gonzalez. After several weeks of consistent evidence in this direction, it is possible to imagine the Colonel feeling the impulse of taking over the steering wheel and start imposing his own pace and planning. He was probably waiting for the opportunity to walk onto the stage to play a new, stronger role when the Pinardi affair took place. He seemed to have surmised that this case gave him a good chance.

On August 7 Gonzalez sent a note to Bariloche addressed to "Prof. Richter and his group" with the indication that the addressees had to sign it to prove they had received the message -a blunt signal, perhaps a bit clumsy, of a new style-. It said: "Please be advised that Prof. Giovanni Pinardi's appointment has been discontinued and that he will be put on trial for having disclosed secret information to foreign officials on research currently under way in this country".

The stern tone was not casual. Gonzalez wanted to test the extent of his authority and instructed his informer to report back on Richter's reaction as soon as possible. Dated August 14 the answer was: "Your communique caused an excellent effect. Dr. Richter immediately summoned his staff. It was apparent that Dr. Richter was impressed not only by the content of your note but also by the formal letterhead and seals. He said that Dr. Pinardi had made a bad impression on him when they had met in Buenos Aires and for that reason he had been careful not to make sensitive comments to him about the project." [56]

Gonzalez' note elicited a prompt reply from Richter. He emphasized the importance of keeping everything secret and insisted on security. At the same time, he pointed out the important progress achieved at Huemul. He wrote to both Perón ("Hochverehrter Herr Praesident") and Gonzalez ("Hochverehrter Herr Oberst"), gently apologizing for not doing it in Spanish. He said he was certain that no valuable information had been leaked out. Yet he recommended that internal and external security be reinforced. "If the secret is guarded until the necessary facilities to produce atomic energy are completed, the practical success is assured. In recent weeks, important experiments have been carried out yielding important results, so that success is not a mere possibility now but the certain outcome." In his letter to the President he also adds: "Thanks to your foresight, the Pilot Plant at Huemul will soon be recognized as one of the most important research centers in the world."

Encouraged by the President's unfaltering support, Richter acted very much on his own. It made Gonzalez uneasy. Gonzalez' informer felt the same way. His comments and descriptions in the routine "Secret and Strictly Confidential" reports to Gonzalez, reveal data which never come to the surface in an official document of public nature. These confidential messages contain information of particular value because they provide a naive picture of the growing personal conflicts developing in parallel to the atomic adventure.

Soon after, Gonzalez sent another note to Bariloche, also on official stationary, indicating a strict schedule for the experimental program; an obvious reference to the frequent delays which according to Captain Pasolli were entirely due to lack of planning. The Colonel also warned against invading other people's areas of responsibility. He was indeed testing his muscle, reaching further out than ever before. He was obviously unimpressed by Richter's claims of new results; he wanted proofs, and suspected -correctly- that the erratic way the project seemed to follow had to have a negative effect on the anticipated program. By that time Gonzalez appears to have assumed that he had to reach the point of setting down a schedule by himself.

Again, according to the informer in Bariloche, the effect of this new memorandum was that "Dr. Richter became aware that his superiors had decided to alter their policy, limiting his power of decision". It is obvious that the informer knew that this was his boss' main concern. The report also indicated that Richter blamed Pasolli for the delays, claiming that the modifications he (Richter) had proposed were minor ones and could never be invoked to explain the slow progress. He also accused Monti and other people of not telling the truth and spreading rumors which only produced distrust "and an unhealthy atmosphere of doubts and ill feelings in Buenos Aires".

Furthermore, Richter was quoted as saying that his recent small scale experiments indicated he was on the verge of success and that he could carry out his project "anywhere else, so he does not care whatever charges may be pushed against him here." At this point, the informer stressed that "Prof. Richter suggested abandoning the project and he said that now more than ever he would not tell anything about his secret experiments".

Somewhat contradictory, the report continued: "The situation has improved sensibly. For the time being though it would not be advisable to insist on warnings since this might make matters worse". It was clearly a case of a very delicate equilibrium and the informer tried to do his best to keep the balance.

The following paragraph further illustrates this point: "From time to time, through formal notifications, Dr. Richter must be told clearly what he is supposed to do regarding various aspects of his work. Such notifications will have the effect of checking his rebellious nature and his tendency to act as if he were lord and master. They will make him feel that he has a task to accomplish of which he is responsible before the law. He will curb his verbal excesses and will be more willing to follow instructions. In conclusion, Dr. Richter has begun to understand that his superiors reward him but also expect results from him." But this was of course mostly wishful thinking. The author of these lines, eager to please his boss, was far from making a realistic judgement of the situation.

Both Perón and Gonzalez worried that Richter might decide to leave the country and quit the project. Just the kind of worry Richter was probably trying to induce. In the occasion of one of Richter's trips to Buenos Aires, the informer remarked: "There is no problem with this trip provided, of course, his daughter remains here." [57]

Actually, the fears were not completely groundless. It was already known to Perón and Gonzalez that when Richter came to Buenos Aires, he frequently paid a visit to the US Embassy. It was natural to wonder what business he had there.

After the war, Richter had tried to go to the Unites States. When Germany surrendered, Richter was in Berlin working in his own laboratory which was funded by his father, a wealthy industrialist [58]. According to his own version [59] when the Russians walked into Berlin, he destroyed the laboratory with Jaffke's help and, aided by the Americans, he fled into West Germany. There he met Lieutenant Colonel Elmer G. Stahl, who took an interest in his work. In Stahl's own words [60]: "During the summer of 1945, when the Russians and the Allies tried to recruit German scientists, I heard about Richter and met him. At that time Richter wanted to come to the US and I tried to get him a visa. Later Richter went to Argentina, and we exchanged letters somewhat regularly for some time".

Stahl does not explain why he failed to get a job for Richter. In 1951, Richter told Argentine reporters his own version,[61] calling it "a funny incident". The story is not quite credible but it gained popularity: "The American Consul, who questioned me at length, asked whether I had children. I said no but I have a cat. The Consul then replied that I could not travel to the States with a cat, and since I loved my cat dearly, I came to Argentina instead."

However, Richter never abandoned the idea of getting a US visa. His correspondence with Stahl had this purpose. In spite of the unlimited support Perón gave him, and his own insistence on keeping a tight lid on his secrets, Richter actively pursued the goal of heading North. In this connection, it is illustrative to quote from a letter written by an official of the US Embassy in Buenos Aires, on August 11, 1950 [62]: "Dear Dr. Richter, Captain Bergeson has indicated to me that he has taken your case to the Navy and he believes they will be able to do something about your visa to travel to the United States and make arrangements for your patents. He has asked me to contact you and ask you a copy of the contract Mr. Stahl sent to you. He suggests you write him a letter explaining briefly what you promised to Mr. Stahl and indicating that, since Mr. Stahl could not meet his part of the contract, you are making an identical proposition to Capt. Bergeson, in case he should be able to do so within a reasonable period of time. He would also like to have a copy of your letter to Mr. Stahl. This is not essential, but it would help. A copy of Mr. Stahl's contract, plus your letter to Capt. Bergeson, will allow Capt. Bergeson to submit an application for your visa and arrange the commercial and official aspects of your inventions, for mutual benefit. It would also be convenient to have a list of all your inventions ready to be patented, and their commercial use. Capt. Bergeson left Buenos Aires on July 26, and promised to look into this matter upon arrival in the United States. Looking forward to an early reply, yours sincerely. A. J. Sforza"

It is a striking coincidence that this letter should be written on the very same day Richter wrote to Perón and Colonel Gonzalez assuring them that there was no reason to worry about possible leaks of classified information in connection with the Pinardi espionage affair.

Richter Becomes More Independent

Besides the intelligence agent, Colonel Gonzalez had another good informer in Bariloche: his own son. Lieutenant Gonzalez Jr. had been acting as Richter's secretary and interpreter since the day the scientist came to work on Huemul Island.

In September 1950, Lieutenant Gonzalez Jr. wrote to his father [63]: "Dear Dad, together with this note you will receive a letter from Ricardo to which I should like to add a few comments. As you will see he insists on going North. I tried to persuade him otherwise, but he paid no attention. He claims that the project will not suffer if things are well organized in time. I could not change his mind. He also insists in bringing Mrs. M over here at any cost. It might be convenient to tell him that if he wants her as private secretary, he better pays her from his own pocket and she makes her own lodging arrangements. This might help to quiet him down a bit for a while. We also talked about his scientific assistants. I told him that you wanted to know the fields and levels of expertise required, so that in case these people could not be brought from Europe, we could try to find appropriate Argentine graduates. He did not want to answer and quickly changed subjects. It is very difficult to deal with him. I tried to make him understand that in spite of our efforts, because of the present situation in Europe, we may be unable to trace these two people after all. It was useless. He argued that our people lacked experience and that the matter was urgent. Then I asked him again to name the specialties, out of sheer curiosity I said, but he just rambled off in another direction. In short we are just like in the beginning. That's all for now. Warmly, your son, Goyi."

The letter is a genuine testimony of the growing difficulties involved in the relationship between Richter (none other than `Ricardo') and the Colonel. The latter had shown his cards perhaps too soon, while Richter kept his winning ace as long as the President was on his side. The letter shows that by that time Richter's intentions to go to the United States were openly known. This did not make the scientist any more giving in other matters such as his demands for a new secretary (perhaps someone recommended by his Swedish friend?) or two new - non Argentine - assistants.

Not only the authority conflict remained unsolved but Richter acted increasingly as "lord and master" (as the Bariloche informer had put it) giving explanation of his actions to no one.

This attitude became more apparent in a long report he sent to Buenos Aires some months later, written in German, entitled "Organisationplan Projekt Huemul", which shows the extent to which he wished to secure full independence for himself while at the same time he was obsessed by secrecy, actually two aspirations amounting to practically the same thing.

The plan was contained in a single spaced, four-page report marked `Top Secret'. [64] An organizational chart in the first page indicated that the Director of the Project exercised direct control over the operations group working at the Atomic Plant as well as over the information service. Everything else - power plant, constructions, personnel, purchases, health protection, etc. - fell under the responsibility of the Secretary General of CNEA (i.e. Colonel Gonzalez), who - it was made clear - was subordinated to the Director of the Project.

The first and longer part of the report dealt with security procedures. It stated: "An essential condition for the successful operation of the Huemul Atomic Plant is that the island be completely isolated from the rest of the world. There will be a special guard with precise instructions to open fire against any person who fails to heed the first warning to stop. Likewise, guards will open fire against any vehicle drawing near the island without previous notice." All personnel were required to carry guns "to prevent secret agents from entering the premises". The mainland guards would forbid anybody, civilian or military - whatever the rank- to cross over to the island, adding as a gesture towards Perón, "the President may grant special clearances."

A watch tower with a beacon and a long range machine gun was to be installed at the highest point of the island. Two guardians had to be there at all times. They were to be able to watch the lake during the night but illumination should be cycled at irregular intervals "so as to confuse foreign agents". Patrol boats were to circle the island in opposite directions at the slightest signal from the watch tower. "This is how it should be done in order to save fuel", Richter pointed out.

The report also indicated that "ultra-secret laboratories" were to have double guard and that the set illumination plan was to be kept "top secret to avoid difficulties in case secret agents manage to come to the island", and for such circumstances an "assault" boat must be permanently on the alert to transport troops. The main task of the Bariloche garrison in this case was to "cut off the escape route of foreign invaders helped by gun boats on the alert".

The document then specified what to do in case of an atomic explosion. Among other indications, "everyone was to follow the Director's boat to avoid serious atomic injuries", because the Director's boat was equipped with Geiger counter to measure radiation. It is pointed out that "it is very unlikely that the town of Bariloche may be affected by the danger of radioactivity or explosion", and detailed instructions of what to do in such a circumstance follow.

The last part of the plan deals with the organization of the Project, though concern for security is always present. For instance, it is stated that "an independent administration will help to keep the work on the island totally isolated", and it is recommended that all information about fuel consumption, salaries, electric power, rank of employees, etc. be kept classified. The big reactor must be continuously illuminated to avoid the risk of sabotage. It is interesting, in this regard, that Richter should indicate the order of priority for constructions: first the watch tower, second, the big reactor, third, the power plant.

Finally, the report emphasizes the urgency with which all purchases have to be carry out. "The administration must make sure to meet the delivery terms. Purchasing agents in the United States and England must be notified that delivery of materials must be given first priority and most urgent attention following the President's personal orders. Otherwise the production of atomic energy will suffer considerably."

Since the plan assigned the Secretary General of CNEA the responsibility for all administrative duties, it followed that Richter not only looked upon Gonzalez as his subordinate (and not the other way round as the Colonel liked to believe) but also placed him under the spotlight as the likely target if there were delays. A wise move: Gonzalez had tried to force Richter to follow a strict time table; now if progress did not follow the schedule it was going to be Gonzalez´s fault.

This conflict, which began in mid-1950 with the demolition of the reactor structure, then with the Pinardi affair and later with other incidents, finally forced Perón to adopt drastic measures in an ineffectual attempt to conform both men.

Probably, Richter suspected that Gonzalez would not be happy with this "Organisationplan", so to avoid misunderstandings, he cleverly finished off the report with a definite remark: "It must be borne in mind that the Director, as heretofore, is solely responsible to the President. CNEA will provide assistance without interfering or curtailing the Director's independence previously agreed upon with the President."

By late 1950, the virtually complete autonomy exercised by Richter was particularly apparent by the frenzied pace with which he ordered equipment and supplies. The role of Gonzalez had merely become limited to channel these orders and... pay the bills.

At that time Richter's main supplier was Mr. Heriberto Hellmann, a German electro-mechanical engineer. He was responsible for the heaviest equipment installed in Huemul. Hellmann was a former employee of the German company AEG and had been sent to Argentina in 1937, with a three-year contract. War hampered his return home and he took residence in Buenos Aires. When he was introduced to Colonel Gonzalez by a mutual friend in mid-1949, he had already established himself as the prosperous owner of HAMAC Co., the Argentine substitute for AEG.

Shortly afterwards Hellmann met Richter. "Richter was looking for someone to advise him on electrical and mechanical installations. He knew little of electricity. While in Germany, Richter had worked mostly in chemistry. He had specialized in catalyzers and knew chemistry as well as physics. Richter told me that his work in Germany had made him famous and for that reason he had been taken to England. His working style was odd. He was suspicious of almost everybody and did not have scientific collaborators in his laboratory. There were assistants but they were not scientists", Hellmann remembered years later. [65] "Richter indicated to me the things he needed, an electromagnet of such a diameter and such magnetic field, etc. I was probably the only person with whom he discussed his ideas. Once he told me that in order to achieve high temperatures, he had to build a small sun. I asked him how he would control it and he replied: `that's why I need the magnet; to hold the ball in place'. But the question of the magnet came later, in the second half of 1951. It all started differently."

On December 9, 1950, Hellmann and Richter signed an agreement in Bariloche stating that a previous order for an 800 Ton electromagnet -quoted at about 5 million pesos (1.25 million dollars) - was dropped and that Hellmann was to build instead 10 coils of 3 ft. in diameter capable of managing 150 Amp, a matching power generator, a couple of large inductance coils and a few other smaller items including carbon electrodes for a spark gap and 1500 ft. of high frequency cable. The cost balance was about even as the new items compensated the electromagnet.

Hellmann had already been working for Richter a few months and he had become used to the frequent modifications in his purchase orders. They were a nuisance of course and the document signed on December 9 was just a subterfuge which Hellmann thought could help to stop the streak of changes. But he was wrong.

Actually Richter seemed to feel proud about this trait of his: "I hope that you have grown accustomed to the heavy load of my orders", he had written a few days earlier, on November 21, "I am anxiously expecting the first test coil." He closed here and then added, "URGENT NEW ORDER: Two new coils will be necessary. See Colonel Gonzalez for funds."

Then on December 1 Richter wrote saying the coils should have no iron cores. He explained: "The design is more difficult than I first thought. Jets of hot gases must go through the coils´ axis and the walls must withstand temperatures of 300 to 600 degrees centigrade. Probably they must be made of copper or porcelain."

In that same letter Richter asks Hellmann to fly urgently to Bariloche as "we have achieved some very interesting results and I would like to talk to you personally about them." It was during this trip that the above mentioned agreement was signed in order to define an entirely new package of experimental equipment.

It is possible that Richter had another reason to ask Hellmann to go to Bariloche. He had learned that Colonel Gonzalez had offered Hellmann a contract as advisor. Hellmann was already working for the project as Richter's advisor, why would Gonzalez also wanted his services? Was it necessary to make a new contract? Was Gonzalez perhaps trying to secure the loyalty of the man who knew about the intimate details of Huemul Project more than anyone besides Richter?

The letter of December 1 reveals Richter's uneasiness: "I should also like to discuss with you the contract Gonzalez is preparing for you." Indeed, Hellmann knew a lot, the power requirements, the specifications of the voltaic arc, the technical difficulties, the changes, the ordered equipment which was no longer needed, etc. These were details which not even Ehrenberg or Jaffke knew. Hellmann's loyalty was of crucial importance for Richter to avoid interferences from Gonzalez. The conflict between the scientist and the Colonel was taking a new turn which disturbed Richter. It was like a chess game and the offer to Hellmann was Gonzalez' latest move.

Richter's letter of December 1 was longer than usual. It included a request for another insulator and announces the need of more coils. Also he asks for a high power switch (to handle 10 million watts!) for "a huge voltaic arc" of up to 50 thousand volts and 200 Amp DC. In this connection, he says "recently Jaffke almost killed himself from an accidental discharge". Towards the end of the letter the excitement grows and new ideas pop up: "it just occurred to me that you could make the new coils similar to the large coil you already sent me although perhaps there is no enough room to accommodate them."

It is understandable that after reading this letter Hellmann would wish to hold his client's "creativity" down to within manageable limits. The making of a document precisely defining what was wanted, had this purpose, and Hellmann got it, as indicated, on December 9. But with little success.

After the meeting in Bariloche, there were other letters. One dated December 30 was labelled SECRET. There Richter describes his ideas on how to reach even higher currents and asks Hellmann's opinion. He suggests that instead of 200 Amp the generator delivered 2000 Amp. "With this we could achieve more than 4 million watts a second. I need your opinion on how to have the coils reach this value". And he asks, "how much iron, what gaps and which quantity of copper would be necessary?" There are other technical details which end up confusing Hellmann, as he finds it difficult to follow Richter's spry thinking.

There were also problems with the buildings, some of which were almost ready. Richter worried that the new generator will require a new building. "However a new building could be ready by the time you deliver the new equipment", he says. "Another possibility is to get a 3000 Amp generator," he adds. "I would be satisfied if we go beyond one million watts a second. I am anxious to hear your opinion on this. In case these ideas are feasible, we should act quickly so that Colonel Plantamura, who is already in Europe, gets whatever you need. Possibly you could use copper pipes to cool the coils with water. We shall not be limited by the size of the plant. All previous requests stand as they were, just in case these ideas cannot be implemented."

On January 9 Richter wrote again indicating that it was better to have only one coil. As a justification he says: "In order to make it easier for you I reluctantly agreed with the construction of 10 coils, but after January 1 we have restudied the problem and have concluded that one coil is best." He also indicates that is better to replace the generator by a rectifier. "I do not want to go below 3000 Amp. I regret to alter concepts again but we are in the midst of a flood of new data. You will be pleased when you learn to what purpose your equipment has been used."

It was clear that Hellmann's understandable effort to put an end to the frantic cascade of new ideas was unsuccessful. Actually it seems to have excited Richter's imagination into an even more frenzy state. Hellmann found himself not only incapable of following the pace of orders; he actually found himself paralyzed. What could he do? He did not do much for a while and then something quite unexpected happened.

In a letter to Gonzalez, by mid-January 1951, Richter denounced spurious dealings between Commander Blason and Hellmann. Richter claimed that there was an agreement between the two men and that Blason benefitted from unlawful commissions. Colonel Gonzalez proceeded to question the engineer about it. Was Blason receiving bribes? Hellmann forcibly denied that anything like that had ever occurred. He was really shocked by such an unjustified accusation. Richter had seemed well disposed towards Blason, and certainly towards Hellmann. Why should he wish to cast on them the shadow of suspicion?

Hellmann immediately wrote to Richter demanding a prompt clarification of this most unpleasant situation. "If you fail to do this I shall not be able to continue our collaboration."

He got no answer. But Hellmann never knew that Richter did write to Gonzalez on the back of the very letter he (Hellmann) had sent Richter a few days earlier demanding an explanation. Richter wrote: "When Dr. Hellmann visited Bariloche, he intimated that Commander Blason had been after him with insinuations which could be interpreted as a gesture towards obtaining hush money. There were no witnesses, unfortunately. I would have imagined that Dr. Hellmann was an honorable man." [66]

There was never any substantiation of these charges and they were most probably unfounded. What could have led Richter to do something like that just at that time, when things were progressing -at least for Richter- so well?

One may only wonder, could this have been Richter's next move to discredit his friend and prevent him from becoming Gonzalez' advisor?

"Definitely Positive Results"

The incident with Hellmann was just one more of a long series which included Dr. Greinel, Captain Pasolli, Prof. Pinardi, noncommissioned officer Rodriguez, optic expert De La Fuente and commander Blason, among others, but it was undoubtedly the most serious. Hellmann was the man in charge of supplying the equipment for Huemul. Without his collaboration it was like going back several months. A lot of planning would come to nothing without him. Extremely annoyed by Richter's attitude towards Blason, and even ignoring that the scientist had also tainted him, Hellmann stopped all work for Huemul.

Obviously this meant a heavy additional burden for the project management, and the bewildered Gonzalezes - father and son - who were committed to please Perón's wishes, found it increasingly hard to cope with Richter's eccentricities.

When the situation was reaching unbearable limits, and even though the equipment supply had been discontinued for some time, the news that Richter had achieved success, reached Buenos Aires.

It was in the afternoon of February 16, 1951. Jaffke had been performing a series of experiments that day in Laboratory 2. He had triggered a voltaic arc inside a cylinder containing a mixture of lithium and hydrogen. A spectrograph and a couple of Geiger counters were used to register the electromagnetic radiation emitted by the elements in the arc. On the spectrograph focal plane, a photographic plate was readied to record the spectrum of the burning elements. Once developed the spectrum on the plate appears as a series of thin vertical lines, unless very high temperatures are reached in the arc in which case the lines should broaden. The purpose of using a spectrograph was just that: to obtain evidence of very high temperatures. If this occurred, it would mean that the temperature of the burning material had reached the required value to unleash thermonuclear reactions, and the thermonuclear radiation should trigger the Geiger counters.

As soon as Jaffke had the plates developed, he took them over to Richter. When Richter saw them, he jumped excitedly and left to see Captain Gonzalez Jr. Prieto remembered that memorable day [67]: "That afternoon I was talking to the Captain in his office about my transfer to Buenos Aires. I was tired and discouraged and wanted to leave for the Capital. Richter rarely came to this office. That day, he unexpectedly showed up. Then I left the office. They must have been talking for about half an hour. When they finished I went back to see the Captain and he said to me: 'Come on Prieto, lift up your spirit. Look what Dr. Richter had just brought me: definitely positive results!'".

Colonel Gonzalez was vacationing in the hot springs of Copahue when he got the news. He immediately went to Bariloche and once there - according to Gonzalez' testimony [68] - Richter told him that a few days earlier thermonuclear reactions had been achieved in the course of an experiment. He invited Gonzalez, his son and Colonel Plantamura to witness a similar experiment. He took them to the "small reactor" - a cylindrical reflector 10 ft. high by 6 ft. in diameter with cement walls 2 ft. thick. "At the time of the explosion, we observed that all control devices, oscillographs and detectors reacted strongly and were triggered into action. The spectrograph did likewise; the lines moved, there was a change in color and a very strong light on the plate." From this description, it would seem that for demonstration purposes Richter replaced the photographic plate in the spectrograph - which is opaque - for a semitransparent one, probably ground glass. Thus his visitors could observe the spectrum from outside the instrument. Colonel Gonzalez remembered seeing something just like it in a photographic plate that Richter later brought to Buenos Aires. That plate showed a "whitish round halo, to which Father Bussolini assigned great importance." [69]

A few days later, Colonel Gonzalez had a meeting with Perón. According to his own recollections, he proposed to hold a demonstration in the presence of experts "which I insisted should be all Argentineans". Perón agreed. However, it was not carried out. A new incident interrupted the brief span of hope and joy; technically, of lesser importance than the crisis involving Hellmann, but far more dramatic otherwise, it forced Perón into an unprecedented move.

According to some witnesses [70], the garrison commander in Bariloche decided to visit the island. Major Monti was no longer in charge. He had been relieved of his command as a result of having imposed sanctions to an officer who had cheered the name of Perón and Evita while waving his beret during a political gathering. A colleague tried in vain to dissuade Monti to do that, aware that his action would backfire in Peronist circles. Eventually the officer got a minor punishment and Monti was transferred to Buenos Aires. He was replaced by Colonel Fox by the end of the year 1950.

Apparently Colonel Fox was not told in time of Richter's strict regulations concerning visitors to the island. The Colonel surmised that being the island part of his jurisdiction he was naturally entitled to take a stroll through it. He was not, and Richter gave him notice in a rather rude manner. The story was told by Richter to Hellmann, not without the bit of salt Richter was bent to add to his stories. According to this testimony Richter would have pistol pointed the officer upon his arrival at the island's pier to force him to back up and fall into the freezing waters of lake Nahuel Huapi. "The colonel´s beret was left floating", pointed Hellmann when recalling the incident.

In a society used to look upon the military as a privileged cast, it does not take much to guess the consequences of such action by a civilian. However, the episode fortunately did not leak through the public or the military establishment, but only because Perón himself - a general of unquestioned leadership - acted promptly, showing once more, his unequivocal commitment to Huemul Project.

On February 28, the President handwrote to Richter: "My dear friend, thank you for your kind letter of February 27. My congratulations for the results already achieved and I look forward to congratulating you personally for those which shall follow. I regret what happened. I have just been informed about it. The Minister explained it as a result of the rigid military style and of a misunderstanding; it has been overcome now and it will not happen again. Colonel Gonzalez will explain it to you in more detail. My wish is that you may work in quiet and peace there, without any worries. For this purpose, I am enclosing an Executive Order for you to use at your own convenience. In addition, I am taking action to make sure that you have all you need at the island, without having to depend on anything or anyone. With my best wishes, a warm hug and my congratulations for your success so far. Juan Perón."

Richter's complete independence was thus definitely established. The letter from Perón put an end to whatever hierarchical ambiguity might have still existed between Richter and Gonzalez. The text of this letter was invoked by Gonzalez, years later, to detach himself from responsibility when charges were made against the Project, after 1955. [71]

The Executive Order which Perón enclosed in his letter to Richter is a rather unusual document and must rank among the most unconventional ones ever produced. By this Order Richter was endowed with presidential powers, an unprecedented - and possibly unconstitutional - privilege. The document is characteristically handwritten and betrays rush. It is also possible that Perón was annoyed at his subordinates for creating problems instead of solutions and it is thus very likely that he wrote it without consulting anybody; just following his impetus and natural tendency to get things done. He wrote: "To Mr. Prof. Dr. Ronald Richter, Bariloche. Herewith you are designated my sole representative on Huemul Island, where you will exercise, by delegation, my full authority. The atomic research conducted there fall under your exclusive authority and, if the need arises, I shall explicitly indicate in every case if an official will interview you in my name. Colonel Gonzalez, Secretary of the Atomic Commission, will act as liaison in compliance with this order. Also, you will explicitly authorize in every case any person who comes to see me in your name. Buenos Aires, March 1, 1951. Juan Perón."

The President took immediate and forceful action and averted a crisis which could well have killed the project. The equilibrium was reestablished, or, more precisely, the ambiguities, if any remained, were definitely removed. Richter enjoyed full independence and full powers now. It was perhaps a timely reward for his achievements now that positive results had been obtained.

Officials associated with the project got down to analyze what should be done about the sensational discovery. Richter was consulted several times. He and Perón met to decide on a text for the official communique, and the extent of the inevitable press conference. It was a singular, extraordinary, circumstance: what had been achieved on Huemul Island had never been attained anywhere on Earth.

The press conference where it was announced that controlled thermonuclear reactions had been carried out, took place, as described in the first chapter, on March 24, 1951.

The Argentine press reacted in different ways. Some media published exaggerated, distorted versions of the announcement. Most mass oriented or pro-government newspapers - such as El Mundo, Noticias Graficas and particularly Democracia and El Lider - gave ample space to print every favorable comment they could fish around, and used their boldest characters for headlines. There were misleading references to the atomic bomb, to the new Argentine power, and to the very pleasant reaction abroad. Other newspapers were restrained and cautious. Notably the conservative La Nación occupied only a fraction of the first page to report the news under the insipid headline: "The President of the Nation described the work on Atomic Energy".

Some of the popular newspapers played down the tone of disbelief which greeted the news abroad, particularly comments from experts such as Enrico Fermi, Werner Heisenberg and George Gamow. Others, like Clarín, La Nación or El Meridiano (from Córdoba) kept an independent, unbiased, stance and reproduced the foreign dispatches, which were numerous and important, faithfully.

For example, according to Democracia, the International News Service reported that the White House had refused to make any comments on Perón's announcement and that a spokesman for the US Atomic Energy Commission had said that there was no reason to doubt General Perón's or scientist Richter's statements [72]. El Meridiano offered a more honest and complete version of the same press release [73]: "The US Atomic Energy Commission refused to make any comments regarding the Argentine announcement. An official associated with atomic research at an international level said `he did not believe' the Argentine report and another expert called it `suspicious'".

Statements by Senator Johnson, which were skeptical, published in The New York Times, coincided with the version in Clarín. El Mundo, on the other hand, indicated that Johnson expressed his hopes that the announcement was true and, recalling that many European experts had taken refuge in Argentina after the war, he had added that "it was only natural that those scientists should devote themselves to atomic research". [74]

In general US government officials as well as diplomatic circles showed considerable interest. They were inclined, however, to wait for further information before risking an opinion.

Associated Press quoted the opinion of two scientists from the Office of Naval Research. Dr. Lidel said that while a hydrogen bomb could be improved, it was unlikely that a thermonuclear reaction could be used for the controlled liberation of atomic energy for practical peaceful purposes. Dr. Lapp was a bit ironic: "I am surprised that the Russians have not pulled that one. Perhaps the Argentineans are trying it on for size."

The agency also reported other comments. "It is impossible for me to make a statement on the basis of such incomplete information. However, I will say that according to what President Perón has announced, the whole claim seems rather strange", said Enrico Fermi, the man who achieved the first atomic chain reaction in 1942, and had visited Argentina in 1934 reportedly to explore the possibility of settling down in this country. [75]

Prof. Heisenberg, who had agreed to come to Argentina four years earlier invited by Gaviola and Beck, and had been named as a potential atomic advisor to Perón by Mr. Mizelle, also showed skepticism: "I don't think something new in atomic research has been developed in Argentina which American scientists would have not known for a long time." [76]

Other opinions were even more conclusive, perhaps too much, as it became apparent later on. Some scientists believed that temperatures of 20 million degrees up, as in the Sun, could never be realized on Earth in a controlled manner, but only through an atomic explosion. "Even if the Argentineans had achieved the impossible and had found a way to produce these high temperatures, they could not find an appropriate material container to hold these temperatures for some time without melting the container."

Indeed, when Perón made the atomic announcement in 1951, controlled fusion (or thermonuclear) reactions were deemed impossible. Shortly after, however, the subject started to be analyzed and investigated. Study groups on this field of Physics were formed during that decade and journals such as Review of Modern Physics, Scientific American, Nucleonics, and some books, began publishing articles on the subject. Within a few years, controlled nuclear fusion changed from "impossible" to "thinkable", and people started to talk about it as "difficult, but possible".

As early as 1955, the distinguished Indian physicist Prof. H. J. Bhabha, who was chairman of the First International Conference on the Peaceful Uses of Atomic Energy in Geneva, ventured the opinion that the problems of controlled nuclear fusion would be solved in twenty years [77]. That same year, the chairman of the US Atomic Energy Commission officially announced the launching of the Sherwood Project, the first long term research program in the US aimed at studying controlled nuclear fusion for peaceful purposes.

The Swiss Newspaper Die Woche, in a reference to Bhabha's statements in Geneva, pointed out on August 14, 1955, that "such possibility had been mentioned years earlier by atomic expert Richter, who had then been regarded as a quack, because in those days the general opinion was that the high temperatures required could only be obtained through a uranium bomb explosion."

The New York Times continued publishing comments on Perón's press conference almost daily for a week, following the announcement. The April 1, 1951, Sunday edition carried an article signed by Waldemar Kaempffert, of a slightly less skeptical tone than previous ones as it admitted the remote possibility of attaining controlled nuclear fusion reactions. Entitled "Argentina lacks development resources even if in theory its atomic tests are possible", the article gave a most thorough evaluation of possibilities in favor of Perón's atomic claim.

After a brief review of Richter's ideas - "an able Austrian physicist who is now a citizen of Argentina" - Kaempffert recalled the relatively optimistic opinion of Sir John Cockcroft. Prof. Cockcroft was at that time the Head of Harwell Research Establishment in England. In 1932 he and Dr. Walton had devised the first operational particle accelerator and obtained the first artificially induced nuclear reaction with it. In June 1950, at a conference in Oxford he had said: "Someday, we will find the means to obtain temperatures high enough to fuse deuterium nuclei and produce helium."

In his article Mr. Kaempffert also quotes some calculations of Dr. Lloyd Motz, from Columbia University, based on a purely speculative model. The essence of Motz's model was a fast compression of deuterium gas. If this compression could yield pressures of up to 100,000 atmospheres, the gas temperature could reach the minimum required value of one million degrees, explained Kaempffert. In such a circumstance, deuterium nuclei could come together and generate the fusion reaction, releasing energy as they become helium nuclei. A very strong expansion would subsequently occur, together with a sharp decrease in temperature. By this mechanism the vaporization of the container walls could perhaps be avoided. One could then compress the gas again and keep the cycle going this way. Was it possible, though, to get these pressures?

Kaempffert mentions the work of Percy Bridgman, from Harvard, who was able to reach 20,000 atmospheres. Not enough but not too far either. "It just may be that Richter is thinking along these lines", says Kaempffert. "Dr. Motz would not dismiss Richter's project as a technical absurdity." The remaining question was whether Richter could control the process. The article concludes with a note of caution and warning: "Even if all this is theoretically possible, Richter faces tremendous metallurgical problems and mechanical difficulties which are probably beyond Argentina's industrial resources. If we have tried to present the case in the most favorable light, it is not because we accept President Perón's much too optimistic announcement, but to indicate what may be in Richter's mind and why President Perón says scientists in the United States and Europe are on the wrong track. American and European scientists are well aware of the works we have referred to above."

Among the supportive statements published in the press in those days was the report that French physicist Funet-Caplin claimed that the methods described by Richter were quite similar to experiments performed by himself in June and September 1950, in which he successfully attained fusion of atomic nuclei. Funet-Caplin did not specify the methods employed but echoed Richter in that uranium or plutonium were not used, neither large installations such as Los Alamos were required. [78]

Apart from the question of the scientific validity of Richter's results, Perón's announcement did have a non-negligible influence on the origins of a scientific activity devoted to the study of the technical feasibility of using fusion as an alternative energy resource. In particular, the United States Government initiated an effort in this direction already in July 1951. Precisely on July 26, the Atomic Energy Commission met to consider a research grant for Princeton University, proposed by Dr. Lyman Spitzer "for the investigation of transport and reaction phenomena in light elements". The Commission approved a grant of 50 thousand dollars to this effect. In the minutes of that meeting [79] one reads that "it was pointed out that the work to be done was in the area in which physicist Ronald Richter, working in the Argentine, had claimed success."

In that meeting an assistant of Chairman Gordon Dean reported that "as yet it had not been possible to arrange for a visit by an AEC representative to the Argentine to discuss Dr. Richter's finding", to which Mr. Dean said that "he felt the Commission should renew attempts to secure further information on Richter's work."

Dr. Spitzer, a distinguished astrophysicist, was stimulated to think about this problem after reading about the "claims of Argentine researchers" [80] in the March 25, 1951 issue of The New York Times reporting on Perón's press conference the day before. He was just about to leave for a short skiing holiday and reportedly [81] he conceived the first magnetic confining device for hot plasmas, which he called "stellarator", while on the snowed slopes.

The grant awarded to Dr. Spitzer by the AEC on July, 1951 marked the beginning of the US research effort on controlled nuclear fusion.

German aircraft designer Kurt Tank presents the new jet fighter *Pulqui II* to President Juan Perón and others, at the Buenos Aires City Airport, the day of its inaugural flight on February 9, 1951, just one month and a half before Perón´s atomic announcement. Tank escaped to Argentina in December 1947 under false name and immediately was hired by the Government to develop modern aircrafts. Upon arrival he recommended Perón to bring Richter to Argentina. Tank had briefly met Richter in Europe and was impressed by the latter´s ideas on nuclear propulsion for planes.

Trucks loaded with bricks for Project Huemul on rafts crossing Lake Nahuel Huapi in 1950 from Playa Bonita to the island.

At that time and for several months, tons of bricks, cement, and gravel were brought to the island reportedly generating shortages in the construction industry in the country. *Courtesy of H. Campos.*

Between three and four hundred soldiers of the Second Engineering Corp from Neuquén worked in the Island in 1950. *Courtesy of H. Campos.*

Ronald Richter, his wife, their daughter Mónica (born in Bariloche in mid-1950) and their cat Epsilon, in their house on Lake Nahuel Huapi. Their cat became somewhat famous because when journalist interviewed Richter in July 1951 he teased them saying that he had come to Argentina, instead of the US, because US custom would not allow the cat to enter the country.

Formwork for the large reactor when the top was still in progress. Later a large building, named Lab 1, was built surrounding this structure. Picture is from April 1950 when Perón and his wife Evita visited the island. Four months after it was finished this structure was demolished.

Hand written letter from Peron to Richter of March 1,
1951 by which Peron entrusts Richter with presidential
powers within Huemul island. It was after Richter had a
row with the Commander of the Bariloche garrison

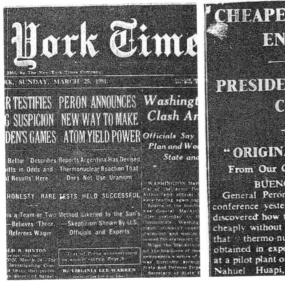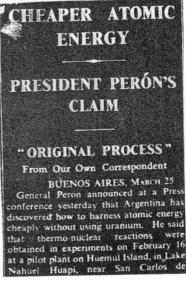

Left: News of Perón´s announcement were printed in the front page of The New York Times of Sunday, March 25, 1951. Under the headline "Peron announces new way to make atom yield power", it says "Reports Argentina has devised thermonuclear reaction that does not use uranium …Tests held successful… Method likened to the Sun´s – Skepticism shown by U.S: officials and experts."

Right: Column published in The Times (London) on Monday, March 26, 1951.

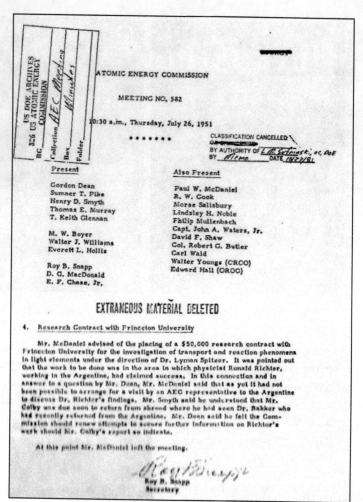

Minutes of the 582nd meeting of the US Atomic Energy Commission, July 26, 1951, in which a research contract with Princeton University of 50 thousand dollars was granted to Dr. Lyman Spitzer. It is pointed out that "the work to be done was in the area in which physicist Ronald Richter, working in the Argentine, had claimed success." *Courtesy of P. Dean*

NOTES TO CHAPTER 3

[1] Interview with Brigadier Medardo Gallardo Valdez, on January 15, 1982. Other quotes of Gallardo Valdez in this chapter are also taken from the same interview.

[2] Interview with Brigadier Cesar Ojeda on March 16, 1981. Other quotes of Ojeda in this chapter are also taken from the same interview.

[3] "...he intensely wished it had never involved him..."

Gallardo Valdez refused to comment on this episode and actually denied having to do anything with it in a telephone conversation with the author in March 1981. After Ojeda confirmed to the author that Gallardo Valdez had been sent to this mission by himself ("I told him it was secret but not for this long", Ojeda joked when the author mentioned Gallardo Valdez's forceful silence), Gallardo Valdez admitted talking about it without concealing his discomfort.

[4] Letter to the author by Dr. Enrique Gaviola, dated April 2, 1981. Author's archive

[5] Ibid. 4.

[6] "...precipitated a spectacular atomic adventure..."

When the author interviewed Gallardo Valdez on January 15, 1982, the retired Brigadier said he was not aware that Mattheis had turned out to be Kurt Tank. Moreover, he ignored the connection between Tank and Richter.

[7] Ibid. 2

[8] Statements by Perón to reporters in Casa Rosada on June 29, 1951, taken from Los Principios, June 30, 1951, and Mundo Atomico, year 2, number 5, pag. 5, 1951.

[9] Statements by Richter to reporters in Bariloche, taken from Noticias Graficas, June 27 and 28, 1951.

(10) Casos de la Segunda Tirania, Vol. I, Editorial Integracion (1958), pag. 76 onwards. The salary of $5000 monthly (U$S 1250) was increased gradually to $20,000 in 1952. The increase followed approximately the inflation rate at that time. For comparison we may recall that 2 years before Gaviola offered Heisenberg U$S 800 a month, 3 times his own salary as Director of the Observatory.

(11) ".. his hypothetical biography..."

Autobiographical index prepared by Ronald Richter for Peter Alemann. Some of the entries are intriguing: "A Sudden Explosion", "Shocked-induced fusion: a hobby", "Encounter with the Gestapo", "On Suspicion of Being a Spy", "The Gestapo Strikes Again", "Twilight of the Gods", "Being a Guest of the British Secret Service", "A Decisive Encounter in London", and others. The author is grateful to Jorge Sabato for a copy of this material.

(12) Secret intelligence report dated August 21, 1950. The author is grateful to Colonel Gonzalez for this material.

(13) Ibid. 2.

(14) Interview with Colonel Enrique Gonzalez of June 27, 1979. Other quotes from the same source also correspond to the same interview.

(15) Interview with Heinz Jaffke on July 6, 1980.

(16) Ibid. 15.

(17) Bailey Willis, El Norte de la Patagonia - A History of the Hydrological Studies Commission, Public Works Ministry, 1911-14. Published by the Agriculture Ministry, National Parks and Tourism Bureau, Argentina, 1943. The author is grateful to Alberto Boselli for having brought this book to his attention. The book describes an ambitious project sponsored by Minister Ezequiel Ramos Mexia at the beginning of the Century, aimed at transforming the Nahuel Huapi area into an industrial and commercial development pole.

(18) "...The island's name was Huemul..."

According to Juan Martin Biedma in Toponimia del Parque Nacional Nahuel Huapi, National Parks Service, Buenos Aires, 1978, the real name of the island was "Huenul", which means "on top". In the original letters to Perón and Gonzalez, Richter correctly referred to it as Huenul. In the translation from German to Spanish, the translator changed it to Huemul, a more familiar term in Spanish (an animal). The term became "official" when the island was mentioned in the 1951 Decree # 9697. On the other hand, Emilio Morales in Lagos, Selvas y Cascadas, written around 1910, already referred to the island as Huemul. He enclosed, however a map drawn by Emilio Frei where the island is shown as Las Gallinas. The island which bears this name today is called Las Cabras in Frei's map, and lies next to Huemul.

[19] Interview with Lieutenant Colonel Carlos A. Monti on March 3, 1981.

[20] Ibid. 19. Also Brigadier Ojeda told the author that by that time Tank no longer talked about nuclear propulsion for planes as he had earlier when he recommended Richter upon his (Tank's) arrival in 1947.

[21] "...A winding trail was opened to the first plateau..."

While this work was underway the soldiers uncovered pieces of a wooden box containing human remains. Dr. Hellmann who was nearby when this happened told the author that there was an inscription bearing the name "Chief Huenul" and the date of his death, 1902. In Toponimia, author Biedma (see 18) states that the name Huenul corresponds to "an island settler - Bernardino Huenul - who by 1919 used to live in Puerto Panuelo". Mr. Maldonado, an old native of Bariloche told the author in 1983 that Bernardino Huenul had lived in San Pedro Peninsula. In 1984 journalist Francisco N. Juarez, searched the archives of Bariloche City Hall and found a death certificate dated December 21, 1904, issued to the name of Pedro Nolasco Guenul, 105 years old, Chilean, and fruit grower. His son Bernardino Guenul and a friend Fernando Carbul signed the document along with the Justice of Peace. Thus it seems that the coffin found in 1949 belonged to Bernardino's father Pedro Nolasco and the island's name comes from him who inhabited it with his family probably since the 1880's. Around 1965 the author saw the canoe which reportedly belonged to "Chief Huenul" in the bottom of the lake by the rocky promontory of La Florida. The canoe is now in the hands of Parques Nacionales. The author is grateful to Mr. Maldonado and Mr. Juarez for their testimony.

[22] Interview with Fernando M. Prieto on August 10, 1979.

[23] "...Bertolo..had the following story to tell..."

Interview with Bertolo on January 28, 1979. Bertolo kindly guided the author through the island in a most instructive visit. Some episodes of Bertolo's life seem taken from a fiction novel. A native of Italy, he came to Argentina on February 27, 1950. His first home in the New World was the Immigrant's Hotel by the Buenos Aires harbor; his second, was Huemul Island. His coming was a direct consequence of Perón's policy of stimulating the immigration of Europeans. His oldest son was born 24 hours before he departed for Argentina and his family joined him only one year later. During the war he was in Russia and for six months his family believed he was dead. In his own words: "The Italian government paid my father a pension because a comrade told my family that I had been run down by a Russian tank. He could escape but I couldn't. But the tank actually made a turn just before hitting me. When Perón opened the immigration, in Italy there was poverty and a lot of misery. The US did not help because they said there were many communists. The Russians didn't help either because they said there were many Christian Democrats. Then we had this opportunity to come to Argentina. It started in 1947. The Italian police were after thieves and murderers from the partisan period. A lot of people went to jail. Each day we had less freedom, so many of us grabbed the opportunity to come to Argentina, and both good and bad people came." Bertolo was killed in a car accident in 1983 after returning from a visit to his folks in Italy. He was then employed by the Bariloche Atomic

Center where he had gone after the Richter's years. He is warmly remembered as a dedicated and very kind person.

[24] Letter to the Editor of Scientific American, by Richter (unpublished), dated June 5, 1963. Since this is a rare, unpublished, sample of Richter's thinking written by himself and it is also a good example of his lively imagination, its full reproduction seems justified (English is from original):

"Sirs:

"In his article `Ball Lightning' (Scientific American, March 1963) Prof. Harold W. Lewis presents a rather inconclusive approach to one of the most interesting problems of plasma physics.

"Since I am not only one but, to the best of my knowledge, the first one who put forward the concept of a ball-lightning-controlled fusion reactor and even got some interesting experimental results (in 1948/52), I should like to contribute to the basic problem of ball-lightning by putting forward an even more exciting (so I hope) concept.

"What we want to find out about ball-lightning in the first place is (a) whether it presents something like a dynamically stable, self-confined, plasma system, and (b) whether it stores electrical energy electrodynamically.

"The extreme rarity of the ball-lightning phenomenon makes it most unlikely that any vital information about its structural stability and its source of energy will ever be obtained by observation alone. It is therefore my considered opinion that we better should concentrate on laboratory-made plasma balls.

"First of all, this gives us the advantage of subjecting the plasma ball to rigorous laboratory testing. For example, by photographing and photometering its spectrum, by analyzing the energy exchange between the plasma ball and the given source of energy, by bombarding the plasma ball with shock waves, and by the excitation of (cavity-) sound resonances, we get a set of conclusive data about its stability and the buildup of stored energy. One of the most conclusive data, for example, concerns the self-induction of the self-confining plasma ball.

"By establishing feed-back loops between some of these analyzers and the plasma-ball-generating process variables, stability and buildup of the plasma ball can be studied under controlled conditions.

"All this we can never do with natural lightning balls.

"From what I have found experimentally, it may be assumed that ball-lightning comes into existence by the interaction of two (or rather several) lightning bolts, one generating a powerful magneto hydrodynamic shock wave which, interacting with the plasma of a close-by second lightning bolt, induces violently twisting, `frozen-in' magnetic fields which, in turn, give rise to intense electrodynamic interactions. In other words, it is the violent interaction between powerful magneto hydrodynamic shock phenomena which provides the most suitable conditions for self-confinement and the electrodynamic storage of electrical energy.

"In another experimental approach, I got rather large plasma balls by inducing powerful short-circuits at an extremely small time constant. (Then, I was actually studying inertia phenomena).

"On the 3rd of October, 1949, when testing a self-confining plasma system, a tremendous but quite unexpected flash of visible and ultraviolet radiation for the first time revealed the existence of a suddenly collapsing, energy-storing plasma configuration. Large voltage peaks induced in given detector coils revealed the existence of collapsing magnetic fields, thus giving proof of the electrodynamic origin of the collapsing storage system.

"It was by these experiments that I became definitely interested in the development of energy-storing plasma configurations.

"As I can see it now, controlled ball-lightning, i.e., controlled plasma electrodynamics, will play a decisive role in the development of energy sources of highest energy density for processing, power generation, and especially for propulsion.

"One interesting approach will be the controlled conversion of a chain-reacting fission plasma into a chain-reacting lightning ball, feeding on its own chain-reacting source of energy.

"By storing tremendous amounts of electrical energy, controlled ball-lightning will become the ultimate `fuel' for rocket propulsion, for booster and for outer space vehicles. It might be used as an orbiting storage system, or even as an orbiting mine against attacks from outer space.

"As an explosive, it might turn out to become superior to fission and even fusion bombs, without producing any radioactive fall-out. But, there is a chance, so I hope, that its most promising aspects as an unmatched propellant will overrule any military thinking so that controlled ball-lightning will become a powerful tool for reaching the stars.

"Of course, its feasibility depends in the first place upon how accurately we can define, analyze, and control its build-up.

"In 1958, Wolfgang Ehrenberg, a former assistant of mine, was publishing some papers*) in which he describes some of our experiments on controlled fusion, based upon ball-lightning phenomena.

"The present paper, for the first time, gives a brief account of the storage concept.

"(Dr.) Ronald Richter.

"*) Dr. Wolfgang Ehrenberg, `Probleme und Moeglichkeiten der Atomkernfusion', Moser-Verlag, Garmisch-Partenkirchen, (Westdeutschland). Dr. Wolfgang Ehrenberg, `Die verschiedenen Wage zur Kernfusion', Technische Rundschau, Nr. 18 (25 April 1958), Bern, Switzerland."

Reference to the first paper by Ehrenberg is made in 26 below.

(25) H. W. Lewis, Scientific American, March 1963, pag. 107.

(26) "...were recorded in a long report..."

W. Ehrenberg, Probleme und Moeglichkeiten der Atomkernfusion (Problems and Possibilities of Nuclear Fusion), 1958, Moser-Verlag, Archiv 921. Ehrenberg was the only physicist to write about Ronald Richter's ideas under a favorable light. While in Bariloche, as Richter's assistant, he held frequent discussion sessions with his boss and in his report he presents some of the ideas which were likely topics in these exchanges. In particular, Ehrenberg describes the use of a magnetic field perpendicular to the voltaic arc axis as a mean to increase the plasma temperature by increasing the electrical resistance of the discharge current. (See also W. Ehrenberg, Atompraxis, vol 4, 1958). The author is grateful to Mario Della Janna, who was Ehrenberg's assistant, for the description of some of the scientific exchanges between Richter and Ehrenberg in the latter's laboratory in what is today the housing area of non-commissioned officers in Bariloche. The author also acknowledges Walter Scheuer for having brought to his attention the reference of Atompraxis.

(27) "...both met again in Bariloche..."

In August 1949 Richter asked the Government to bring his friend Ehrenberg. Ehrenberg was part of a list including other 9 German technicians who were to come to the Aeronautical Institute in Córdoba. From a secret memorandum dated August 21, 1950, provided to the author by Colonel Gonzalez we learn that Mr. E. M. received $25,000 (about 6,000 dollars) for his assistance in getting the exit permits for these people from the authorities in Germany.

(28) "...Dr. Greinel..did not last long.."

One of the secret reports which Colonel Gonzalez received regularly from Bariloche, dated August 14, 1950, said: "Dr. Greinel has fallen in disgrace with Dr. Richter, so it may be convenient to send him somewhere else." In turn Richter wrote to Kurt Tank on October 19, 1950: "A few days ago I received a letter from Colonel Gonzalez indicating that Dr. Greinel had been requested by Brigadier Ojeda to work with the Pulqui II project. Unfortunately, Dr. Greinel was uncomfortable with us, probably because he is not interested in the kind of physics we are presently engaged in. His is more interested in aeronautics. In Physics he did not go further than basic principles and since he knows mathematics, he may be more useful in your area. If you care to know my personal opinion, I would say that Dr. Greinel lived too long in France and this has weakened his will". (Author's file)

(29) From secret memorandum to Colonel Gonzalez, dated October 18, 1950. (Author's file).

(30) Ibid. 14.

(31) "...And there were many of these meetings..."

Admiral Oscar Quihillalt, who attended a couple of these meetings, told the author that in one of them a geologist from Córdoba, Father Bussolini, Gamba and Richter, gave talks. After Richter's talk Perón said that the scientist deserved a "golden statue" and Richter said that it was Perón who deserved it. This became later known as "the famous dialogue of the golden statues". Richter also said that Argentina would soon be able to produce steel using atomic energy, for export. By sheer coincidence Quihillalt and his comrade in arms, then Captain Pedro Iraolagoitia, met in this meeting without guessing that later on they were to share the same destiny: assume top responsibility for Atomic affairs in Argentina.

(32) From Mr. Francisco González, during a visit to Huemul Island on January 28, 1979.

(33) "...to increase the soldiers' wage..."

Bertolo explained to the author: "When Perón and Evita saw the soldier's hands, they ordered that they be paid a mason's wage: $300 a month instead of $20. At the end of the month the soldiers expected to cash this amount, but they didn't. When they finished their military service, however, Prieto gave each one a saving account with deposits amounting to $9000 (about 2250 dollars)". When the author asked Prieto about this episode, he neither recalled nor denied it.

(34) "...he ordered the iron tubes to be replaced..."

Data on the reactor demolition was obtained from Prieto's testimony (August 10, 1979) and statements from Richter, Prieto and others to the Inquiry Commission headed by Dr. Teofilo Isnardi after the 1955 revolution (see ref. 40 below).

[35] Interview with Heriberto Hellmann on May 1, 1980.

[36] "...and returned to Buenos Aires not knowing what to do..."

Contrary to Prof. Isnardi's Inquiry Commission report (see ref. 40), Colonel González's written records indicate that he did go to Huemul Island to observe the big reactor prior to its demolition. (Author's files)

[37] "...nearly killed Behrens, the famous German pilot..."

In a letter to Richter dated August 2, 1950, Tank bitterly comments that Brigadier Ojeda had ordered Behrens to take a fresh 420-hour flight course, as a result of a serious accident while testing Pulqui II. "To inflict this sort of punishment to one of our best German pilots, deserves no comments", Tank said. About this episode Ojeda told the author that Behrens indeed needed some refreshing. A second accident a year later, took Behrens' life. (Author's files).

[38] "...it is most likely that a report dated June 20..."

Part of this document is given in Prof. Isnardi's Inquiry Commission report (see ref. 40). Since this is one of the few documents describing the work done at Huemul based on Richter's own data it is reproduced here:

"The process to obtain nuclear energy proposed by Dr. Richter, currently in progress, consists in triggering the thermal transformation in a different way (from that used in the Hydrogen Bomb). While in Germany during the war, Dr. Richter discovered the possibility of making the nuclear structure quasi-stable by the isomerization of nuclei using magnetic fields. Interaction of this state with an adequate magnetic field frequency, gives rise to a resonance process by which nuclei become unstable state and go to another state when radiation energy is supplied. By selecting appropriate elements, it is possible to achieve temperatures of 20 million degrees, using this process of nuclear transmutation. The process can be kept going after ignition, by adding light elements. The problem is to find control procedures adequate to handle these processes. Dr. Richter's efforts have been mainly focused, up to now, in the development of control procedures and they have reached the anticipated success." (Author translation from Spanish original)

The physical ideas contained in this report constitute an odd blend which make little sense. The process of exciting atoms with magnetic fields into isomeric states corresponds to the Zeeman effect discovered towards the end of the last century; it is not a process of nuclear transmutation as Tank puts it. The magnetic field has the effect of splitting a given state into several of slightly different energy. Nuclear excitation into these states can be induced through external radiation of appropriate frequency. It is a gross mistake (as the Isnardi's report points out) to equal this Zeeman energy with heat energy or temperature. The resonance process mentioned in Tank's letter is associated with Larmor's precession and is further discussed in the last chapter.

(39) Letter to Kurt Tank by Ronald Richter dated October 19, 1950. (Author's file)

(40) Report of Inquiry Commission headed by Prof. Teofilo Isnardi, Casos de la Segunda Tirania, Vol I, Integracion, Buenos Aires, 1958.

(41) To be precise Colonel Gonzalez tendered his resignation as Secretary General of CNEA in March 1952 and was replaced by Navy Captain Pedro E. Iraolagoitia. As of November 1952, when the island was placed under government control and Richter left the laboratory, he ceased, in fact, as member of CNEA. The legal existence of CNEA according to Decree 10936 of 1950 finished in 1955 when the DNEA (Direccion Nacional de Energia Atomica, created by Decree 9697 of 1951 - see following chapter) was renamed as CNEA.

(42) Ultima Hora, La Paz, Bolivia, June 15, 1950.

(43) Folha da Manhã, São Paulo, Brasil, July 14 and 15, 1950.

(44) Colonel Gonzalez description of events in answer to the publication of the Inquiry Commission (ref. 40), and prepared for the judge who was in charge of the investigation of

Huemul Project, written in 1956-57. (unpublished, author's files).

(45) Letters of Enrique Gaviola. Archives of Bariloche Atomic Center.

(46) Esto Es, number 96, week of October 18-24, 1955, pag. 28.

(47) Ibid. 45.

(48) Ibid. 14.

(49) Letter to Dr. Bengt Paul, Stockholm, Sweden, by Ronald Richter, dated October 19, 1950. (Author's file)

(50) Ibid. 39.

(51) Letter to Enrique J. Th. Halberstadt, England, October 19, 1950. (Author's file)

(52) Ibid. 49.

(53) Secret memorandum to Colonel Gonzalez, dated August 14, 1950. (Author's files).

(54) Letters of Sergeant-Major Federico Rodriguez to his friends Leloup and Inaraja, both dated August 24, 1950. (Author's files).

(55) Secret memorandum to Colonel Gonzalez, dated October 16, 1950. (Author's files).

(56) Ibid. 53.

(57) Ibid. 55.

(58) "...When Germany surrendered, Richter was in Berlin..."

Richter was born in Falkenau, in February 1909. His father, a well to do businessman, gave him financial support to install his own laboratory, already before Ronald Richter went to Prague University, where he graduated in 1935 and this support continued until the war years (see La Razón, June 28, 1951). Richter's contact with nuclear physics research was limited to using a van de Graaff proton accelerator for six months in 1942-43, at Manfred von Ardenne's Institute in Berlin. While at this Institute Richter studied the effect of proton bombardment on fulminating pellets, as described by his colleague and friend W.

Ehrenberg (see ref. 26). Besides this job Richter did not have others before coming to Argentina in 1948, except for two brief, temporary, contracts with AEG at the end of the war and, shortly afterwards, at the Institut du Petrole in Paris (from December 31, 1947 to August 1948). Both were related to the development of catalyzers.

[59] La Razón, June 28, 1951.

[60] La Razón, March 28, 1951.

[61] Noticias Gráficas, June 28, 1951.

[62] "...letter written by an official of the US Embassy..."

Letter to Ronald Richter by A. J. Sforza, dated August 11, 1951. Richter's version of the incident was different. To Mr. Peter Alemann he said: "This is an interesting story. It started in 1950, when I was building up in Huemul. An Assistant Naval Attaché of the US Embassy in Buenos Aires with the name of Sforza invited me to his house and drinking coffee he asked me bluntly: `Tell me, Mr. Richter, something about your atom secrets'. I told him that this was not my intention, not being in the interest of Argentina and myself. But I should like, so I told him, to make some statements on the hydrogen bomb, having brought the subject of secrets into the conversation. In those days, the American hydrogen bomb was still in a mysterious twilight at least for the general public. Sforza took paper and pencil and began to note down. With the time he got a little pale and asked me whether he could really give those details to the State Department and the Atomic Energy Commission in Washington. He did it and some months later I got and invitation from the Embassy to `high level conferences' in the United States. I had to postpone the trip because I was just in the middle of building something interesting. In 1951 this invitation was repeated and this time even more urgently. In this connection, a letter of General Perón is very important. He wrote me with his own hand on the first of June 1951: `Concerning your trip to the United States, you are absolute master of your decisions'. I had the freedom to go, the President declared that there was only a moral commitment between us (in spite of a contract that lasted until August 1953). It was a noble gesture of the President that had the effect of keeping me in Argentina. I could not possibly betray Perón and wanted to respect his friendship. You cannot even say that his wish was almost an order, because this wish was not even pronounced!" (From Peter Alemann's original notes in English). (Author's file)

It is fortunate that the letter from Sforza was not lost. The contrast with the version given by Richter is startling and indicates the tendency towards fantasy of the Director of Huemul Project.

A similar result had an application which Richter submitted to the American authorities in Berlin, before coming to Argentina. Mr. F. J. Biermann, Chief of the Scientific Section of the Military Government, wrote to Richter on May 19, 1947: "This office regrets that after careful examination of all the materials submitted, we are unable to undertake any steps in your case". (From Peter Alemann's original notes in English). (Author's file)

The author is grateful to Peter Alemann for making these documents available to him.

[63] Letter to Colonel Gonzalez by his son, dated September 27, 1950. (Author's file).

[64] Organisation plan Projekt Huenul - Top Secret, by Ronald Richter, dated February 27, 1951. (Author's files).

[65] Interview with Mr. Heriberto Hellmann, May 1, 1980. The letters, documents and other data quoted in this chapter in connection with the equipment requested by Richter, correspond to this same interview.

[66] "...I would have imagined that Dr. Hellmann was an honorable man..."

Comments written by Richter for Colonel Gonzalez in the back of the letter Hellmann himself had written him. Hellmann never knew of them. (Author's files).

[67] Ibid. 22.

[68] Ibid. 14 and 40.

[69] "...whitish round halo, to which Father Bussolini assigned great importance..."

Inquiry Commission report (see ref. 40). Father Bussolini is also quoted: "In addition to the visible spectrum, there were strange, inexplicable halos which presumably corresponded to ultraviolet radiation." As the Inquiry Commission Report correctly pointed out, "halos such as these commonly occur when too much light enters the spectrograph. Halos are caused by reflections on the faces of the lenses. A photograph shown in the Smyth report (see ref. 16, The Early Years), shows a circular halo at an angle due to this effect."

[70] Ibid. 65 and 44.

[71] Ibid. 40.

[72] Democracia, March 25, 1951, pag. 3.

[73] Meridiano, March 25, 1951, pag. 1.

[74] The New York Times, March 25, 1951; Clarín, March 26, 1951; El Mundo, March 25, 1951.

[75] Evolución de las Ciencias en la República Argentina, 1923-72, Física, Volumen II, by Jose F. Westerkamp, 1975, p. 180.

[76] The New York Times, March 25, 1951.

[77] Proceedings of the First International Conference on the Peaceful Uses of Atomic Energy, Geneva, August 8-20, 1955.

[78] The New York Times, April 1, 1951.

[79] Minutes of AEC meeting on July 26,1951. This material was kindly provided to the author by the US Department of Energy after being declassified by the Department of State. The author is grateful to Prentice Dean and Jack M. Holl of the Historian's Office at the Department of Energy and to Joan Bromberg and Lewis Pyenson for valuable assistance in this matter.

[80] The Princeton University Plasma Physics Laboratory - An Overview. January 1979. The author is grateful to Dr. Martin Crespi for this valuable reference.

(81) FUSION, Science, Politics and the Invention of a New Energy Source, by Joan Lisa Bromberg, The MIT Press, Cambridge, Massachusetts, 1982.

4 | Crisis (March – December 1951)

The Press Conference

On Easter Sunday, March 25, 1951, Richter held a press conference on his own. Perón put the presidential residence in suburban Olivos at his disposal, a wonderful setting especially that day in which the weather was nearly perfect. A score of journalists gathered around the scientist to hear further details on the fantastic experiments at Huemul announced the day before.

Colonel Gonzalez and his son, who as usual, acted as interpreter, accompanied Richter. The Information Secretary Raul Apold, Plantamura and other senior officials were also present. A picture in the newspapers the following morning shows the group standing outdoors around Richter who, in shirtsleeves, looks much more relaxed than the day before besides Perón at the Casa Rosada.

Richter was evidently at ease: he talked for three hours. Without Perón he was master of ceremony. He could run the show as he pleased. Nobody would rush him. Abundant credit he enjoyed to have everyone's ears eager to listen to him. His speech was published in full by most local newspapers. If the importance of a topic can be measured by the space given to it by the press, then that was the day for nuclear physics. In essence, Richter's speech was a good lecture in basic nuclear physics. For he did show uncommon ability to explain the intricacies of nuclear science to the non-initiated, a trait which had served him well two years earlier when expounding his ideas on atomic fusion to Perón.

He started explaining that Atomic Energy stemmed from the famous mass energy equivalence discovered by Einstein. He then described the structure of the atomic nucleus. He spoke slowly and used his hands to help shape his ideas. The translation, with its regular pauses, made the discourse seem even more academic. He explained in some detail how to obtain energy by splitting nuclei of uranium 235 or plutonium 239, or conversely, by fusing light elements such as hydrogen or lithium.

After a while, the lecture became a bit monotonous. It did not help when he rambled off and started talking about mesons, which have little to do with thermonuclear reactions. But it was only a short detour. His audience must have been relieved when he reconsidered, "this, however, is an extremely complicated story, we could go on talking for hours."

Journalists tried to concentrate on everything he said, waiting for the moment he would turn to the experiments done on the island. Yet Richter continued to elaborate on isotopic numbers, multimillion figures and chain reactions. He mentioned related developments carried out by the US, England and Russia, "where factories a mile long are presently being built", adding that "the sole factor which can explain the need for such huge factories is the demand imposed by war".

Richter repeated what he had told Perón: the path elected by the US to produce tritium for the first hydrogen bomb was wrong. "Had Argentina decided to follow such a path, we would have been forced to travel the long way of uranium. To decide otherwise represented a considerable risk. Fortunately, our decision proved to be correct. The central idea is this," - he said producing an instant of great expectation – "to begin with, is it possible to obtain the extreme temperatures needed in the reactor? Secondly, provided we obtain such temperatures and inject into the reactor the appropriate elements, what should be done if the chain reaction started developing too fast?" Now he was shifting into high gears. Would Dr. Richter continue further and satisfy the curiosity of his audience? How had he managed to achieve the high temperatures? How had he controlled the reaction? But again, Richter turned back to uranium.

From time to time, he sprinkled his talk with intriguing comments. While referring to the secrets of the hydrogen bomb, he said: "This is something we could verify whenever we wish. Nevertheless, we will not do so because we like to keep the secrets of our friends." Later on, he indicated that "experts will easily infer from our experiments that our people were continually exposed to mortal dangers." He also exaggerated: "Once at Huemul, a single experiment was repeated every day for eight months. Kilometers of special paper were used to register and verify one single result." Astonished, the Information Secretary Apold, could not refrain from asking: "Where did that happened, in Bariloche?" Richter replied, "Yes, sir. Foreign scientists may be amazed at our results but the fact is that there are only two ways to achieve success: either by following a certain method, or by making a discovery. Anyone who knows of a method is able to follow it, but the essential thing is to make a discovery. We have been very fortunate in making two discoveries. Our project is based on them." Now it was perhaps the moment he would disclose some of his secrets. But he added (ironically?): "I trust I have made myself clear."

It was difficult to establish the seriousness of his assertions. At times he was solemn and precise; the next instant he was childish. He seemed as fascinated by the atomic adventure as a child after watching Star Wars. Reporters were at pains to tell truth from irony or just kidding. He had a subtle sense of humor. While explaining that due to security reasons the Bariloche work group was small "the larger the group, the easier it is for secrets to leak out" Richter pointed out that its members carried a considerable work load and tended, therefore, to become exasperated. But then he spoke of "electronic brains" which "did the work of five hundred men", and said the man in charge of the equipment was frequently annoyed with it and that the electronic brain "was often annoyed at the man."

The press conference acquired a new rhythm as Richter moved from scientific concepts to more domestic aspects of his activities. Obviously aware of critical remarks made by technical staff from Philips when he ordered some very expensive and very inefficient photocells of gold, he explained that he needed them to be inefficient on purpose. ("Now they will understand the reason..."). Then he became more personal. Like a motor warming up, he grew more excited, less solemn. He spoke about his dear Prof. Rausch von Traubemberg, one of the first scientists to take an interest in the hydrogen/lithium reaction. Prior to falling prey to Nazism, von Traubemberg had been a professor at the University of Prague during Richter's earlier years there as a student. He was probably responsible for planting the seed of atomic interest in the Chief of Project Huemul. Richter remembered him with affection.

Only a few disclosures were made regarding the work carried out in the Huemul laboratory. "The Bariloche pilot plant is equipped with the best instruments available. We have altered some of them to fit our needs". "In Bariloche, we have one of the finest spectroscopy laboratories in the world..." He mentioned a "huge solar furnace" that was being built, but said nothing about the first version of such installation (still waiting, since previous August, to be demolished!).

He also remarked that "we are very interested in isotope production" (a topic which later that year would become particularly controversial when Colonel Gonzalez demanded to see some results) but he added, – "just as with the uranium piles in the US and England, this is ashes for us and we are therefore studying the possibility of avoiding these ashes completely."

Richter was definitely enthusiastic about the emerging automatism of those days and liked to remind his audience of how modern his installations were. Though neither cyclotrons nor van de Graaff accelerators were used on the island as they were elsewhere, he said somewhat naively that "thousands of partial measurements are taken regularly, but we wished to save time and have therefore installed instruments which are able to analyze directly the particles and quanta originated in the core of the reactor so that months of work are saved."

"The material employed in the early measurements was irrelevant. We worked, for example, with deuterium or lithium hydrate. A lot was learned and this subject is closely related to the hydrogen bomb. It may be interesting to note that during our Huemul experiments on thermonuclear reactions great gas speeds were attained. In forthcoming publications, we shall demonstrate that speeds up to 2,000 miles per second roughly equivalent to a thousand times the speed of gases in explosives and rockets were reached. These results were obtained without difficulties." Richter then explained that the expansion velocity of an explosive mixture can be determined using the Doppler effect. What he said on this occasion turned out to be of decisive importance later on. "In a reactor, where there is gas continually expanding, the masses of gas move toward the instrument. As a consequence, spectral lines shift toward the violet." [1] Again, he promised written reports describing the results in detail, "without mentioning how these processes actually take place but presenting the evidence."

The press conference was drawing to a close. Richter had provided explanations of a general nature, yet a large number of specific questions remained unanswered. He admitted it: "I do realize this presentation provides an incomplete and almost incomprehensible picture, but there are secrets we must keep for security reasons", adding, "we cannot break customary conventions by disclosing our secrets."

Richter then said he was ready to answer questions. Some portions of the ensuing dialogue are revealing of his personality. [2]

-Journalist: Dr. Richter, could you please tell us as far as you can within security limits what actually happened on the island on February 16th?

-Richter: "For a while, our efforts were directed at producing nuclear reactions within high temperature zones. At other times, we were similarly engaged in producing high temperatures without a nuclear reaction. On February 16th, all parts of this research program were brought together in one major experiment which, by rare coincidence did not fail."

Rare coincidence? Did he actually mean that? Perhaps he was just adding a bit of salt to his description, or merely trying to be modest. However, Richter once did tell a friend about trying with unwavering stubbornness, even blindly, seemingly impossible experiments. They might be merely unlikely, not impossible, he would argue, and a strike of luck might yield success. Was the result achieved in Huemul such a case?

What followed was a peculiar exchange. Possibly, Richter was trying to evade straight answers, or perhaps the translation process posed certain difficulties. (Somewhere along the press conference, Capt. Gonzalez was replaced by another interpreter. The conference had turned out to be a sort of translators' marathon).

-Journalist: "Was there an explosion?"

-Richter: "Yes. For example, in a uranium pile there is also a tendency to an explosion, though dwindled and controlled in intensity so as to establish a dynamic equilibrium."

Understandably, the journalist was not satisfied, so he insisted: "Was there a big noise?"

-Richter: "Yes, there was a huge explosion."

The journalist wanted further details: "Could it have been heard beyond the island?"

No luck. Richter replied: "That depends on whether there is a storm."

The journalist tried again: "What I meant is whether the people in Bariloche could have heard it."

-Richter: "No, they did not. They live six and a half miles away."

At this point, another correspondent intervened. The nature of the explosion remained unanswered.

-Journalist: "Which is the exact difference between nuclear fission and a thermonuclear reaction?"

-Richter's reply was brief: "Nuclear fission is an explosion and the thermonuclear reaction is a synthesis."

-Journalist: "I should like to ask you what is the relationship between our method and that of the hydrogen bomb."

-Richter: "What produces an explosion in the hydrogen bomb we seek to control."

-Journalist: "Is it possible, then, to control a conventional or H bomb atomic explosion?"

Richter then went into an involved explanation on controlled and explosive liberation of atomic energy. What in a bomb occurs explosively, he said, in a laboratory takes place in a controlled manner, adding: "Yes, sir, for the very first time a thermonuclear reaction has been produced in a reactor."

Someone asked what the comparative cost between the Argentine and foreign methods was. Richter evaded a straight answer but pointed out that "our method is infinitely less expensive. We do not need great uranium factories, nor do we use tritium." The journalist tried to make him quote a figure, but Richter answered that the issue had still to be settled. "Relative costs still need to be analyzed in the large reactor now under construction. We shall determine the most convenient material when is finished." The ambiguity remained. It could mean that the cost of the method as well as the optimum material to employ were still unknown. This posed a weighty question. Unless Richter was referring to relatively minor improvements which normally occur in the course of all scientific developments, surely a rough estimate should be available. Were these aspects which allegedly still needed to be determined of secondary importance, or Richter did not want to disclose valuable information? The journalist inquired no further.

A reporter asked about possible applications of atomic energy to industrial technology; specifically, to mineral casting. "Would it be technically and economically feasible to use atomic energy instead of coal or electricity?"

Richter replied: "Yes, it would be possible since extremely high temperatures take place within the reaction zone. Precisely one of the problems we had to solve was how to prevent the furnace from vaporizing from the resulting heat in the reaction zone. We have managed to do it perfectly well."

The unsatisfied reporter rephrased his question. Richter replied: "Atomic energy could be used in smelting furnaces and in power plants. Other technical applications would be much more complicated since special equipment would be required. But in smelting furnaces and in power plants, it would be simple and direct. The material to be used may be totally disassociated; it could be reconstituted or condensed later on. At 700 degrees, for example, water disassociates itself in hydrogen and oxygen, but condensation at lower temperatures brings it back into water through an explosion. Metals could thus be obtained by vaporizing mineral ores completely. This could be a fairly inexpensive technology."

A journalist asked how long it would take for the February 16th discovery to be implemented in practical terms. "That's difficult to say, since there are other factors not directly related to actual implementation. It cannot be determined yet. Experiments depend on constructions that need to be built, on certain installations and on the large reactor which has to be completed. To put it differently: a chemist, for instance, may conduct a test tube experiment with positive results. If he repeats the experiment in a container a hundred times larger, he may arrive at the conclusion that the principle of scaling up does not apply. This is why one has to study the correspondence between results and size of the experiments. Tests would have to be repeated over and over again." Then he added emphatically: "What is certain at this point, is that a thermonuclear reaction took place, and the process for its future application is already known to us. I would like to stress the fact that we have been extremely fortunate. A great deal of luck is needed in order to solve this type of questions in merely three years, a comparatively short period of time."

Someone asked the inevitable question: "Would it be possible to produce an atomic bomb in Argentina?"

-"As far as being possible, indeed it is; but from all I know, the President of the Republic is against it."

-The reporter's tone was apologetic: "I was referring to the mere possibility... and, what about the hydrogen bomb?"

-"A hydrogen bomb would pose no advantages for us. We know about the processes involved in building an H bomb and how tremendously expensive they are. If we wished to build a hydrogen bomb, we would need to make investments of a comparable magnitude to what has been done in other countries. But that's not what we want to do."

-Journalist: "Though I realize you cannot list the materials involved in producing the first reaction, I would like to know whether those materials are found in Argentina or imported from abroad."

-Richter: "Yes, there are no imported materials."

The reporters were not satisfied yet. It was not much what they had as far as hard data were concerned. The next question pointed in that direction.

-"So as to have a general idea, is it a large place where the reaction actually takes place?"

- "I prefer not to comment on that, but soon I think we will be able to show some pictures of the installations."

The journalist tried a different approach: "Is there danger of radiation in the area next to the facilities, like in other countries?"

-"No, but there's danger of an explosion", Richter replied, (he had told friends in Bariloche a different story about radiation risks such as men losing their virility, and others unpleasant possibilities, a few months earlier).

A member of the audience wanted to know what sort of temperatures had been achieved in the reaction zone. Richter had already gone over that but it was interesting to learn the exact figure. Intriguingly, the scientist replied: "Several million degrees, but as far as our project is concerned the temperature concept should be disregarded. I shall explain why." His reasoning involved the well-known Maxwell law which predicts the distribution of molecule velocities in a gas. At a given temperature, molecules have different speeds. "If you take, for instance, a relatively cold gas, some molecules still move at high speeds." He argued that those molecules might initiate a thermonuclear chain reaction even though the gas temperature might not be exceedingly high. Nevertheless, he admitted: "It is necessary, however, that the number of particles with great kinetic energy be large."

When Richter finished, it was already noon. Satisfied or not, it was time for the press conference to adjourn. A journalists asked a last question: "And what do you do to achieve such 'millionaire' temperatures? Do you use electricity, or some heating up process, or other explosions?"

He had hit the nail straight on the head. Richter replied: "Ah..., that's precisely the secret."

The Peronist Medal

Both locally and abroad, the echo produced by Perón's announcement lasted well over a week. In general, the reaction had more to do with the political rather than the technical aspects of the announcement. At a time when Peronism was enjoying its finest hour, it is not surprising that some sectors within the Party were exuberant with the atomic success and indulged in all sorts of declarations. Meaningless expressions of obsequiousness and cheap nationalism were not uncommon in the pro-government circles of those days.

On Monday 26th, legislator Jose Emilio Visca proposed that the Lower House declared its "enthusiastic support for the patriotic concern of the President of the Republic, General Juan Perón, aimed at finding a solution to the peaceful use of atomic energy, as a contribution toward the greatness of the Argentine Nation and all mankind."

A similar spirit prevailed at the ceremony held in the White Room of the Casa Rosada on March 28th. Richter was to be awarded the Peronist Medal and the diploma of 'Doctor Honoris Causa' of the century old University of Buenos Aires. Ministers, provincial governors, legislators, generals, brigadiers and admirals were present at the ceremony. Oddly enough there were no physicists.

First, a member of the Governing Council of the University of Buenos Aires read the resolution appointing Dr. Ronald Richter 'Doctor Honoris Causa'. Then, the Minister of Education Mendez San Martin, addressed the audience. His speech was most disappointing for it had little to do with either Richter or his work. It was unctuous, full of platitudes and wholly devoid of substance. It revealed, moreover, that neither the Ministry of Education nor the prestigious University of Buenos Aires had taken the trouble to find out about Richter's background. No reference was made to his achievements nor to his scientific past. The whole extent of the Minister's words on the scientific achievement was: "Dr. Ronald Richter already deserved such an honor as a result of his prominent services." He remarked also that Richter actually deserved the medal for "his Peronist faith, which he professed from the very first moment he set foot on Argentina."

Except for one or two words at the beginning and at the end of the speech, nothing more was said about Richter or his work in Huemul. The major part of the speech which might have been delivered anywhere else or in anybody else's honor evolved around "our great President and Leader", "the glorious history of Peronism in our New Argentina" and "the unique and inspiring presence of Eva Perón."

Evita had just presided the closing ceremony of the Third Inter American Conference on Social Security. Mendez San

Martin saw fit to dedicate a considerable portion of his speech to the "remarkable gifts of this exceptional woman who accomplished such outstanding work". Obviously, he was referring to the Conference, not to atomic research at Huemul. "It is not surprising" he added clumsily – "that Mrs. Eva Perón has offered us her singular and wondrous presence as the first woman in the world to conduct with amazing efficiency a Congress of such extraordinary importance as the one which ended yesterday."

When Mendez San Martin finished his speech, the Secretary of the Peronist Order, Major Aloe, read the resolution awarding Richter the Peronist Medal "for his merits and extraordinary services rendered... particularly considering that in the course of his experiments Dr. Richter and his men have been permanently exposed to death hazards."

At that point, Perón stepped forward to reach the large table where so many ministers had sworn allegiance to the Motherland in the past. He was flanked by Minister Angel Borlenghi and Speaker of the House Héctor Cámpora. The overpowering bust of Liberty loomed behind Eva Perón and Ilse Richter. Capt. Gonzalez Jr, between Richter and his wife, was ready to translate the President's words.

"For a man of action, whatever his activity, the driving force is always success. Napoleon used to say that success must be constructed, that it is not given freely by Fate or Fortune. Sheer luck or coincidence may sometimes originate success, but its effects are temporary and those chosen by luck are elected at random."

"There are men, as well as certain man made organizations, who believe that great ideas or momentous discoveries are sufficient to attain success. Far from it. There are no short cuts to success. It is achieved through hard and continuous labor. A strong man builds his own success. By the same token, it becomes worthless in the hands of those who are not prepared to work for it."

Perón spoke of success with deep conviction. Undoubtedly, it was a subject dear to his heart. When he spoke of Richter, he was speaking of himself as well. He was spelling out his own doctrine as a man of action. His words had substance even if the philosophy behind them was questionable. A good contrast with the senseless blabbering of his Minister of Education. His definitions had at least a ring of commitment and that made them interesting.

"For success to actually deserve such a name, it needs to be conscious. Success results from genius plus hard work, often accompanied by self denial and sacrifice. When success is achieved easily, it seldom lasts. First you have to dream of success, then you have to prepare yourself for it, next you have to work hard, and finally you have to learn how to use it and profit from it. That's the perfect success."

After mentioning the moral values which the Peronist Medal stood for, Perón bent over Richter and pinned the medal on his lapel. Many flash bulbs from the cameras were triggered at once making the marble bust of Liberty shine. The scene was registered by photographers of all latitudes. The New York Times published a good picture of this moment in its Sunday edition of April 8th. [3]

Richter returned to Bariloche on the following day. A singular week in the history of Argentina had just ended. News of Perón's announcement reached most newspapers in the world. The impact of the announcement went beyond the scientific factor to reach its possible political connotations, as evidenced for instance, in the Conference of foreign ministers in Washington. Yet the scientific validity of the announcement was widely discussed by specialists including a few Nobel Laureates. Some powerful media like The New York Times disposed of resources to analyze possibilities and eventual consequences of Richter's work. As mentioned earlier, a distinguished US scientist was even motivated to submit a research project on controlled fusion to the US Atomic Energy Commission.

Some sectors within the government displayed a rash and senseless enthusiasm. As noted earlier, some local newspapers rendered distorted versions of foreign commentaries in order to make them seem favorable to the government.

Perón exhibited the same degree of personal commitment toward the Huemul project as he had shown with Kurt Tank's modern fighter plane Pulqui II baptized a month earlier. The idea of the New Argentina which the Government actively fostered, was obviously strengthened by these technological achievements. These two projects achieved success almost at the same time. The results were spectacular. Pulqui II was indeed at the frontier of aircraft design. Controlled fusion was even beyond that. Argentina was competing in the international technological race. People felt proud and the government profited from the credit acquired by these achievements. No one could dispute Perón's principal and decisive influence in these projects. Therefore, it should not be surprising that the atomic development rendered, for a while, the services of a resonance box used to produce noisy political propaganda.

Beyond these considerations however, controlled nuclear fusion was indeed an extraordinary development. "If it were true, it would constitute one of the major discoveries in the history of mankind", declared a renowned scientist. The Austrian physicist Hans Thirring wrote to a journalist: "If Richter had actually cleared the path toward controlled nuclear fusion, the Nobel Prize would be small for him." [4]

Yet by the end of that week, legitimate doubts remained on the validity of the results obtained in Huemul and also on Richter's own scientific background. Despite the space devoted to him by the press, the truth was that nobody knew much about him. The newspapers had been unable to reach beyond some vague references. And, as indicated earlier, not even within the Ministry of Education which encompasses most scientific and high learning institutions in the country much information had been gathered.

Meanwhile, where were the Argentine physicists?

None had attended the ceremony at the Casa Rosada. None had been approached by the press in search of an authoritative opinion on the subject. Indeed, times had changed. The remarkable influence on Argentine political life which the Argentine Physics Association had until 1947, had simply vanished.

That year (1947) Gaviola had resigned as Director of the Córdoba Observatory and was now with Rigolleau, a private company. In September 1950, Gaviola had finished his third term as President of the Physics Association, and had been succeeded by Richard Gans. The same Gans who 35 years earlier at La Plata had inspired Gaviola to turn to physics. Gans had returned to Argentina in 1947, still surrounded by the aura of prestige he deservedly enjoyed back in 1916. Time, however, had taken its toll. He was no longer as enthusiastic and inspiring to the young and did not appreciate Gaviola's and Beck's efforts to achieve a level of excellence for the new generation of Argentine physicists. Neither did Gans feel as strongly toward the Physics Association, nor consider its activities as important as those who founded it. In one word, he had been elected but his heart was not in his job and shortly afterwards he resigned. The presidency remained vacant for the next two years.

The Association continued to exist thanks mainly to Secretary Galloni, whose principal contribution was to keep the scientific meetings going, but the old influence on public life was lost. Such was the situation when Perón issued the atomic announcement; the Association was acephalous and there was no reaction from it.

Minutes of Association meetings at the time indicate, however, that its level of scientific activity had neither stopped nor diminished. Physicists had simply turned their backs on public issues. Without publicity, meetings kept going regularly and new members joined the Association, not only young graduates but also senior physicists both Argentine and foreign. During the 16th meeting held in Tucuman in September 1950, a few distinguished personalities signed up as new members. Among others there were Oscar Quihillalt (who later became chairman of CNEA), Italian physicist Luis Moretti and Otto Hahn's brilliant disciple Dr. Walter Seelmann Eggebert. Manlio Abele had also become a member shortly before. (In 1948, Abele was the man in charge of the storeroom at the Córdoba Aeronautics Institute who provoked one of Richter's furies for not delivering instruments promptly). He was a good Italian physicist who had worked with Moretti in Milan, and had come to Argentina after the war. The Association also hosted prominent visitors such as Dr. Kowarsky who attended the same Tucuman meeting. Together with Joliot in Paris, Kowarsky had almost beaten Hahn and Meitner in discovering nuclear fission in 1938.

Argentine physics was neither dead nor dying at the time Perón and Richter captured the attention of the news media on that particular week in March 1951. The then considerable number of physicists in Argentina, however, remained completely removed from the Huemul project, and the Government did nothing to alter this situation. The first time that the subject was ever brought up in the Physics Association was in 1956 when a motion was approved "to appoint a commission to study the Richter case and its effect on Argentine physics and the role of physicists and the Association in this connection."

In 1951, the Physics Association turned mute. One of its most conspicuous members Gaviola attempted to do otherwise: he wanted to air his views about Project Huemul. As departing President in September 1950, he had still to write a report covering his tenure. (In the meantime, as already noted, Gaviola had offered his services to Gonzalez but the contract never realized owing to Gaviola's strong views about Richter). In March 1951, Gaviola considered that the pending document offered him the opportunity to say something about the atomic announcement. The report was completed on April 12th and sent to "Ciencia e Investigacion", an Argentine scientific journal which had published his earlier reports. On this occasion, however, the editors refused to print it. The report included an implicit criticism of Huemul seasoned with characteristic

Gaviola's acid style. It was dangerously close to openly declaring war on the Government and the editors did not want that.

It began: "If we should examine such items as the increase in the membership of the Physics Association, the level of scientific contributions, etc., we might feel satisfied with ourselves and face the future of Argentine physics confidently. However, should we enlarge our scope of vision, we would probably perceive certain disquieting signals that would make us uneasy regarding the immediate future. On the average, the level of scientific teaching in the Universities has dropped. The imbalance between theoretical and experimental physics has broadened, while quackery has grown alarmingly everywhere in Argentina." The report continued with a passionate discussion on the importance of intellectual honesty within an institution of physicists such as the Physics Association. "The worst crime a physicist may commit is to fake or forge results. The penalty for such a crime ought to be expulsion from the scientific community; scientific death. For the Physics Association, there is no alternative but to maintain intellectual honesty at all costs."

Finally, Gaviola went straight to discuss "the noxious effects of secrecy". At this point he recalled his 1946 memorandum which dealt with this subject, while emphasizing the possibilities of attracting top scientists to work in Argentina in an atmosphere of academic freedom. In his view, "secrecy is an all powerful, corrupting influence. It acts as a shield covering up mistakes, failures, frauds, lies, deceit, illicit transactions, embezzlement and all manner of corrupt practices. Secrecy constitutes an effective screen for hiding intellectual dishonesty. Quakery thrives on secrecy."

To illustrate the idea Gaviola resorts to Christian Andersen's story "The Emperor's New Robes", according to which the Emperor of Persia hired the services of a foreign tailor who promises special robes made with magic cloth. The cloth was woven with a secret formula which made it so sheer, so fine and transparent that only persons of noble birth, clean reputation and outstanding intelligence could see it. "The Emperor hired the tailor, assigning him a special area within the palace so that he could work in absolute secrecy, protected by a powerful guard," Gaviola said. "When the Emperor donned the new robes, everybody including himself saw him naked. No one, however, dared to utter a word. Nobody wished to acknowledge failures in ancestry, reputation or intelligence." Gaviola finished his personal version of the story thus: "The Persian Tailors' Association denounced the impostor, but the government proceeded to annul the Association's legal status. The government appointed a probing commission, and finally closed the Association down while knighthood was conferred upon the magic tailor, who was also appointed President of the Imperial University."

"The moral in this story" continued Gaviola in his report, in which he also apologizes to the author of the story for not being faithful to the original – "is that instead of hiring a swindling magician, the Emperor ought to have consulted the Persian Tailors' Association, or at least, some native Persian tailor worthy of his trust with a sound reputation for intellectual honesty."

The analogy of Gaviola's story was far too obvious for the editors of "Ciencia e Investigacion" to dare publish such a report under the prevailing political circumstances. Consequently, this unorthodox yet thought provoking document was never published. It constituted a frontal attack on what the government was trying to accomplish in Bariloche. It could be argued that it was disrespectful toward the President, since it compared him to the obstinate Emperor who walked naked through the streets of his realm, and that its publication would not have helped the Physics Association's position. It could also be argued that the Association had to display prudence, as befitted a scientific institution since little was actually known of the work carried out on Huemul and there was no hard evidence on which to pin down criticism.

True, there was little information and therefore a margin for doubt, but Gaviola and Beck had taken the trouble of finding out as much as they could about Richter. Owing to their experience and foreign contacts, it was relatively easy for them to learn in a short time far more than the Ministry of Education and the Ministry of Technical Affairs put together. They knew that the first thing to do when finding out about a scientist is to have a look at his publications, and that it is not necessary to ask the scientist himself to get them. The information can be obtained from a specialized library by screening the index of authors. Gaviola and Beck checked through the twenty preceding years. There were no publications by Dr. Ronald Richter. The only reference they could find of Richter's research work at the University of Prague where he had studied was a paper published in `Annalen der Physik' in 1937, by physicist Felsinger who thanked Richter for lending the equipment he had used to measure photoelectric effects of "soft" X rays on various samples. [5]

The Dutch Connection

On the very day Perón announced that Argentina had achieved controlled nuclear fusion, Prince Bernhard left The Netherlands for a South American tour. It was just a coincidence; the trip was of a commercial nature and in no way related to the work in progress at Huemul.

The distinguished visitor arrived in Argentina on Tuesday, April 3, after visiting Rio de Janeiro and Montevideo. Two days later, Prince Bernhard was received by Perón. This meeting eventually turned out to be of paramount importance for the development of atomic energy in Argentina. Capt. Pedro Iraolagoitia, who was the Chief of Staff at the time, greeted the Prince at the doorsteps of Casa Rosada. Iraolagoitia was completely removed from atomic matters at that time. In view of what happened later it is an incredible coincidence that precisely in a year time he would be in charge of CNEA and that in that capacity he should be the one to dedicate a powerful

Philips synchrocyclotron purchased as a result of Prince Bernhard's visit to the Casa Rosada that day.

It is not surprising that Perón and Prince Bernhard should spend some time talking about the recent developments on Huemul Island and that Bernhard should have offered to sell Dutch manufactured equipment. Upon leaving Buenos Aires on Monday 9th, the Prince frankly acknowledged to the press he had come to do business. There is no evidence on whether Bernhard was knowledgeable in nuclear equipment, nor whether his entourage included an atomic expert. Was he aware that Amsterdam University in collaboration with Philips had recently built one of the most modern particle accelerators in the world? In any case, the illustrious visitor offered to sell Philips products and services, as well as to send over a specialist to help decide on actual purchases.

On May 17th, The New York Times informed: "Dutch physicist takes model of cyclotron to Buenos Aires." The information was from Amsterdam. "The leading Dutch nuclear physicist Prof. C. J. Bakker is leaving for Buenos Aires tomorrow with a model of the Dutch cyclotron. Dr. Bakker pointed out that his visit had been arranged by The Netherlands Government. It is believed to be the result of discussions between President Juan Perón and Prince Bernhard during the latter's recent goodwill tour to Argentina. Dr. Bakker, Amsterdam University professor of experimental physics, said he hoped to 'study the development of atomic energy in Argentina.' He added that he did not know whether he would have an opportunity to study the work done by Dr. Ronald Richter. President Perón said last March that the Austrian born Dr. Richter, now an Argentine citizen, had achieved 'controlled release of atomic energy.' With Prof. F. A. Heyn, Dr. Bakker supervised the construction of a cyclotron in Amsterdam that is said to have made The Netherlands independent of Great Britain and the United States in the supply of radioactive isotopes."

Since Bakker visit was imminent, Perón felt he had to put Richter at ease and avoid misunderstandings. Perón wanted to assure Richter he was not meddling in his affairs, nor seeking foreign aid "which we do not need". Some press releases had been worded in such a way that Perón felt uncomfortable. They could be interpreted as intimating that Bakker's visit was for technical assistance.

Perón proceeded to write a long letter to Richter which was, as usual, handwritten. Once again, Perón expressed his respect, his regard for atomic research and his genuine faith in obtaining results which should greatly benefit the Argentine iron and steel industry. In this unique relationship between the politician with power, and the scientist with his secret, the latter wins. Perón does not issue orders; he suggests, asks, explains and even apologizes. His attitude is that of a person dreading a sanction. Perón was used to ruling with a heavy and sometimes arbitrary hand, yet with Richter he was extremely careful.

On May 23, 1951, Perón wrote: "My dear friend: When Prince Bernhard of The Netherlands visited us last month, he placed at our disposal the products and services of the Dutch firm Philips, in addition to whatever assistance might be useful to us. I accepted the offer and he promised to send a representative to materialize such collaboration. I wish to make perfectly clear that what he offered and I accepted was industrial cooperation, not scientific collaboration, which we do not need. I was unpleasantly surprised at the distorting publicity prior to Prof. Bakker's visit. It implied that the professor was coming to participate in a scientific endeavor which is and will be under your exclusive responsibility. You are the sole head of all atomic energy work conducted in Argentina. We ought to be very careful with what we tell Prof. Bakker. My suggestion is we should act with great reserve while trying to obtain Philips to provide us with what we may need for our work, but that is all. I am certain, Prof. Richter, that you will know how to handle this better than I. My feeling is that we may benefit from the industrial technology being offered to us, and that we can use Philips to speed up our work, particularly considering that Dutch industry is good and that we have trade surpluses which can be put to good use. Prof. Bakker and Colonel Plantamura are going south today to meet you. As stated earlier, the mission is more commercial and industrial than scientific. As you well know, I have always tried to cooperate in your work and have offered my full support. This visit serves that purpose. If useful, we shall make the most of it as far as industrial cooperation is concerned. If not, we won't have lost anything. Please take care of yourself and do take a rest from time to time. I'm planning to pay you a visit as soon as the demonstration Colonel Gonzalez is talking about takes place. Considering current progress, I will probably have the pleasure of seeing the large reactor and the other facilities practically completed as well. If I can manage to get some time off during the winter, I may go down there to rest for a few days and accompany you in your work. If the visit could be made to coincide with the demonstration, so much the better. I have placed great expectations in the electric power production process. It would give a tremendous impulse to our steel production plans. I have everything worked out already, but the waiting period is a real torment for people like us, who anxiously look forward to the rapid growth of the New Argentina. You alone can act as a bromide to my frayed nerves by accelerating the process. When engaged in the art of governing, I know well one must be prepared to wait, but I also know how hard it is. Well, my dear friend and professor, I leave the Bakker question in your hands, knowing you will decide whether Philips' offer is convenient to us. It all resulted from a kind offer by Prince Bernhard of Netherland, and I shall eventually reply to him according to your advice. Greetings from my wife to you and Mrs. Richter, to whom please extend my best personal regards. A warm embrace. Juan Perón."

It is a long, carefully written and highly revealing letter. One pictures Perón sitting at his desk, taking well over an hour to write his friend to whom he felt indebted. Perón insists repeatedly that Bakker's visit is of industrial' nature, not technical or scientific. He goes as far as advising Richter to be careful in giving Bakker details of the project. Was it necessary? Had Richter not prepared his huge `Organisationplan Top

Secret' a few weeks earlier? It seems as if Perón worried that Richter might feel underrated by this unexpected visit on which he had not been consulted in advance and took pains to calm him.

Further on, the letter becomes even more personal: Perón asks him not to work so hard, to look after his health. While telling Richter he hoped to visit him soon to see the reactor, Perón seems to do so more to please Richter rather than to satisfy his own curiosity. As he says: "to accompany you in your work."

The expression of his genuine desire to use atomic energy to hasten the development of the metallurgic industry, constitutes an eloquent historical document of Perón's real intentions, hitherto unknown. The candid, unaffected manner in which Perón describes his worries to his friend is truly moving. His support for Project Huemul was not designed at building atomic bombs (as Rodriguez Araya and others believed), but to peaceful uses in industry.

When Bakker visited Richter in Bariloche in May 1951, the man he met was confident in his work and proud of his recent success, though disinclined to speak about them. Bakker remained four days in Bariloche discussing various forms of collaboration with Richter, yet he was unable to make much progress. Richter mentioned his plans for a great solar furnace and listed certain equipment that Philips might supply. But made it clear that the final decision depended exclusively on Philips' ability to comply with requirements within the shortest possible terms. A promise to send catalogues of various instruments was as far as negotiations actually went. On Sunday 27th, the unhappy Dutch envoy returned to Buenos Aires; he had not even been allowed to visit the island. He had managed, however, to plant a seed which was to be of utmost importance, though not for the Huemul project: the purchase of a synchrocyclotron similar to the one recently completed in Amsterdam.

After Bakker's visit, Richter wrote to Perón: "Dear Mr. President: I should like to express my sincere gratitude for your kind letter which was brought to me by Lieutenant Colonel Plantamura. Your unfaltering support of our atomic energy project is extremely gratifying. The content of your letter, moreover, has given a new impulse to the situation in Bariloche. Prof. Bakker was received with utmost courtesy and we tried to make his stay in Bariloche as interesting as possible. He repeatedly expressed a desire to visit our facilities, which of course we had to refuse. He was told most amiably that as soon as our installations were ready to be visited by outsiders, when the great atomic energy furnace starts operating, then we shall have the pleasure of inviting foreigners for a tour of the island. "Evidently, Prof. Bakker came down here with the purpose of working with us in the reactor. He was surprised that you offered him the possibility of industrial cooperation only. I explained to him that our scientific research has reached such a stage of mature development, that we no longer require any foreign assistance. I also told him that we are now building a particularly high output furnace with the sole purpose of studying technical problems related to atomic energy production. Therefore, collaboration with Philips would be of interest to us only insofar as they can provide us with the instruments and equipment we may require. I made it clear that short delivery terms would be decisive in order to maintain our interest in such a possibility. I also said that, later on, we may be interested in having Philips build for us, for instance, the complete instrumentation and control equipment for atomic energy furnaces. This possibility would become even more interesting should Philips consider the feasibility of moving over to Argentina. Prof. Bakker expressed fears that if Philips facilities moved to Argentina they might someday be nationalized. We finally agreed that Prof. Bakker will be sending us a complete catalogue so that I may decide which apparatus, equipment, special electronic tubes, etc. are of interest to us. As you can see, I made no commitments. I stated clearly that all purchases would require very short delivery terms. We also discussed the possibility of purchasing the Philips Synchro Cyclotron, an equipment which made a very good impression on me. I would recommend buying it for the planned nuclear physics training center in Argentina since it's easy to operate. Ultimately, however, it is a question of price; therefore, I leave it in your hands. When our visitor returns to The Netherlands, surely the press will question him regarding his impressions. It will be interesting to learn what he has to say. This is all, then, regarding Prof. Bakker."

In another paragraph Richter also informs Perón about the latest developments on Huemul, saying he was looking forward to the presidential visit. To a certain extent, however, he seems to prefer the visit to take place after the large facility is completed: "On my return to Bariloche, the Experimental Plant was completely overhauled. We still need to finish some pending work, but want to do it in a modernized facility with a greater capacity. We are heading apparently to some very interesting developments in this respect. You can rest assured: we are doing everything within our power at the Pilot Plant to transform Argentine leadership in atomic matters into a practical success of great significance. The fact that you should wish to visit us in Bariloche makes me extremely happy. I agree that your forthcoming visit will be even more interesting when the great atomic energy furnace is ready. It will make us very proud should you decide to christen it yourself. Whenever you decide to come, however, I am sure you will see some extraordinary things. According to our present schedule, we estimate that atomic energy production experiments will be resumed within three weeks."

It is likely that Prof. Bakker, who remained three more days in Buenos Aires, took the opportunity to insist before Argentine officials on the purchase of the cyclotron. This piece of equipment was one of the most powerful and modern particle accelerator of its time. A few days later, The New York Times carried the following headlines: "Netherlands, Argentina Near Atom Accord; Dutch said to Offer Technical Assistance. The Netherlands is understood to have offered technical assistance and facilities for construction of equipment. Word is being expected from Buenos Aires on an offer to build a cyclotron at a cost of US$ 790.000. A model of the Amsterdam cyclotron, largest in Europe, was left in Argentina by Prof. C. J. Bakker, director of the Netherlands Institute for Nuclear Research, during his visit there last month, which was undertaken after preliminary discussions between Prince Bernhard and President Perón." The article continued saying: "An authoritative source emphasized tonight that the cooperation would cover only peaceful nuclear research and that the primary Dutch interest in the arrangement was commercial." It also pointed out that the arrangement was not directly connected with special research conducted by Prof. Richter on Huemul.

The purchase order for the synchrocyclotron was signed on June 30th, 1951, thirty days after Bakker's visit.

The National Department of Atomic Energy (DNEA)

If the purchase of the synchrocyclotron was not directly connected with atomic research on Huemul, where would it be used? In his letter to Perón, Richter said: "I would recommend to buy it for the planned nuclear physics training center..." What was he referring to?

In May 1951, the Government issued a rather intricate decree # 9697. One of its purposes was to define the composition of the National Commission for Atomic Energy (CNEA), created a year earlier without naming its members. Now it was established that Perón himself would preside the Commission whose other members were Richter, (Minister) Mende and Gonzalez (acting as Secretary).

The other purpose of this decree was to create three new entities, all related to Atomic Energy, and with seemingly overlapping objectives.

At first sight the content of this decree looks like a superfluous multiplication of bureaucracy and one wonders what was the real purpose of it. Was the National Commission for Atomic Energy (CNEA) not sufficient for taking care of all problems related to this field? As mentioned earlier, the CNEA had been created to coordinate and advance nuclear research; to control its development and to offer suggestions to the government regarding its best practical uses.

The new bill stated that "recent experiments conducted at the Atomic Energy Pilot Plant on Huemul where highly satisfactory results were achieved emphasize the need to adopt early measures for the Argentine Government to channel, plan and make the best possible use of this new source of energy."

The new entities were: A National Plant of Atomic Energy (PNEA) in Bariloche for conducting atomic research, and assuring prompt and efficient exploitation of this type of energy; a National Laboratory of Atomic Energy (LNEA) operating within the Plant and finally a National Department of Atomic Energy (DNEA) to "carry out, monitor and coordinate all activities related to the exploitation and utilization of atomic energy in addition to performing such tasks whenever necessary." As we see, all with the same ultimate aim.

The reason for this multiplicity appears to lie somewhere else. Richter was appointed head of the Laboratory and responsible for the Plant; his category was to be equivalent to a National Director, reporting directly to the President of the Republic and having under his control as many governmental agencies as might be called for (more yet?). He was granted official status plus land and property (which to all practical purposes had already been under his jurisdiction since the second semester of 1949 anyway), essentially following the guidelines of the organizational chart prepared by Richter himself a few months earlier: "...it must be borne in mind that the Director is solely responsible to the President."

Land and property under Richter included Huemul Island, Gallinas Island, Gaviotas Island (the last two being merely rocky promontories east of Huemul), Playa Bonita (on the mainland facing the island), part of the military area and a few houses of the Bariloche Garrison (in time, this area became the premises where the Bariloche Atomic Center stands today) and the Peninsula de San Pedro Hotel, located some twelve miles away to lodge visitors.

Up to that point the document seems aimed at providing an institutional framework for Richter's work and at satisfying his wishes of full independence.

On the other hand, DNEA, with headquarters in Buenos Aires, was placed under Gonzalez. The Colonel authored the draft of this decree. He knew Richter wanted independence and he did not mind that. On the contrary, he liked the idea of relinquishing his responsibility for what Richter did in Huemul. At the same time Gonzalez wanted an institution he could control. So a piece for each one seemed to be the answer to the problem. The potential conflict owing to the overlapping objectives was not a concern, at least in those days. Gonzalez went with the draft to Perón and since Perón was willing to satisfy both the scientist and the Colonel, he signed it.

As far as DNEA was concerned, Gonzalez's intentions were wholesome. He believed young people needed to be trained in atomic matters. It annoyed him that Richter refused to accept graduate students at the Bariloche laboratory. This attitude is clearly apparent in the letter of September 1950, already quoted (ref. 63, previous chapter Project Huemul), which he received from his son.

Gonzalez knew next to nothing about atomic energy and made no bones of it. Consequently, his efforts to create an Argentine institution separate from Huemul to train students and organize working teams, in a gradual, earnest and more conventional way, were praiseworthy.

Among other functions, DNEA still had to "provide for the needs of personnel, materials and elements" for the Bariloche Plant, a service Richter had requested. He refused having anything to do with administrative or accounting matters; he had already stressed the need for this type of service in his organizational plan. There was nothing Gonzalez could do about it since Perón had summoned him to fulfill precisely that task. It was one of those inevitable burdens. Thereafter, Gonzalez's participation in the Project Huemul was limited to administrative dealings exclusively. It had never been otherwise anyway, but now it was in print.

The other tasks of DNEA provided a more distinct profile to the new institution. It had to train personnel and control production, marketing and exploitation of all atomic energy related materials in Argentina. Despite the apparent duplication of objectives with Bariloche, the DNEA was entrusted with a large and significant scope of action. It also had to take care of radiological protection and safety not merely in connection with the use of radioactive materials within Argentina but also regarding the control of radioactive effects of atomic explosions beyond Argentine borders.

Also DNEA had to study financial strategies, to divulge technical and scientific aspects of atomic energy so as "to create a national awareness on the subject" and organize a Scientific Library.

The plan had been well outlined. Beyond the partial overlap with the Bariloche Plant which was doomed to produce inevitable conflicts, the DNEA constituted a new and significant step. It carried the seed of a well-conceived institution capable of producing significant achievements in time.

"I was a good friend of Dr. Cruz, at the time President of the University of Cuyo - recalled Colonel Gonzalez. [6] He once mentioned they had in Cuyo a fine group of students, whose leader was an extremely able, serious and enthusiastic professor by the name of Otto Gamba. Cruz offered to ask Gamba to come and talk with me if I were interested. Since I know nothing about physics, I wanted to have knowledgeable people around me. So, aided by Father Bussolini, Capt. Beninson and Dr. Gamba, I concluded that we could offer courses not only in common physics but also in nuclear physics. We used to meet at first in an apartment on the Barolo Arcade, which belonged to the Migrations Bureau. There we made plans, discussed who could come, etc., and when I realized all this might work, I asked Perón to purchase the building at 25 de Mayo Street and Rivadavia."

Gonzalez remembered Gamba with affection. "He had all the drive; Gamba was quite extraordinary. He kept pestering me all day long, he wanted so hard the project to succeed."

In April 1951, while Gonzalez drafted Bill 9697 he encouraged Gamba to recruit young students for DNEA. He also turned to the `the old guard' Prof. Teófilo Isnardi, and José B. Collo. Gaviola was also summoned but as it had happened the previous year, Gaviola denounced the Huemul "fraud" and, according to his own testimony, offered to act as "a member of Richter's firing squad". [7] Hence Gaviola was left out.

As soon as the decree giving birth to DNEA in 1951 became official, a group of selected graduates in Physics – Carlos A. Mallmann, Ernesto Bertomeu, Horacio Bosch, Adulio Cichini, Juan Roederer and others - started to work in the old building at 25 de Mayo Street.

The beginnings of this novel and vigorous activity coincided with the purchase of the Philips synchrocyclotron. Gonzalez never knew, however, that the powerful equipment had first been offered to Richter and that he had recommended it for the new research center under Gonzalez in Buenos Aires. Events related to atomic development in Argentina evolved fast in those weeks. On May 17th, the PNEA, the LNEA and the DNEA were created. Richter's letter to Perón describing Bakker's visit and the offer of the synchrocyclotron was dated a few days later, on May 28th. Gonzalez got the offer of this accelerator via the general manager of Philips in Argentina, and the decision to buy it was probably helped by Gamba's enthusiastic support. Gonzalez recalled these events in this way: "It was not a proposal which had been submitted to Perón. No, I undertook it myself, on my friends' advice." He was obviously ignorant of the role which Prince Bernhard, and later on, Dr. Bakker and Richter himself, had played in this connection. His testimony, however, seems to stress the fact that Perón gave some kind of general approval and then it was up to Philips in Argentina to conclude the deal.

An instrument such as the synchrocyclotron needed to be housed in an appropriate building. Minister Ramon Cereijo had recently expropriated the Massone Institute, which manufactured pharmaceutical products, to install in its place the state run Chemical Industries. The expropriation had been poorly conducted and it became widely referred to by anti Peronists as a typical example of the government's authoritarian style. As DNEA needed space, government officials thought of letting Gonzalez use half of this building. "I first inspected the building", remembered Gonzalez with a touch of pride, "then told Perón: 'Look, either you give me the whole building or none at all.'". Perón agreed: "Ok, it's yours. Go and tell Cereijo to keep out of it."

In early 1952, the headquarters of the National Department of Atomic Energy moved to the new premises, where they have remained ever since.

An Independent Witness

Meanwhile life with all its wealth of human interactions was going on at the Atomic Plant in Bariloche. Richter's relationship with Pasolli and Prieto had become strained from the time of the reactor demolishing affair. Pasolli was reluctant to continue working for Richter, and Richter was against having the Army Engineer Corps working on the island any longer.

Consequently, Richter insisted before Perón on the need of having a non military construction company. On the strength of his recent success and its impact on government circles, Richter obtained what he sought, at least in part.

During the late Thirties, while in Italy, Perón met the Marquis de Incisa, who later emigrated to Argentina and by 1951 had a construction company of name SACES operating in the country. Undoubtedly Richter would have preferred a German company not Italian as Perón suggested but he accepted it. The contract with SACES was signed on May 8th, and its first task was to demolish the great reactor which was still standing, eight months after the historical decision of tearing it down.

In the meantime, the reactor's huge cement structure had been surrounded by walls three ft. thick and 48 ft. high with a roof on top. The demolition work took place inside these walls. The effect of the explosives on these walls are still visible. When in 1979, Bertolo, the mason, accompanied the author on a most instructive tour of the island, he exclaimed [8]: "Can you imagine what it was like when the dynamite exploded with the roof still on?"

Bertolo, who continued working for SACES, recalled the excitement of those days: "When we were about to complete the demolition, orders came that the reactor had to be built underground. So we had to construct a large platform made out of 2" planks in order not to destroy the whole roof structure. You can't imagine what it looked like at the time: it was 18 ft. higher than what you now see and with the roof. Later on Dr. Richter ordered the walls to be lowered so that a slab might be placed instead of a roof with girders. The girders were used afterwards on the workshops down the hill."

An accidental witness to this hectic activity was Mr. Ricardo Rossi, an engineer from Philips/Buenos Aires who visited the island in June with the catalogues promised by Bakker.

He arrived on the island precisely when Richter had ordered a new reactor to be built underground and construction squads were beginning to pierce the rock.

Instructions to visit Huemul came as a complete surprise to Rossi, since he knew nothing about Bakker's visit. Philips/Buenos Aires had maintained previous contacts with DNEA for some time. "They were first rate clients" Rossi recalled – "a large number of purchase orders kept coming in from Huemul; they included photoelectric cells made out of gold and that sort of thing. We kept sending them brochures all the time."[9]

"I was indeed surprised at being asked to visit Huemul. On whose orders, I didn't know. Possibly, it was due to Gonzalez, who was a friend of the president of the company." The visit seemed to be premeditated. Before the trip, Gonzalez summoned Rossi and told him he had a son down there, but he needed additional confidential information on what was going on. He added that Richter, as a rule, allowed no one on the island unless he fully trusted the person or was a close friend of his.

Rossi's testimony is valuable because it determines the approximate date when Gonzalez (despite the recent announcement and the accompanying euphoria) began to nurse increasing doubts regarding the Huemul activities. Since May, and as a result of Decree 9697, his responsibility regarding the project had been substantially reduced, Gonzalez was no longer involved in technical decisions. His interview with Rossi, nonetheless, revealed he still felt some degree of commitment and wished to be kept informed. Also, despite the fact that his responsibility had been curtailed, he still had to provide funds for the project. He could not continue extending checks for ever increasing amounts without at least hoping they would render some fruit. Ordinary incidents the kind that never reach the newspapers or are publicly disclosed had him worried. He received odd bits of information from sources of all sorts; construction workers, electricians, members of Gendarmeria (Border Guards), and other people living next to Richter in everyday life and for whom Richter's actions were plainly visible. For instance, it was disturbing that the reactor demolition work took more than a year to begin. Was it really necessary to hire a private company for such a simple task? Or was it merely a whim? Richter decided to take 18 ft. off the wall to have the roof lower. Could he not have anticipated this need before it was built to 48 ft.?

Many other changes were being proposed at the time: the photography laboratory, the power plant and several other buildings were to be relocated. In certain cases, like the power plant, Richter justified his decision by invoking potential radiation hazards. In a letter to his son, Gonzalez groped for answers: "...another thing I don't understand is the relocation of the power plant. If there is actually danger of gamma radiations, then the whole island would be endangered, not just the power plant." Naive statements are often full of logic. Gonzalez suggested that the matter should be given further thought. Nevertheless, his suspicions had not reached the limit, so he added: "yet, if Richter says he wants it that way, let it be: change the location of the power plant according to his instructions."

Morena, commercial manager of Philips, accompanied Rossi to Bariloche. They stayed at the Tres Reyes Hotel on the boulevard bordering lake Nahuel Huapi. Cane, a senior official of the National Parks Service came with the safe-conducts to cross over to the island. Since March, the secret of Huemul had become an everyday topic of conversation in town, though nobody knew what was going on. "All we knew, was that they were trying to obtain the H bomb", Rossi recalled. The opportunity of visiting the island was a privilege shared by very few. Rossi and Morena listened avidly to the stories Cane had to tell about the private life of Richter, his coming and going when he visited Bariloche, the influence wielded by one of his Austrian lady secretaries, the noise resulting from explosions, the island's illumination at night which was three times brighter than that in the whole town of Bariloche, the guards who kept watch round the island, the countless railway wagons arriving daily in Bariloche full of bricks and building materials, etc., etc. It was evident, that local residents looked down on what was going on at Huemul. Few gave credit to the reports on atomic research conducted on the island, an attitude based on simple intuition, and some like Cane thought the end of the project was near. "I have a feeling he (Richter) won't be seeing the first snows this winter", Cane remarked aboard the taxi that took them along the winding road by the lakeshore toward Playa Bonita. It was the beginning of the winter season and snow had yet to fall on the lowlands.

The road connecting Bariloche and Llao Llao was flanked by exuberant vegetation. The summit of Mount Lopez, covered with fresh snow, emerged from woods of pines and coihues a truly impressive sight to the visitor's dazzled eyes. "We had an opportunity, then, to take a good look at the place where Richter worked." - Rossi recalled – "His office was not too large. I was very much impressed by the library: the books were all high school level. He had a beautiful Nestler slide rule which he didn't know how to use; he was clumsy with it. After talking to some of the people down there all of them of low scientific level it seemed to me that the man had impressed them with a mere explosion of a hydrogen oxygen mixture, induced with a spark. He had a Geiger counter according to what I heard him saying to other people while I waited. Our interview lasted less than an hour. We spoke in basic technical English. He had little to say on the items in our catalog and advanced no technical opinions in connection with what we had to offer. The conversation was trivial enough. He restricted himself to translating the information contained in the catalogues. It surprised me very much that as a scientist he didn't even try to evaluate how much I knew."

Another casual remark closely related to the above came up during his conversation with the author in August 1979: "...while speaking with Cane, he told me that a German of name Tank, who worked on the Pulqui had been there a little earlier... Apparently, this man had come to study thermodynamic aspects involved in Richter's work. Well, according to Cane, when this man left he said that 'he couldn't continue talking with Richter because he lacked the required technical level'."

There is evidence that by August 1950, Tank still supported Richter. At about that time Tank sent Brigadier Ahrens the memorandum Richter had asked him to produce on his way to Buenos Aires, when the issue had arisen whether or not to demolish the reactor. Tank wrote then a letter to Richter which reflected his appreciation for the German scientist. [10] In that letter, Tank showed his distress over a couple of failures with the Pulqui. He had been curtly reprimanded by his Argentine aeronautics superiors, and his pride had been badly hurt. "Once the cause was detected, the accident became unimportant" Tank had written "It's a pity, however, that in cases such as these your `fellow-citizens' lack the required expertise and to make matters worse, now Ojeda is set on making Behrens take a fresh training course before being allowed to fly the Pulqui again. That this kind of punishment should be imposed on one of our best German test pilots deserves no comments. Just imagine you had a slight problem in your experimental work, or a deficient installation, or some kind of difficulty and, after cursing you at will, you or some of your men were sentenced to take a ten semester physics experimental course at some Argentine university before being allowed to continue doing research."

By June 1951, Tank had changed his mind. Perhaps, judging by Cane's comments, Tank would not have considered ridiculous by then to send Richter back to school. Cane had told Rossi that Tank did not wish to continue being involved in a project which lacked scientific level. Tank's opinions on the Huemul project were disclosed to Gonzalez only a year later.

Again, according to Rossi: "We tried time and again to discuss the matter at hand but it was useless. The Cockcroft - Walton accelerator was mentioned, but Richter was uninterested. I believe the purchase of the synchrocyclotron was already decided by then. All during the meeting, Richter maintained an extremely wary attitude; he expressed practically no technical opinions. When we tried, for example, to discuss photoelectric cells a subject which I know well since I have had previous experience with it in Philips we were discussing the work function, that is, the relationship between a certain electronic emission and a given amount of illumination. Richter took no part in the discussion. He refused to offer any explanation while insisting doggedly on the gold cells. If what he wished was some relatively inefficient cells, there are other materials less expensive than gold to make low efficiency cells. Morena and I were allowed to visit the island accompanied by someone who had practically no technical knowledge. All along, I kept trying to figure out how they could prevent an explosion caused by hydrogen and oxygen. In what way could they avoid the presence of oxygen within the reaction chamber, without having created a vacuum before? I recalled that in The Netherlands a plant had blown to pieces when trying to produce hydrogenated iron. The accident had always stayed on my mind to such an extent that once, while working with hydrogen in Buenos Aires, I was actually terrified. We took every conceivable precaution. I was telling the person who was accompanying us all this when we came to see an enormous hole that was being dug out of the rock. It was a monumental undertaking of staggering dimensions; we were deeply impressed."

It was actually surprising that Morena and Rossi should have been allowed to tour the island with such liberty. Shortly before a technician of Westinghouse had come to Huemul to fix one of the power generators and had been forced to walk blindfolded all the way to the power plant. [11]

About this episode and without too much conviction, Rossi said: "I don't know, really. Perhaps Richter trusted people from Philips..." (yet Bakker had not been allowed to set foot on the island). "My impression is that Richter was deep at the time in some inner problem or personal conflict, and he was simply uninterested in everything around him. He was utterly indifferent to everything he did or ordered to be purchased. Huemul was such a monumental undertaking that I in his place would have run like mad all day long checking plans, verifying measurements, doing a thousand things."

Immediately on returning to Buenos Aires, Rossi was summoned to Government House. Colonel Gonzalez was eager to learn what he had to say. Rossi told Gonzalez everything he thought about Huemul, disregarding what the Philips President had recommended: "Be cautious. Don't forget, Rossi, that you are a Philips employee." Rossi thought he had to give priority to his duty as citizen and, as such, he could not withhold information that he deemed important for the country.

As soon as Rossi finished talking, Colonel Gonzalez said he would immediately call upon the President and Mende, and asked Rossi to please wait in case Perón required any further explanations. Whether the meeting actually took place, and if it did, what the President's reaction was, we do not know. Mende and Gonzalez returned to thank Rossi and he went home at rest with his conscience. Rossi was only thirty years old and had a taste for daring adventures. "I was happy about the meeting with Colonel Gonzalez. After feeling one is up against a monolithic wall at least that's what I thought of the circle around Perón, with everybody paying homage to him it was refreshing to find someone in the Government who wanted to know the truth. He was worthy of applause. Yes, it's comforting to find someone who cares, who worries about defending our dignity. It was an encouraging experience; it made me feel good that there should be someone like Gonzalez at the Casa Rosada."

Reaction to International Response

"Richter seemed to be deep at the time in an inner problem or in some personal conflict, and was simply uninterested in all that was happening around him on Huemul...", Rossi had said. Was this remark significant? Was there any reason for Richter to be worried, or was it merely a temporary, albeit unusual, state of mind? Prieto's earlier remarks on the peculiar personality of the German scientist come to mind: "...occasionally, Richter turned his gaze inwards, as if staring into a vacuum, completely oblivious of everything around him. One would think he was daydreaming, or in a trance..."

When Rossi visited the island, perhaps he found Richter in one of those trance like moods for which he was not prepared and therefore was surprised by it. Yet Richter acted differently on this occasion: he might have pretended disinterest to avoid technical discussions with the Philips people but this does not explain his quite abnormal permissive attitude towards Rossi and Morena who were allowed to walk around the island like no other visitor ever.

In those first months of 1951 a lot of things had happened. The experimental discovery in February, the worldwide press coverage of March followed by citations and honors, the visit of Prince Bernhard and his scientific envoy, the official creation of the Atomic Energy Pilot Plant in Bariloche, the formal appointment of Richter as head of the Huemul Laboratory with almost unlimited authority, the SACES contract, the initiation of the much delayed construction work for the new reactor underground... all these were indeed auspicious events. Could there be something disturbing Richter to such an extent that it caused him to lose his characteristic poise and self assurance?

Perhaps there was. Richter did not expect the string of unfavorable comments that the announcement had elicited from the international scientific community. Convinced as he was of the validity and importance of his scientific findings, he probably hoped to earn sound international prestige. He had failed to get recognition in Europe after the war when he wandered about seeking a respectful job. [12] Perón, however, had granted him the opportunity of testing his ideas. Now that these were starting to bear fruit, it was time to reap the credit he deserved from his colleagues overseas and that he had sought for so long. And along with it, his ultimate goal: a US contract to work beside the world famous leaders of nuclear research.

Such was not the case, however. Quite the contrary: comments by Fermi, Heisenberg, Gamov and other prominent scientists had not been gratifying. As a matter of fact, the tone of their remarks had been definitely skeptical. And now on top of that, two months after the first reactions, the editor of United Nations World came up with a disturbing challenge. Professor Hans Thirring, head of the Theoretical Physics Institute at the University of Vienna, upon the editor's request had written a pointed, acrid commentary on Perón's announcement, which was published in the May 1951 issue. The editor was now offering Richter the opportunity of exercising the right of reply.

In the editor's own words: "When news about the Argentine atomic bomb broke, the editors of United Nations World realized its importance in the international scene and decided to investigate the unexpected event. The first result was a statement by Prof. Thirring which will be forwarded to Mr. Ronald Richter with the request to comment on it. If such a reply arrives, we shall be happy to publish it in our next issue." (13)

The article by Thirring was entitled "Is Perón's A Bomb a Swindle?" (14). It was not a very elaborate work. Over half the article dealt with a crank who had visited the University of Vienna in July 1950, claiming he had built a miniature atom bomb. Thirring explains in detail the demonstration that took place, which was also witnessed by Lise Meitner who happened to be there at the time. The point Thirring makes of this episode is that this strange character had an Austrian passport with an Argentine visa stamped on it. The story, of course, had nothing to do with Richter, who was living at the time in Bariloche. Perhaps Thirring was trying to associate a couple of ideas as an introduction to the analysis of Perón's announcement: atomic energy, fantasy, Argentina, delusions, illegal refugees, etc.

The analysis which followed was brief and the conclusion implacable. According to Thirring, there was a 50% chance that Perón had fallen victim to a crank suffering from self delusion; a 40% chance that Perón had been taken in by a sly swindler; a 9% chance that Perón, aided by Richter, was attempting to bluff the world, and finally, the remaining bit, a 1% chance, that Richter's assertions were true. (15)

An inset carried a brief biography of the author: "...a scientist of exceptional stature, born in Austria in 1888. Among his books are a basic study of Einstein's theory, and a History of the Atom Bomb published in 1947. An outspoken liberal, after the war he was ardently wooed by the Russians, but gave them a rude shock with his emphatic declaration of faith in the principles and ideals of Democracy at the Conference on Intellectual Freedom last June, in Berlin." Consequently, Thirring enjoyed an enormous prestige (helped by his political views akin to western intellectual circles, to which the journal aimed). Therefore, even though his opinions could be regarded as somewhat presumptuous and subjective, they had an unquestionable impact.

Richter had never written anything about his scientific work. International indices of published scientific works register not a single paper of his. [16] His PhD thesis was never published. The August 1950 report to Brigadier Ahrens had been written by Tank and the "forthcoming publications" promised at the March 25th press conference had not materialized. What to do with this challenge? To pick up the gauntlet and proceed for the first time to write down his ideas? He could not neglect the challenge nor take it lightly. If he refused to answer, his credibility would be definitely ruined in the eyes of the scientific community, and his chances of reaching a place in leading scientific circles would be nil. If he accepted the challenge, everybody would read his reply. United Nations World was one of the most widely read and respected magazines of its kind in the post-war years. Moreover, some of Thirring's statements were difficult for Richter to ignore, as for instance, the assertion that Richter's results were "pseudo technical achievements which so irresistibly lure the imagination of power-thirsty dictators", or the subtle reference he made to the Nazi scientist collaborator image, which Richter detested so strongly.

According to available data, the United Nations World editor's letter and Rossi's visit to Huemul seem to have occurred at about the same time ("the first snows had yet to fall", Bakker had already been there). It is therefore likely that the visit took place while Richter was facing the painful dilemma of replying to Thirring.

Richter finally wrote a long letter which includes some interesting paragraphs, although it does not reveal technical details which were not known. [17]

Both the beginning and the end of the letter contain political remarks. After expressing his thanks to the editor for giving him the opportunity of replying, Richter bends the full force of his fury on Thirring: "Unfortunately Prof. Thirring's article contains not facts, but infamy. The reactor operation crew and I are deeply sorry for Herr Thirring, because he revealed himself to be a typical text book professor with a strong scientific inferiority complex, probably supported by political hatred". Further on he adds that "perhaps he is suffering from unwelcome political circumstances in Europe" (a counter attack for the insinuation that he was Nazi?).

Leaving politics aside, he then turns to subjects of a more technical nature. Richter categorically denies the fact that an atomic explosion had ever occurred, or that a bomb had been built, or that there was any intention of doing so in the future. "Therefore he points out there is no atom bomb secret in Argentina."

Richter explains that in Europe he had worked on extremely high temperature related problems, and that at first, he had planned using thermonuclear fusion reactions exclusively as a research tool in connection with extreme temperature conditions. While doing so, "I made some discoveries concerning the control of `extremely hot plasma zones'. Later, I learned how to produce a zone of tremendous heat."

"Perón never asked me to study atom bomb problems. He gave me the chance to carry on in the development of thermonuclear reactors (while) the whole world seemed to be fascinated exclusively by the nuclear fission process." He avoids going into technical details, but points out that he possesses the most modern instruments and apparatus.

In connection with H bomb related problems that came up during the course of his experiments, Richter says: "...this enabled us to understand why in an H bomb one must use tritium produced in a fission reactor." [18] This, as well as the following comment, has a special historical value: "One year ago, I reported to President Perón on the explosion disintegration of the Lithium 6 isotope and the new type of neutron chain reaction, so decisive in thermonuclear bombs."

Further on, he emphasizes: "...It is my personal opinion that in our pilot plant we probably have more knowledge about thermonuclear reaction kinetics than have the United States and Great Britain at the present moment." [19]

Regarding the experiment of February 16th, Richter emphatically claims to have achieved the first controlled thermonuclear reaction at a technical level. "Scientists in the United States, in Great Britain, and in other countries are waiting for detailed information about our processes and" -he underlines- "the Russians are waiting for the same information."

Richter's letter is written in forceful style but the statements remain ambiguous and difficult to evaluate from a scientific point of view since, as expected, no hard data are provided.

Richter suggests holding scientific discussion with foreign colleagues and with a touch of style, he proposes leaving aside `psychological warfare' methods as employed by the press and engaging in "a sportsmanlike race under fair conditions with everybody trying to win for the West".

Precisely in those days, the international press committed a sensational gaffe. A Brazilian newspaper reported that on May 24th Richter had been arrested. (The German scientist was at the time acting as host to Prof. Bakker in Bariloche). With sense of humor Richter remarks in his letter that he had read with much interest in `Time' magazine the news about his arrest being kept in absolute secrecy. "It must really have been the deepest degree of secrecy because I only knew of it through the newspapers".

Journalists on the Island

Another problem bothering Richter during that month of June 1951, was the difficulty in obtaining a US visa. Richter had not changed his mind about this, and now the matter was being openly discussed with Gonzalez and Perón, an uncomfortable situation for both of them. It was indeed disturbing that the holder of the Argentine atomic secret, endowed with extraordinary powers and enjoying almost unlimited support from the President, should wish to take a temporary leave of absence in the United States! And precisely at a time when expectations stemming from his recent discoveries were at their peak ...! Why did Richter insist on travelling to North America? Perón and Gonzalez kept turning this and other questions over in their minds, while trying to figure the best way to deal with Richter on this issue.

Perón wrote to his protégé on June 1st, resolutely addressing the problem. In a straightforward manner he tells Richter that he is aware of his intentions to travel north. The news had obviously been transmitted by Capt. Gonzalez Jr. to his father, and through him to Perón.

The President felt no qualms about writing to Richter on this matter, even though he might be placing himself in a delicate position should the news spread. Perón had committed himself and the country as a whole too far already to afford running the risk of being asked why Richter was leaving Huemul, even if temporarily. Despite this, Perón's attitude as reflected in his letter was admirable: he took a straight, clear and noble stand. Perón wrote: "As you well know, there is only a moral commitment between you and I. Insofar as your personal actions are concerned, you are free to do as you please. You are an Argentine citizen and, as such, entitled to the same rights as I am. Under no circumstances will I be the one to limit those rights. At this moment, I am merely taking the liberty of transmitting to you some information through Gonzalez. Should you decide to travel, however, we shall be ready to help you do so." [20]

Richter never left for the United States. Perhaps Gonzalez managed to persuade him, or perhaps he was unable to obtain the visa since the work contract he had been trying to secure never came. Whichever the reason, Richter recalled the episode in the following way: "The letter which General Perón wrote to me on June 1 represented a great deal to me. The President stated I was at liberty to leave whenever I wished, and that only a moral commitment existed between us (despite the fact I had signed a binding contract until August 1953). Such a noble gesture on part of the President had the effect of making me stay in Argentina. I could not betray him. I wanted to honor his friendship. Since he didn't even express a wish, he cannot be accused of suggesting somehow that his wish was an order." [21]

There are reasons to suspect, however, that the decision was not wholly Richter's, as he failed to obtain a visa. [22]

Apparently, this incident had a positive influence on Richter's mood, as by the end of that month for the first time since operations began the Huemul project chief allowed the gentlemen of the press to visit the island. He even went as far as acting as their host for four complete days. The journalists, somewhat under the influence of official propaganda, arrived at the island prepared to witness extraordinary sights. They were deeply impressed when they left. News and articles were constantly dispatched from Bariloche to the Buenos Aires newspapers bearing impressive titles such as "Spectacular Experiments Are Imminent in Bariloche"; "From Huemul Island, a Surprising Development Will Rock the World"; "Richter was a Russian Prisoner in 1945"; "The Atomic Experiment Can Continue Even Without Richter". Also, there were others as exaggerated as, "Our Country is the Leading Nation Worldwide in Atomic Energy Research".

On June 25th, the fifth edition of the evening paper La Razon published an interesting account of the first day of the visit: "It is raining. As of yesterday, journalists have been staying at the Pistarini Hotel. They are now waiting for Dr. Richter, though probably the visit to the island will be cancelled because of the weather. Although it is cloudy, the slope of Mount Lopez can be seen all covered with fresh snow. At 11.10, Richter makes his appearance driving his own car and apologizing for having been unable to greet the journalists yesterday evening, as he was sick. The rain has stopped and Prof. Richter invites the journalists to cross over to the island." When Richter assures them that they will not get wet, the reporter notes that "the scientist cares not about himself, but thinks of the others. While concentrating exclusively on his work, Richter has an outlook on life which is only attained by people who live intensely. His reactions at times remind us of a young boy having fun."

Admiringly, the journalist quotes some of Richter's remarks: "It's not at all surprising that I invented this new atomic process. Since I have done nothing else all my life, I had to invent something of the sort ...and it's not much". The reporter describes Richter breaking into laughter, happy to have said something "he is intimately convinced of and which he trusts everybody will be able to understand."

The article continued: "Visitors arrive in Playa Bonita where a barge is waiting for them. The island a mile offshore, covering 60 hectares seems like a fortress. Again referring to foreign slander, Richter remarks `I'm sorry I can't give you the pleasure of taking my picture behind bars'. Coihues and Arrayanes (both local species of trees) are all about us. Journalists disembark on the shore slithering in deep mud. As they start climbing, it begins to rain again. They are concerned, knowing that Richter has been sick but the German scientist continues to climb at a good pace with his head uncovered, while talking incessantly. He has a large forehead, brown eyes under bushy, light eyebrows, a well drawn mouth and a resolute chin. His height is above average, he is strongly built and obviously healthy. One cannot help being impressed by his reactions. He is the kind of person one trusts instinctively, just like one trusts anyone devoid of evil. His expressions, gestures and smiles, which light up his face frequently, suggest he has a happy disposition and is inclined to take life as it comes..."

"Noises of machinery in motion can now be heard. A large, unfinished building appears before our eyes. A shed full of workers can be seen at a turn of the road. The group comes to a low building with a metal door (probably Lab #2, where the experimental reactor was mounted). Somebody asks: 'How many Argentine citizens work on the island?' Prof. Richter replies: 'It might be better to ask how many foreigners work here ...there are three foreigners, the rest of us are all Argentines'. Replying a reporter, Richter apologizes for not showing them the small reactor, "which no one is supposed to see since it constitutes the core of the secret. Its special characteristics make the fundamental elements on which it operates too visible."

The group reaches the highest part of the island where Lab #1 is located. A huge hole, 33 ft. deep, has been blasted in the rock. 'We plan to begin work on this reactor within six months. By that time, you may look forward to some extraordinary developments. In addition, we are engaged in biological research; we shall start producing isotopes within two months. They will be used to fight cancer.'

The various articles appearing in Noticias Graficas were even more enthusiastic. They stressed the revolutionary consequences of the new atomic method, Richter's unlimited regard for the ability of the Argentine citizens working with him, the manner in which Argentina had taken the lead in atomic matters, the atomic power plants which were to be built, and the splendid business that Argentina could derive from all this by signing cooperation agreements with more industrialized nations.

This last piece of news did not slip by unnoticed to the Associated Press. Under the title "Argentine Hints at Atomic Trade", the New York Times on June 26th informed: "Atomic scientist Ronald Richter hinted today that Argentina might be willing to sell her atomic secrets 'if she can make a good deal'.

He told reporters visiting the Huemul atomic plant, 850 miles south of Buenos Aires, that there was also a possibility Argentina might exchange the secret for machinery and raw materials needed for atomic industrial development."

The first foreign journalist to visit Huemul was Mr. J. Zugschwert, who was able to talk with Richter in his native tongue. He arrived on the island just a few days before the Argentine journalists. Zugschwert pointed out in his report [23] that atomic facilities on Huemul were different from similar installations elsewhere. He was impressed by the fact that everybody was able to walk to and fro unhindered. "It is not true that there are thousands of people here, only two hundred perhaps. Trains do not arrive in Bariloche loaded with minerals nor carrying huge containers."

His description is captivating: "I am standing right in the center of the facilities area. A freezing wind keeps blowing. Richter raised no objections to my taking as many pictures as I wanted. I couldn't see, however, the inside of any building, except the house with the most secret center. Richter walked over with me. He commented that up to then, he had always protected the atomic furnace from curious glances. 'You are the first journalist to know something about it', Richter told me."

"A deafening noise was coming from down deep: the foundations were to be placed 36 ft. down below and barely a quarter would rise above the surface. Eventually, this will become the largest furnace operating on the island; an enormous concrete cylinder whose seemingly plain thick walls will lodge a great variety of scientific processes. When completed, it will turn out to be quite a complex building, with some hundreds of cubic meters of concrete guarding the ultimate secret."

"We then returned to the vantage point from where we could see all around. Four constructions of interest were visible: the building where the furnace is located, rising about three stories high; two one floor labs, none of them over 500 m2. As far as can be estimated, the facilities cover approximately 2,000 m2 in all." (Zugschwert was probably standing on the second terrace, within sight of labs # 1, 2, 4, and the power plant. When he visited the island, personnel lodgings and equipment warehouses had already been built on the first terrace some distance below.)

"While standing there in the center of the island, the secret seemed even more unreachable, as one had the impression of being in the midst of a small industrial facility. There are no chimneys in sight, no high tension power structures, no deafening noises typical of large industrial processes."

"Labs seem to be something special. We have been told they are equipped with the most modern instruments available, yet nobody knows what goes on behind their walls. However, labs are the only buildings surrounded by barbed wire, with iron doors, double guards and searchlights at night. "

"There are, in addition, four assembly barracks, guards' headquarters, a photo lab and a canteen. I was allowed the unheard-of liberty of looking around as much as I wanted, but always accompanied. What actually hampered me from seeing most of the island was the rugged landscape and abundant vegetation."

"Ronald Richter was waiting for me by the main lab. 'What have you seen?', he asked me. 'I have seen nothing', I told him. Richter laughed. 'I haven't seen anything, either', he replied."

"We walked again toward the site of the great reactor. He showed me a photo of the furnace where the world's first thermonuclear reaction had taken place. It was just a plain concrete structure with no equipment in it."

"We headed then for the pier. A truck passed us and then a jeep. Is it possible that there might be other things hidden on the island? Or in other places in Argentina...?"

Zugschwert adds a few interesting remarks: "In any exchange of opinions, not only scientific arguments count; skeptics get the most when they ask pertinent questions. Who actually observed what in connection with the decisive atomic experiment? Was Richter alone when as initiator, observer and scientific discoverer he performed this highly controversial experiment?" And he goes further: "There is doubt as to whether the experiment actually took place, and if it did, whether it was successful. There is no evidence. No other laboratory can repeat the experiment or analyze results since nobody knows where to begin." Significantly, and unfortunately, these were interesting questions indeed, which Argentine journalists failed to risk.

Zugschwert continues: "The Argentine government has created a special atomic energy commission, of which Richter is the only physics expert. I met Richter for the first time shortly after this commission was created. He was standing in front of his house, a house just like all others, except for the guard post across the street which kept watch day and night. I was carrying a bundle of newspapers: a collection of sundry criticisms that I wanted to discuss with Richter. Among others, there were accusations of a personal nature suggesting that Richter was a Cagliostro, or an ignoramus. Secrecy, no doubt, constituted the core of the problem. Richter was conscious of this and spoke about it openly. There was, of course, a funny side to it. When news spread that he had been arrested, for an instant he looked astonished, then he laughed. 'You see, he said you have come just in time'. A US press agency had spread the false news. It struck me that this news did not impress him much. He seemed to have other things on his mind. Not knowing him, one would think Richter was an industrial businessman rather than a scientist. He is not fond of exhibiting his degree, he dislikes being awarded public honors and he is not worried about building up his own image."

Zugschwert dwells further into other salient features of the scientist's personality. "People in Bariloche view Richter as a gentleman who walks around in a leather jacket and without a hat. His hobbies? When not working, he is usually seen driving his Cadillac with his cat Epsilon at his side. Richter is not the kind of theoretical physicist who would spend an inordinate amount of time trying to solve one specific problem. There is a practical streak in him that informs all his actions. He looks more perhaps like an atomic engineer than a nuclear physicist. What really moves him is not to discuss a certain theory, but the manner in which that theory can be implemented. He is revolutionary and secretive, and secrets are always surrounded by doubts. 'It doesn't worry me in the least, the final outcome will decide everything', were his words in the end."

And so it would be. The visit to Huemul by the journalists marked the end of a semester as well as the end of the most spectacular chapter in the history of the project. The climax had been reached. From now on, difficulties lay ahead. Based on the local press, however, the future looked promising. Important developments had been announced for the near future; among others, isotope production and construction of industrial atomic plants. On the other hand, suspicions that the project was being conducted erratically kept growing steadily within the inner circles of the project. The scientist's eccentric personality moreover, had already posed problems to the President himself.

However, neither the gradual loss of supporters nor the ungratifying reactions from European and US colleagues seemed to intimidate the resolute disposition of Ronald Richter.

Schizophrenia

The second semester of 1951 was characterized by a series of promises made by Richter to various government officials, probably spurred by Gonzalez's pressing demands. The Colonel was becoming increasingly restless: he had still to provide the requested funds for the project. [24]

On August 20, Gonzalez wrote to his son asking him for "a careful analysis of the situation with Richter, while conveying the urgent need of providing concrete evidence after all this time on the authenticity of experiments conducted on Huemul." This was probably the first time that Colonel Gonzalez revealed his mistrust so forcibly.

On September 3, Richter wrote to Minister Mende (now a more likely supporter than Gonzalez himself) saying: "We are now collecting highly interesting data almost daily. We expect briefly to use such data for an atomic energy demonstration to be held in front of a large audience." That same day he also wrote to Gonzalez: "Within three days, I expect to start working in Lab # 2, which has been modified in order to produce radioactive isotopes, particularly cobalt 60. This will constitute unquestionable evidence that atomic energy is being produced on Huemul." This was subject though, to receiving some aluminum tubes. In the same letter, he also mentions the possibility of staging "an explosion in the desert for demonstrative purposes." On that same date, he addressed a similar message to Perón: "Lab # 2 compares now to what it was on February 16 as a fully equipped factory would to a small experimental lab."

On September 12, Capt. Gonzalez Jr. cabled a message to Buenos Aires saying that Dr. Richter was planning to have a heavy water production plant. A week later he informed again that within four or five weeks Dr. Richter would be taking a 'present' to his friends in Buenos Aires, that is, cobalt 60.

On September 21, Colonel Gonzalez repeated his request, though this time addressed to Richter. He asks for a written report by Richter describing the situation of the project to be used for supporting further disbursement of funds. Simultaneously, Capt. Gonzalez Jr. wrote from Bariloche on Richter's behalf indicating that "shortly a momentous announcement is to be disclosed to the President of the Republic which will alter fundamentally the whole situation". Nevertheless, Richter preferred to wait a couple of weeks before setting the definite date of the announcement, as he first needed to receive some specific materials in Bariloche which had just been ordered. That same evening, Colonel Gonzalez instructed Richter to address his report directly to the President, indicating the date and materials which were needed. He repeated the same request three days later.

Mr. Miralles, the Bariloche Post Office chief, and Mr. Nievas, head of the local Radio Communication Service were given no respite. The exchange of telegrams between father and son developed a frenzied rhythm. The messages were so long that they filled four or five typewritten pages of the regular telegram forms. The messages denoted bewilderment and anxiety. The Colonel in Buenos Aires urged for definitions so as to stave off an avalanche of purchase orders. The Captain in Bariloche acted as liaison while endeavoring to achieve the impossible in the midst of an embarrassing situation. In Buenos Aires, tense discussions were held with Hellmann to determine whether the electromagnet requested by Huemul should be built with cast iron parts or with metal plates in order to shorten delivery terms. The heads of major steel industries were contacted by phone continuously. "After having paid two million pesos which we owed as of last year, I have no more money left!" the Colonel complained. The son replied: "Everything is just fine down here. I have discussed the situation with Richter for several hours informing him about the difficulties, but he finds the situation amusing. He feels a crushing blow will be inflicted on his enemies and therefore begs the Colonel to take it easy." Trying hard not to seem discouraged, he adds: "From the tone of the discussion, I gathered the distinct impression that Richter plans to send a great deal more than just a report to the President. Again, he seemed to be absolutely confident that within a few days as soon as yesterday's purchase requests are received in Bariloche he will be able to establish definite deadlines and shall publicly show the enemies of the project that their campaign of lies and slander is absolutely groundless."

Though Richter referred to `enemies' and `a campaign of lies and slander', no names were provided. Yet in his telegrams Capt. Gonzalez Jr. refers to difficulties with personnel on the island. He stressed the need for replacing four of them. A personal letter from Colonel Gonzalez to his son on September 14 was even more revealing. He insisted on the absolute necessity of producing actual evidence, "otherwise, I don't know what I am to do with either question: funds or the basic underlying problem (of managing Richter). If we had the radioactive cobalt to show, there would be no problem whatsoever. I'm telling you again: even the President's situation has become uncomfortable. He is being attacked most of all from his own back yard so to speak. Mrs. Perón keeps harping him on the subject influenced, no doubt, by her nasty little clique." From this casual comment we learn that, by that time, Evita herself was beginning to harbor serious doubts about Huemul and was decidedly against earmarking further funds to the project. This was a major obstacle indeed. "He's being attacked from his own back yard", Gonzalez writes while begging for positive evidence. Until then, Perón had avoided all scholarly advice, yet he could not ignore the opinion of his wife, who constituted a supporting pillar of his political success.

It often happens as in this case that the most significant historical insights result not from official documents but from strictly personal papers written on the spur of the moment. When Richter mentioned his enemies, he was probably far from considering Evita among them, and possibly never learned otherwise. It is likely, however, that Capt. Gonzalez Jr., eager to corner the elusive Richter, did mention to him the difficulties his father had encountered in government circles.

Also the following paragraph in Colonel Gonzalez's letter is of interest: "These last few purchase orders represent an enormous amount of money in dollars, and on top of that we must add (the relocation of) the power plant, which in my opinion still remains unclear and unnecessary. Why do they want to change it from its present location? Couldn't he have thought of it earlier? How come nobody told me anything when I was there?"

Gonzalez explains that the equipment to be built by Hellmann requires 700 tons of copper at a cost of $ 14.700.000 (about 3.6 million dollars), and that "a few days ago the cost of the whole job was estimated at 10 million pesos (2.5 million dollars); now it will go up to 20 at least. I just lack the gall to ask for such an amount only a few days later..."

In this letter Gonzalez also refers to the commercial aspects involved in the project, should the outcome be successful. Richter had obviously expressed some concern in this connection. Gonzalez tells his son: "As to the future, tell Richter not to worry; Perón agrees with the commercial exploitation of atomic energy and, since the President has always been exceedingly generous with him, Richter will receive the benefits he has been counting on. Naturally, all this has to be written down in a contract or an agreement to be signed by both parties. Since I know Perón well I have no concern in this respect."

As confirmed by these documents, Richter had an amazing degree of power over government officials working close to him. In the very same letter where Gonzalez expresses his anxiety over the twenty million pesos that the electromagnet was to cost, the delay in achieving positive results, the difficulties encountered among inner government circles, he also worries about putting Richter at ease regarding the future benefits he was to receive. The letters exchanged between father and son in September/October 1951 showed a pathetic fluctuation between believing and despairing. These sentiments were craftily manipulated by a man of unscrupulous personality.

The rules of this game were varied. One was to increase the number of purchase orders and the demands for short delivery terms. Another was to accuse somebody of espionage in order to force alliances and exact loyalties. Yet another is to keep promising sensational results and to subject schedules and deadlines to the delivery of critical supplies. Finally, claims are always ambiguous and difficult to verify. Undoubtedly, Richter had considerable talent in manipulating people. The Gonzalezes father and son were subjected to an almost schizophrenic rhythm as can be seen from the successive contrasting attitudes they adopted. They were faced with a situation without gray tones. It was all or nothing. The first symptoms of the disease were plainly visible already, yet to admit it would mean the death of Perón's project. Rather than doing so, it was necessary to summon whatever strength remained to continue nursing a fast eroding faith, while grasping desperately at the slightest sign of hope.

In the message to his father, where Gonzalez Jr. mentions problems with personnel, that is, "spies" and "enemies", he finishes with the following quote from Richter: "All these unfortunate incidents which occurred recently have ultimately produced a positive result: we are now in a position to determine exactly who our real friends are. This has enabled us to consolidate the internal front here at the plant, which is composed of the three of us (the two Gonzalezes and Richter) " Gonzalez Jr ends the note admitting he could not avoid being touched by this comment from Richter.

On yet another occasion, the Captain informed Buenos Aires that Richter was aware of budgetary difficulties, especially in connection with unexpected, last minute expenses, adding that "a prove of this is the enclosed request that indicates both the ideal quantity and the minimum quantity required of each item". The purchase order was labelled "Urgent" and it included 6 (minimum quantity) or 20 (ideal number) cathodic ray tubes of a certain kind, and 6 (or 20) of another type. Each new telegram contained further purchase requests. On October 10, 1951, a most unusual telegram reached Buenos Aires. Richter had dictated the following message to his aide: "My dear Colonel: I am deeply sorry to hear that you are currently undergoing a state of depression, which I quite understand. However, I consider it my duty to inform you that here on Huemul there is no reason whatsoever to feel depressed. I'm begging you, consequently, to send your depression to the devil. We are on the verge of launching a most interesting development as soon as the requested nitrogen arrives. Shortly, we shall be in a position to report important news. Much though I would like to, I cannot give you detailed information on these new developments. As you well know, our enemies are extremely active at present and we cannot afford to act indiscreetly. Please bear in mind that I fully understand your situation, therefore, I am happy to confirm once again that ultimate success is just around the corner."

A Partner to Share Success

Perón and Gonzalez had been able to maintain a friendly relationship from the days of their youth, with the sole exception of some slight friction in connection with the GOU leadership issue. Their relationship, however, was now based mainly on Gonzalez' admission of their present roles. Perón gave the orders and Gonzalez carried them on. The latter considered it his patriotic duty to do so; Perón's wishes were respected beyond questioning.

Once before an audience of high ranking officers talking about Huemul, Perón had said: "Dear little Gonzalez, you are the right man for the job: since you know nothing about all this, you won't interfere." [25] This was the way it was between those two men and Gonzalez wasn't bothered by it, quite the contrary: his personal correspondence plus other documents show his wholehearted determination to carry out the mission Perón had entrusted him to the limit of his ability. He managed to do so despite the crucial problems posed by Richter almost daily. Gonzalez' letters, moreover, contained phrases such as, "In times of struggle while fighting for the success of the project, which we carry on for General Perón, our Chief, our friend and our support, who fully relies on us ..."

Despite countless problems affecting these two men - Perón was facing new elections in November, Evita's health had begun to show disquieting signs, the Government had just suffocated a coup headed by General Menendez - they still found time to chat informally like two old pals sitting on a bench in the park. One evening, they engaged in one of those leisurely talks while Perón was having a haircut. The conversation turned to Richter. Perón said he fully trusted him. Gonzalez reminded him of his son's recent messages always promising successful results within a short time. Perón's enthusiasm was genuine; he was looking forward to the opportunity of visiting Huemul to admire the wonderful things occurring down there. He was absolutely certain about the importance of the project and the progress achieved already. Gonzalez preferred not to contradict him. His own doubts would worry his friend and, why would he want to do that? It was pointless. He should be capable of solving the problems by himself; that was the basic reason why Perón had summoned him.

Meanwhile, it was tempting to forget everything and entertain illusions of a prompt success. Yes, Richter had a complex and contradictory nature but, was it not typical of geniuses to be so? In the best tradition of the Buenos Aires coffee shops where people indulge in building castles in the air as a pleasant pastime the two friends yielded to the temptation of imagining the wonderful things which were to take place soon. Ignoring dark forebodings, their enthusiasm grew while speaking about the future of Argentina, feeding on the inexhaustible fountain of atomic energy. Richter was a man to whom Argentina would be indebted forever. Any doubts he might still have regarding the extent of his authority had to be clarified. "You must tell him not to worry about the future of the project", Perón said. Everything was to be carried out according to his will. "He is the master of everything", the President said. "I will not allow anybody to interfere." [26]

But facts were altogether different. The deterioration process leading to the final crisis had already been set in motion. Because of it, Gonzalez would be forced to a violent and inevitable clash within a few months. Richter's closest collaborators including Jaffke who had been his friend and partner from the days of his youth, with whom he had shared hard times in Europe after the war, and with whom friendship extended even to their respective wives had all decided to abandon ship. Difficulties with personnel in general increased daily. Even SACES, the construction company which had been working in the Island for only a few months, was on his way out as Richter was now considering another contractor. No less disquieting was the possibility - a mere suggestion, yet voiced already - of moving the laboratory somewhere else.

Then, a new announcement sparked renewed optimism: "To his Excellency, the President of the Argentine Nation, I have the honor of informing you that on this date, after long months of experimenting, I have performed a new atomic energy experiment which will be of crucial importance for the near future. The significance of this achievement is even greater than the one attained on February 16. I am presently in a position to confirm that what we obtained today in relation to the February 16 development, is like that achievement compared to nothing." The message was transmitted by Gonzalez Jr. on October 26, "with deep emotion and heartfelt congratulations for this anxiously expected news."

A similar message was also addressed to the Colonel with a note saying that due to certain tasks designed to increase safety margins which still had to be completed within two to three weeks, only then the Plant would be ready to invite the President to a demonstration.

The text of the communique Richter proposed releasing to the press arrived next morning. He wanted the information to be precise and to the point, without any additional comments. "A successful, large scale experiment was achieved at the Huemul Atomic Energy Pilot Plant after long months of research. In the course of the experiment, novel and highly complex constructive problems were tested, especially some unusually interesting technological aspects of crucial importance in the building of high performance thermonuclear reactors. As a consequence, the development program for the industrial reactor will be greatly accelerated. Shortly, and in a partially restricted manner, we expect to make the Huemul technical facilities accessible to local and foreign scientific and technical personnel."

Once again, as in the former announcement earlier that year, the communique provided nothing in the way of technical data to evaluate it from a scientific angle. It was a question of either believing in Richter or not. The prevailing atmosphere in government circles was in favor of believing. Capt. Gonzalez Jr. was overjoyed: "At long last, what we've been looking for!" Yet his father was more reticent, his statements were guarded. Yes, the government approved the press communique, though "for special reasons which Dr. Richter will certainly understand, the President wishes the communique to bear the signature of Dr. Richter, as head of the Plant. The information will thus have the scientific validity it deserves."

What made the announcement particularly interesting was that it promised the Plant could be visited by local and foreign scientists within a few days. This was indeed an encouraging sign. Richter had strongly opposed all earlier attempts to have scientists visit the island on the grounds of guarding the secret. Colonel Gonzalez was much relieved. It would indeed be a relief to share his hitherto hefty load with knowledgeable people who could presumably shed light on nagging doubts which harassed him constantly ...! A few days earlier, he had received a telegram stating that Lab # 2, where Richter conducted his experiments, had become contaminated by radiation. It also said that despite this Dr. Richter would continue to carry on with his work. On one hand, it was certainly encouraging to learn that there was radiation (which could only result from nuclear reactions). On the other hand, the news was extremely upsetting due to the grave personal dangers it entailed.

Gonzalez was in dire need of expert advice in order to evaluate correctly its significance and possible consequences. Neither Gamba, Isnardi nor Beninson, who were close to him, could be of any assistance unless they had a chance to visit the laboratory. That chance seemed to be at hand now. As a consequence, the idea of appointing a commission of experts began to dawn in his mind.

November 11, the general election day, was drawing near. The Balbin/Frondizi Radical Party formula constituted the only possible, though not probable, menace to Perón's reelection. The President was far from worried. All that was required of him was to make one or two personal appearances on the radio and TV (the first TV channel in Argentina had started operating a few weeks earlier) to calm down whatever electoral worries he might have. Perón doubled the Radical Party in votes. The women's vote - which Evita incorporated to the electoral system of Argentina - constituted a major contribution toward this victory.

The elections would not have been an obstacle to visiting Huemul. Yet the visit was momentarily postponed due to an operation Eva Perón had to undergo as a result of a most disturbing diagnosis. On instructions from Buenos Aires, Richter was asked to postpone the anticipated presidential demonstration for another twenty five days.

At the end of that period, the visit was postponed again. Instead of Perón going to Bariloche, Richter went to Buenos Aires where he held a series of "secret meetings" with the President, his main advisors and members of the National Economic Council. Finally, the presidential visit never took place, though it was used in the following months as an excuse to justify urgent purchase requests which kept coming from Huemul.

Richter left for Buenos Aires with the purpose of initiating a new and ambitious stage in the life of the project. He insisted being in a position to start producing atomic energy on a large scale for industrial purposes, were it not for the fact that local industry was insufficiently developed to meet his requirements. Consequently, he proposed the idea of signing an agreement with some highly industrialized country for the joint exploitation of atomic energy. Argentina was to provide the know how and the partner country to contribute its industrial capabilities.

Perón apparently believed in the viability of such a grandiose, though delicate proposal, as he authorized Richter to announce it publicly at a press conference in the presidential residence in Olivos on December 11. It is uncertain, however, whether Richter himself believed in this possibility. Certain documents indicate that results allegedly obtained on October 26 had given

Richter a renewed confidence in his method. But beyond technical aspects these same documents revealed not only a strong dose of self confidence, but also an immoderate arrogance, and above all, a sudden and significant contempt toward Gonzalez and his collaborators. From a technical viewpoint, it should be recalled that there was nothing but a huge chasm at the large reactor site at the time. Therefore, no large scale experiment had taken place. As Richter had indicated, the pilot facility in Lab # 2 had been completely upgraded, and the new building was still unfinished. The electromagnet and the gigantic reactance, then under construction, had yet to be sent down south. What kind of experimental testing, then, had actually occurred on October 26? Was it merely theoretical? When trying to analyze these circumstances, personal motivations and technical information become hopelessly intermingled. The recurrent requests by Gonzalez asking Richter to supply undisputable evidence constituted a clear sign that confidence in the project was not unlimited. As far as Gonzalez was concerned, the time for bartering future promises for unlimited confidence was definitely over. Time had come to devise a new strategy. Was this what Richter had in mind in December when he went to Buenos Aires in order to persuade the government to establish alliances with industrialized nations - the United States, for instance -[27]; to be authorized to make the public announcement; to assume the responsibility of negotiating on behalf of Argentina (!); to declare that "our volume of (energy) production will increase ten thousand fold"(!), and to state that Argentina was in a position to claim up to five hundred patents in this connection? [28]

The Hellmann/Richter correspondence, which the latter had managed to re establish a few months earlier, provides a certain amount of information on what was going on at the plant. On November 10, Richter wrote to Hellmann saying the electromagnet had to be mounted in a three to four week period. He also mentioned the installation of an electrical current distribution panel for the labs, which was yet unfinished.

Almost as an afterthought, he "begged" Hellmann to introduce two modifications in the electromagnet: to disregard his earlier indication about not cutting off the polar parts (the parts had already been cut and the pieces had to be welded on again in order to reshape them into the original design), and to drill 10 cm instead of 1 cm holes lengthwise through the iron.

In contrast with the technical aspects, Richter's letter was sprinkled with contemptuous and offensive remarks about Gonzalez and the Argentines who worked with him. While referring to the October 26 "practical success", ("you would be surprised if you knew what it's all about"), Richter said: "It was possible, just for once, to suffer a minimum of propaganda 'non sense', and to have a press release without any additional comments." Actually, it had been Gonzalez who insisted that the communique be signed only by Richter.

Richter continued playing his characteristic swinging game. While insinuating aggravating comments about Hellmann to Capt. Gonzalez Jr., he made openly insulting remarks about Colonel Gonzalez to Hellmann. Unwittingly, Gonzalez almost fell into the trap. In a letter to his son, he said: "I fully coincide with Richter in being wary of Hellmann's requests and his excessive demands for raw materials. In addition to lamination, welding, rolling and other processes, the cost of this equipment (he was referring to the electromagnet) will come to about twenty million pesos, of which Hellmann will keep at least a ten percent. You must also bear in mind that we are paying him advisory fees at a rate of $ 5000 (1250 dollars) per month." [29]

This same attitude was apparent in subsequent letters. The concrete slab to support the electromagnet was finished on November 18. While requesting thermometers, manometers, gas flow meters, and remote control valves to Hellmann, Richter adds that he is trying to finish work as soon as possible while his "team of monkeys are still loafing up the coconut trees." [30]

In December, when Richter met the local and foreign media to announce the beginnings of negotiations with a highly industrialized country, there were contradictory statements. In March, he had already made a distinction between `test tube' and large scale experiments. He had pointed out that when a change of scale occurs, "one cannot be certain whether identical results can be obtained." He repeated the same concept adding: "Research undertaken during these last eight months has shown us how to release large scale atomic energy in a reactor." However, since the large reactor had not yet been built, the experiments could only have been carried out on a `test tube' scale. Precisely in this connection, Richter was asked by a journalist whether he referred to energy produced in large reactors or whether he was speaking of how to build large reactors. Richter answered: "Based on our recent findings, we know already how to build large reactors so as to produce large amounts of energy." Since the reactor was yet to be built, it must be inferred that the October 26 results were of a theoretical nature, and not "a successful, large scale experiment in the course of which novel and highly complex constructive problems were tested" as he had stated.

On December 12, the day after the press conference, The New York Times emphasized Richter's words indicating that Argentina had decided to seek an industrial partner since the country was not in a position to absorb huge amounts of industrial energy which would result from the new method. In addition, it indicated that Dr. Richter had been appointed by President Perón as his sole representative to conduct negotiations. "Dr. Richter declined making any comments when asked whether the partner country might be the United States."

As far as atomic matters were concerned, a rich and eventful year was drawing to a close. This was true not only of Argentina: during the first three months of that year, the US conducted half a dozen atomic explosions and announced the first hydrogen bomb tests within the next nine to ten months. In July, the first official research project on thermonuclear reactions in the US was approved. As mentioned earlier, this project had been inspired in Perón's announcement, and on December 20, the first atomic energy production plant worldwide (based on fission rather than fusion) was set in operation in the state of Idaho.

Above: Dr. Richter (in shirt sleeves) flanked by Coronel Gonzalez and journalists after his press conference held at the presidential residence on March 25, 1951.

Below: At the center, President Juan Perón, Coronel Enrique González and Mrs Perón (Evita). On the right hand side, Mrs Richter and Ronald Richter, the latter holding his *Doctor Honoris Causa* diploma from University of Buenos Aires (March 28, 1951)

View of the Huemul island, showing its main constructions: 1. Lab 1 where the large reactor was built and then demolished to start anew a similar structure underground which in turn later was declared useless and was covered with sand and gravel; 2. Lab 2 where Richter carried out his experiments; 3. Lab 3, warehouse; 4. Lab 4, unfinished, never used; 5. Power station; 6. Richter's desk; 7. Location where construction work was started to build a house for Richter; 8. Photographic lab; 9. Guards station.

<u>Above</u>: Ronald Richter departing from Lab 2, the only one that was actually used and where the experiments seen by the Visiting Committee in September 1952, took place.

<u>Below</u>: Ronald Richter at the control room in Lab 2.

Is Peron's A-Bomb A Swindle?

The chances are 99 to 1 that the atomic explosion in Argentina occurred only in the imagination of a crank or a fraud.

By PROF. HANS THIRRING
*Director, Institute for Theoretical Physics,
University of Vienna*

ARGENTINA HAS NO ATOM BOMB

By Dr. Ronald Richter

Thanks to the fairness of the editors of the United Nations World, I have the ~rtunity to make this statement about the Argentine atomic energy project.

Unfortunately, the article "Is Peron's A-Bomb a Swindle?" published in May issue of this magazine by the Austrian professor Hans Thirring, contained not facts, but infamy.

The reactor operation crew and I are deeply sorry for Hans Thirring, because he revealed himself to be a typical text book professor with a strong scientific in-

Article written by Prof. Hans Thirring from University of Vienna, published in the May 1951 issue of United Nations World magazine, presenting a skeptical view of Perón's announcement (above) and Richter's acid answer in the following issue (below).

NOTES TO CHAPTER 4

[1] This would be so provided the atoms emitting the radiation under observation were all moving in the same direction (as in the case of a star which is moving away). This was not the case in Richter's experiment, where the radiating atoms moved in all directions. What Richter ought to have expected was a broadening, and not a shift or displacement of the lines. As a result of this conceptual error, he arrived at an erroneous interpretation of his February 16th results. (See the Epilogue "The Secret of Huemul").

[2] Argentine newspapers of March 26th, 1951 and Mundo Atomico, March 1951, page 66 onwards.

[3] The same photo was published by the New York Times again on the December 5th, 1952.

[4] Letter dated August 12th, 1954 by Hans Thirring to Peter Alemann.

[5] Hans Felsinger, "Untersuchungen an Sperrschichtphotozellen mit weichen Roentgenstrahlen ("Research on Barrier Photoelectric Cells by means of Soft X Rays"), Annalen der Physik, 5. Folge 29, 81, 1937.

[6] Interview with Colonel Gonzalez of June 27, 1979. Other quotes from the same source also correspond to the same interview.

[7] "Esto Es" number 96, week of October 18 24, 1955, page 29.

[8] Interview with Bertolo on January 28, 1979

[9] Interview with Mr. Ricardo Rossi, August 3, 1979.

[10] Letter dated August 2, 1950, by Kurt Tank to Richter.

[11] Private communications by Colonel Gonzalez.

[12] About Richter's hazardous days after the war, a journalist wrote after interviewing him in June 1951: "When Germany

capitulated, Richter was still working in Berlin. It was the time of the Russian occupation. Prof. Richter decided to keep his secret at all costs and, aided by his friend and assistant, destroyed his laboratory though the Russians, heavily armed, kept watch over the place. Afterwards, he managed to escape to West Germany aided by the Americans. US Colonel Elmer G. Stahl, head of American electrical operations an extremely able and scholarly man, according to Dr. Richter took a great interest in his experiments. But at the time, there were many others who were heading in different directions and the Americans questioned Richter without too much consideration. They were after his secrets. 'Unfortunately, I had forgotten them', the professor told us smiling."

"That was the beginning of a long, hazardous journey for the atomic scientist. The British invited him in 1945 to talk about his theories and his findings. They were more considerate than the rest, but their objective was the same: to learn his secret. He was invited to England, but Richter excused himself. It was too early, he says. Then the French were also interested in him and they invited Richter to Baden Baden, where he was questioned by the military government. He was requested to go to Paris, which he then did."

"In Paris, however, Joliot Curie who had Communist inclinations lead atomic research. Richter considered it against his inner convictions to work there. He managed to leave Paris though he was under surveillance, and returned to Berlin. Soon afterwards, Norwegian experts also paid him a visit. It was amazing how news about Richter's studies had spread throughout a bewildered Europe in the wake of the war. The answer is simple enough: Allied intelligence functioned admirably well. 'It was always far better than German intelligence.'"

"The Norwegians also 'wanted to know'. True to his commitments, however, Richter went to London. He was welcomed there but failed to convince them of his theories. A veritable army of German researchers who had gone over to the enemies of yesterday were working in Britain pursuing different roads. The English were unable to differentiate between scientists on the right track from those who were not. So Richter returned to Berlin."

"The Dutch were also interested in Richter's studies. He received an offer to go to Holland, but refused to travel disguised as a British soldier, which was required of him and his wife. In 1947, he was called back to London, but this time he didn't want to wait in England. He returned to Berlin and a little later went to Holland, travelling always somewhat surreptitiously. On reaching Amsterdam, however, the Dutch informed him that on English instructions he was to leave for Berlin within twenty four hours in an American plane. So they took him back. Then, there was the opportunity of going to America. Richter accepted the offer for the time being; he would see afterwards. But a rather funny incident which he is fond of telling caused the trip to fall through. The American consul who questioned him thoroughly, asked him whether he had a son. "No, I don't, but I have a cat." "I am sorry - said the consul – but cats are not allowed." And Richter, who loves his cat Epsilon dearly, desisted from going to America."

"In December 1947 Richter returned to Paris again. He met some `strange, bright characters' and became involved in the secret service, but eventually managed to disentangle himself. Shortly afterwards, acting on the suggestion of some friends, he embarked for Argentina." (Noticias Graficas, June 28th, 1951, also La Razon, June 28th, 1951).

[13] United Nations World, May 1951, page 2.

[14] Ibid, 13, page 1.

[15] In a letter dated August 12th, 1954, physicist Hans Thirring wrote to journalist Peter Alemann : "In the original German version of my article to the magazine `United Nations World', regarding the first alternative I stated that "Perón had fallen prey to a fanatic who was in turn a victim of his own delusions". The term `fanatic' in the English translation which I failed to see on time became a much stronger term: `crank'. Anyway, I am now convinced that this alternative was correct."

274 | THE ATOMIC SECRET OF HUEMUL ISLAND

(16) The author undertook a bibliographical search in `Science Abstracts' between the years 1935 to 1950.

(17) Letter by Dr. Ronald Richter to United Nations World, the July 1951, "Argentina Has No Atom Bomb"

Following this letter, the UNW published an analysis of Mr. Richter's proclaimed achievements in Argentina, done by a prominent American scientist, Dr. Hugh C. Wolf, Professor of Physics, Cooper Union School of Engineering, and Vice Chairman of the Federation of American Scientists.

(18) During a meeting between Peter Alemann and Richter in 1954, the latter said that in his letter to UNW, they had deleted a `not' after the word 'should'. The sentence should have read: "This enabled us to understand why a pile made tritium should not be used in the hydrogen bomb.". Alemann used this and other data to develop an interesting hypothesis (see ref. 19).

(19) Based on the information referred to in (18) above, and other statements by Richter such as `lithium 6 and the new type of neutron chain reaction.', and `we have probably more knowledge than the United States and Great Britain do', Peter Alemann devised an interesting theory in Richter's defense which deserves to be mentioned. Alemann was a journalist for the Argentinisches Tageblatt. His investigation began as a result of an article published in Time magazine on April 12th, 1954, entitled "The Making of the H Bomb". Among other things it said that the monumental reactor in Savannah River, on the east coast of the United States, built to produce tritium, "possibly turned out to be unnecessary." It concerned the first H "bomb" detonated by the United States in November 1952, which was a huge device weighing 60 tons, and a volume similar to a two story house. The reason for it was that the device operated on deuterium and tritium, both heavy isotopes of hydrogen, which had to be liquefied. The major portion of the apparatus consisted of a liquifier. Hardly a year had gone by when the Soviets detonated their H bomb in a surprising demonstration of how swiftly their atomic program had progressed. The Soviet device was far more manageable than the American. The key to

the difference lay in that the Soviets had used lithium. Alemann recalled what Richter had said in 1951 to the UNW and the local media after Perón's announcement regarding the use of lithium. He started then a long investigation which took him many years, numerous interviews with Richter and countless letters to various people including Thirring himself. When in 1972 Alemann happened to read in Prof. Manfred von Ardenne's autobiography how the Russians had panicked upon learning of Perón's announcement and, knowing Richter's background, he had arrived at the following conclusions: in 1943 Richter was working with von Ardenne, in 1945 von Ardenne went to Russia in order to develop the H bomb.., in 1951 Richter issued his declaration in Buenos Aires.., the Russian H bomb was detonated in 1953 and was copied then by western scientists; which means the Russians had chosen the right method, the one von Ardenne was already exploring in 1943.. Consequently, it was quite feasible that Richter might have known a lot more than the Anglo Saxons in 1951. This finally explained the Russian´s general panic. (See Peter Alemann, "Hatte Argentinien die thermonukleare reaktion?", `Argentinisches Tageblatt', February 23, 1958. Also, Peter Alemann, "Ronald Richter und die Geschichte der H Bombe", `Argentinisches Tageblatt', September 12th, 1972).

[20] Letter dated June 1, 1951 by Perón to Richter. (Author's file)

[21] Statements by Richter to Peter Alemann, who made them available to the author.

[22] Letter from A. J. Sforza, transcribed in previous chapter Project Huemul - "Family life, spies and other worries", and ref. 62 in that chapter.

[23] Article by Dr. Juan Zugschwert, German newspapers and magazines' correspondent in Buenos Aires, June 1951. CNEA file, Technical Information Department.

[24] Quotations in this section were copied from original documents in Colonel Gonzalez' file, provided to the author.

[25] Interview with Admiral Quihillalt, October 2, 1980.

(26) Letter dated September 19th, 1951 by Colonel Gonzalez to his son. (Author's file)

(27) In the course of his interviews with Peter Alemann, Richter stated clearly that the nation he had in mind while proposing an industrial partner was the United States. However, US State Department documents (provided to the author) reveal that in April 1952, Department officials suspected the nation in question was Germany due to a trip Kurt Tank had then made to that country. The pertinent paragraph stated: "Tank was recently in Germany, where he gave a series of press interviews. Major topics were German Argentinean friendship and cooperation between those two countries. Tank also suggested that Argentina was in a position to progress in her scientific endeavors in close collaboration with Germany. This seems to confirm the possibility that Germany might be the highly industrialized nation Richter was referring to. I guess the basis of the negotiation must be found in Tank's recent visit. " (The author is grateful to Peter Alemann for this material).

(28) Mundo Atómico, Year III, number 7, 1952, and various December 12, 1951 Argentine newspapers.

(29) Ibid, 26.

(30) The Richter/Hellmann correspondence. The author is grateful to Mr. Hellmann for showing this material to him.

5 | A New Dawn (1952 – 1955)

Gonzalez Final Act

In early 1952 Richter was of the opinion that the facilities should be moved to a desert area known as Indio Muerto (Dead Indian), 50 miles East from Bariloche. He was also convinced that the construction company ought to be replaced. He had never been fond of the Italians and their company SACES; besides, orders and counter orders had created enough friction between them. When Perón forced him to accept the Italian company of his friend Incisa, Richter had a different idea that he had not yet given up. In fact, contacts had already been initiated – unknown to Colonel Gonzalez - with GEOPE engineers, a German construction company. [1]

On January 3, Gonzalez Jr cabled Buenos Aires inquiring whether there was any news about the GEOPE engineers. Colonel Plantamura (momentarily replacing Gonzalez who was on vacation) replied: " I know nothing about such engineers, nor who was consulted about this. Please inform anything you know about it. I'm inclined to think it has something to do with continuing the works undertaken by SACES in Bariloche. Please clarify what it's all about."

Yet there was no reply from Bariloche. Richter shut himself off and all communications with CNEA officials were virtually discontinued. He proceeded with negotiations for the proposed transfer of the plant to Indio Muerto, without stopping the activities on the island. The electromagnet, at long last, had been installed in January, and Hellmann continued receiving urgent requests with the customary last minute modifications. On January 29, Richter informed Hellmann that now he required 10 million watts and 100 thousand volts DC.

The atomic adventure seemed to be spiraling directly toward the very eye of an inevitable tornado. All sorts of events some decidedly bizarre took place at increasingly shorter intervals. Yet Richter never considered halting; on the contrary, he plunged decidedly into the next conflict. He seemed indifferent to the unavoidable consequences of his actions. His boldness was amazing: he marched resolutely and unwaveringly toward an inevitable clash.

On returning from vacation in early February, Gonzalez was informed by his son that the general manager of GEOPE was in Bariloche. The Colonel got furious. "As soon as I found out, I took the next plane to Bariloche."

Gonzalez was fully aware that he would be facing a difficult situation and that the meeting with Richter would inevitably end up violently. He considered the power of his authority. He recalled Perón's letter giving Richter full powers. The apparently harmless contradictions of Decree 9697 of May 17, 1951, by virtue of which Richter exercised full sway over Huemul while Gonzalez remained responsible for the administration (service contracts, purchases, etc.) now were a matter of great concern.

Gonzalez worried about all this as he arrived in Bariloche on the morning of Friday, February 8. It was difficult to accept Perón's instructions: "do everything exactly as Richter says".

A dramatic sequence of radiograms was exchanged between Bariloche and Buenos Aires that afternoon. "Arrived well but have found fundamental variations in construction schedule" Gonzalez informs Plantamura "Haven't spoken to Richter yet, though I believe work will continue on the island now. Tense atmosphere due to sundry causes stemming from the usual personal conflicts. Planning to call a meeting this evening to clarify situation. President's letter has become increasingly more of a problem; would be wise of you to talk to Duarte (the President's private secretary and Evita's brother) and see whether a direct presidential order might be sent here to clarify extent of my mission and authority. Anticipate difficulties ahead. At 7 p.m. today shall inform you of first meeting's results."

At 5 p.m. Plantamura replies: "Has been impossible to speak with the General due to governors' meeting and other problems. Do not anticipate doing so till Monday. Minister Mende, informed by Duarte of your problem, says he feels you should take things in stride trying your utmost to avoid clashes till you return and situation is calmly analyzed to determine how best to deal with it. Fundamentally, this opinion is based on existence of letter in question which should be modified with utmost care to avoid creating difficulties for the General. Four GEOPE engineers are leaving for Bariloche tomorrow at 7:30."

Gonzalez answers promptly: "Regret the General was not informed of problem. Will take stock of situation at meeting this evening and resolve accordingly. Presumably, will return to B.A." He writes "Regards", hesitates, crosses it out and continues: "I presume Minister Mende could inform the General at his residence and send the requested solution (a new written order from the President) tomorrow in the 7:30 flight. Overall the situation here has reached limits of endurance. Regards"

Plantamura realizes that the situation is getting serious. Gonzalez has implied in a veiled manner that his friend Mende had left him on the spot. Plantamura is eager to help: "I do understand, Colonel, that you are in a very difficult position. Please allow me a heartfelt suggestion: there's nothing to lose and much to gain if you display great patience once again. Showdown ought to be avoided at all costs. Instead, please analyze situation calmly and thoroughly, bringing back all facts of the case so the General may take adequate decision. Kindly try to adopt the forbearing attitude the case demands."

No success. The dialogue ends with an abrupt reply: "Appreciate your good intentions. This is a time to adopt decisions. Regards". Plantamura gives up. He tells the operator: "All right then, tell him I return his greetings and wish him best of luck".

Nevertheless, the meeting with Richter that evening was brief. Probably Gonzalez thought better of it and decided to postpone the confrontation for a few more hours. He only instructed Richter not to take any decisions in connection with the new construction works until they had a chance to discuss it the following morning.

On Saturday morning at 10 o'clock, Gonzalez called on Richter at his home. "I was utterly amazed at finding the GEOPE experts there. They were discussing with Richter how to go about moving the plant over to Indio Muerto", he later wrote in a report to the President. While recalling this incident thirty years later, in an interview with the author, Gonzalez' voice still trembled: "I could barely check myself in time. I wanted to hit him right in the face. Can you imagine? He was secretly dealing with the GEOPE! Whether Perón had an inkling of what was going on, I don't know. Maybe he knew something and I was not informed."

That morning Richter and the GEOPE engineers were actually discussing still a new alternative. Mr. Trimmel, one of the GEOPE engineer present in this meeting, explained that what Dr. Richter was now proposing was different from what they had discussed at their previous meeting. Richter now wanted to set up an intermediate plant prior to building the final one at Indio Muerto. At that point, Richter interrupted blaming both SACES and the Second Construction Corps: "They worked haphazardly, and this occurred thanks to the complicity of Capt. Gonzalez Jr." The dialogue became progressively rougher. Mrs. Ruth Spagat, the interpreter, had difficulties trying not to translate the names they were calling each other. "The Captain lied to me, just as he lied to you!", Richter shouted. Mrs. Spagat translated. Richter continued: "This country is full of long tailed monkeys like yourself up the coconut trees!". Mrs.

Spagat considered for an instant, then translated: "Prof. Richter says he is offended with you." "No" Richter shouted – "translate exactly what I've said!" [2]

Shortly afterwards, still shaking, Gonzalez settled down to write a brief account of his encounter with Richter. He wanted to send it to Plantamura with the recommendation it should be brought immediately to the attention of the President. The ending was predictable: "There is no doubt in my mind that both my mission and Captain Gonzalez Jr.'s are now terminated. Considering Argentina's best interests, the General should not hesitate to accept our resignation to the positions with which he has honored us. We have striven to carry out our responsibilities as effectively as possible, foregoing all personal aims while trying to serve the higher interests of our country." Then he tried unsuccessfully to get Plantamura on the phone. He then cabled the message to Major Mones Ruiz, adding he was taking the train to Buenos Aires that very same evening.

Early on Monday, Gonzalez met with Perón and Mende. He carried a list of facts and opinions from various persons who endorsed his now openly critical stance. A feeling akin to peace pervaded his spirit: at last he was able to shed the heavy burden of looking after Richter's eccentricities. He had finally found the courage to oppose the powerful head of Huemul. No more schizophrenia. He was now able at long last to speak plainly to Perón…and to himself.

A barrage of hitherto curbed doubts – emerging now as certainties began to surface. The long list prepared by Colonel Gonzalez registered all kinds of incidents. An extra $ 19.000 pesos (about US$ 5.000) for instance, had been paid to speed up the delivery of an oscilloscope from Switzerland which, six months later, was still lying packed in a warehouse. Or Richter's instructions to SACES (invoking presidential powers), to build 20 houses and two large constructions at Indio Muerto, when nobody in Buenos Aires knew a thing about changing the location of the plant. Somewhere else on the list, it was pointed out that demolishing the large reactor had cost over a million pesos (about US$ 250.000). Other demolition works were also mentioned. The power plant was indeed a special case: the siting had been modified four times and power requirements had escalated from 1 million to 12 million watts in less than a month.

Gonzalez had also collected opinions from various people. Kurt Tank, who had recommended Richter in 1948, now felt differently. He thought that Richter lacked sufficient training and that he ought to abandon his inclination toward 'occultism'. Among others, Gonzalez cited Rossi's account, Hellmann's views ("Richter is unable to continue this undertaking by himself"), and the testimony submitted by Mr. Beltrami of General Electric (who was forced to walk blindfolded when he went to the island to repair the 1000 Kw power plant generator). Curiously enough, Prof. Isnardi's opinion was very cautious. In reference to Tank's memorandum of 1950, he said: "There is not enough evidence to pass judgment on it."

Gonzalez maintained a firm stand in his meeting with Perón: "Look, you just have to put an end to all this." Perón refused to give up: "No, on the contrary, this must go on Gonzalez, try to understand, it is possible!" After the incident with Richter, it was obvious that Gonzalez could not stay, yet he disliked being rude to Perón. "Regardless of whether it is possible or not, I cannot carry on with something I don't agree with." Then he added in a conciliatory tone: "However, my suggestion is that we should appoint a committee to conduct an investigation. Richter ought to be forced to accept such a committee to visit the island."

Perón nodded: "All right, go ahead and start organizing it." Richter was to come to Buenos Aires to be informed of this decision. Gonzalez had the names of his closest collaborators in mind for the committee. Gamba was in Sweden at the time, so he mentioned Isnardi, Collo and Beninson. Perón objected: "No, no, not Isnardi. I would much rather have Gamba." Gonzalez raised no objection. He immediately cabled Gamba to return to Argentina. Gonzalez respected Isnardi, but he did not like him much. Throughout his tenure as scientific advisor at DNEA, the dean of Argentine physicists had maintained a haughty distance which Gonzalez resented. Rarely had they shared similar opinions on the need to foster atomic research in

Argentina. Isnardi and Collo spent long hours discussing problems of classical physics. Isnardi was a prestigious member of the International Weights and Measures Committee based in Paris. Atomic and nuclear physics interested him far less than metrology. A certain incident, on which Gonzalez was to insist years later, was characteristic of Isnardi's lackluster enthusiasm for the new technologies: Gamba strongly supported a joint project with the University of Cuyo for uranium exploration in the region of the cordillera. It was indeed a good and viable project which later on turned out to be important. However, when the project was discussed at a meeting headed by Plantamura and also attended by Beninson, Isnardi and Collo opposed Gamba on the grounds that Argentina was far from needing uranium and, should the need ever arise, uranium could always be purchased at the international markets.

At another time Prof. Isnardi prepared a Plan of Activities for Gonzalez which again revealed his dislike for atomic matters. The plan stated: "All research in connection with the application and implementation of atomic energy is of a secret nature and therefore is to be limited to the Bariloche National Plant. Not until such research attains practical results in connection with the exploitation of atomic energy, will this Agency (the DNEA in Buenos Aires) become involved in the matter." Further on, it stressed that "not until such time will DNEA undertake training of technical personnel in the atomic field." The plan was therefore contrary to the letter and the spirit of Decree 9697 which clearly established that DNEA should both engage in this type of research and train people. Gonzalez, the author of the decree, could hardly agree with this plan.

It is not surprising, then, that Gonzalez had no qualms relaying to the prestigious physicist Perón's reaction to his name. Evidently, Perón´s reservations towards Isnardi did not stem, at least exclusively from the physicist's blatant anti-Peronism, but also from his biased opinions on atomic matters.

As a result of this veto, both Isnardi and Collo tendered their resignations to DNEA. The investigating committee was finally made up of Gamba, Beninson, Father Bussolini and Eng. Mario

Bancora. The latter did not belong to the group of young professionals who had begun to populate the new DNEA laboratories on Libertador Avenue; his name was probably suggested by Mende. Bancora belonged to the University of Rosario, 200 miles northwest of Buenos Aires. After post graduate studies in the United States, he had built a small cyclotron which earned him well deserved fame (building a cyclotron constituted a considerable achievement at the time), plus a certain standing at the Ministry of Technical Affairs where he had submitted some proposals before being summoned to join the committee.

All arrangements were swiftly carried out. By the second week in February, a plane was waiting at the Buenos Aires city airport to take committee members down to Bariloche. Everything ready except for one thing. Perón had to tell Richter.

The crucial meeting between the President and the head of the Huemul atomic plant took place at the Casa Rosada on Tuesday, February 19. One can imagine Perón being annoyed at having to play a role he disliked, searching for the gentlest terms to break the news to Richter. It was indeed an uncomfortable situation: he had given his word that the secret would not be disclosed. He was not at all certain, moreover, that the time had come to break that promise. Could it be, perhaps, that he had been influenced by an irritable comrade, whose pride had been hurt?

Most likely Perón entertained such doubts when he met his scientific friend. Though the exact dialogue which took place between them is not known, the outcome is. An Associated Press dispatch of that day provides the clue: "President Juan D. Perón today ordered the Minister of Technical Affairs to centralize the work of Argentina's atomic energy project and 'make use of the atomic energy already obtained.' The cryptic announcement followed a meeting between President Perón and Dr. Ronald Richter, head of the atomic project on Huemul island." [3]

The message was clear: Once more, Richter had contrived to get presidential support by persuading Perón that atomic energy had been obtained. This time Gonzalez had definitely lost; Mende would now be in charge.

Vice Commodore Rodriguez Lonardi, who was to fly the plane held ready at the city airport, brought the news that the Bariloche visit had been cancelled on Presidential orders.

The committee, however, was not dissolved; its members met on March 6 at the new DNEA headquarters on Libertador Avenue to prepare a scientific report on the work performed at Huemul. In addition to the members mentioned above Beninson, Gamba, Bancora and Bussolini there was also Dr. Jorge Staricco, a young physicist and an excellent teacher. Though Bussolini later denied having participated, his name appears on the minutes of the meeting. In any case, his signature is not on the report. The Committee recommended "discontinuing all moral and material support currently provided to the project." [4] Yet, to whom was this recommendation addressed? Gonzalez was no longer part of the project and Mende still believed in its ultimate success. The report was filed away for the benefit of historical records.

Surprises for the New Secretary General

During the meeting with Perón, Richter told him about the latest developments, the new equipment recently installed, the rectifier, the electromagnet, the coils, various tasks completed at the power plant and the electrical distribution network. What a shame it would be to lose all that! Richter once again invited the President to visit Huemul. Perón agreed to do so as soon as Richter informed him that everything was ready in a few more days. They also discussed the GEOPE contract. Perón authorized Richter to dismiss SACES and to initiate formal negotiations with the German company.

As far as equipment was concerned, the most spectacular piece was still missing. As soon as the installation of the electromagnet was completed, Richter asked Hellmann to build a gigantic induction coil, that is, a double coil with copper wiring about 12 ft. high and 9 ft. wide, weighing approximately 50 tons. The idea of having such a piece of equipment filled Richter with joy. He wanted desperately to have it ready before the presidential visit. When he wrote to Hellmann again on March 11, he asked whether the coil could be ready in a few days. "I am writing for a very important reason: Will it be possible to have the induction coil soon, so it will be ready by the time the President comes to Huemul? I'd like to show him some truly extraordinary sights." After insisting that Hellmann should speed up the work, he explains that prior to installing the coil the laboratory floor will have to be excavated to provide room for it (he was referring to Lab #2, the only one in operation). Also, he asks for two pumps to carry gunpowder "which are to be used for permanent gunpowder circulation, two to six pounds of fine gunpowder at extremely high speeds", and explains: "this catalytic gunpowder must travel through a chemical reaction zone where it must be swiftly renewed." [5]

On March 15, Richter wrote to Hellmann again: "I received a telegram today from Minister Mende asking me to set a definite date for the President's visit. My reply was that the date depends on you and your news about the coil."

So Mende proceeded to call Hellmann and instructed him to go to Bariloche to clear up all pending matters regarding requirements and delivery terms. (He was starting to tread along the same path that had worn out Gonzalez.) Upon his return, Hellmann reported that Richter's current requirements amounted to some 300 million pesos (U$S 75 millions). Open mouthed, Mende exclaimed: "That's utterly impossible!" [6]

The GEOPE company started working on the island by late March. On Richter's instructions, their first task was to enlarge Lab # 2 to lodge the 47 ton coil. Though work began on April 8, it was not finished until July 7. [7] The delay was unimportant however, since it was naive to believe that the coil could be completed in a couple of weeks as Richter desired. Meanwhile, the long awaited Presidential visit was postponed once again.

The large reactor was another fundamental item in the construction plan of Huemul. What had happened during the eight-month period since the journalists had visited the island in June 1951 and saw nothing but a huge pit?

At the press conference on December 11, 1951, where it was announced that Argentina was seeking a partner for joint atomic energy exploitation, Richter anticipated possible questions from the journalists by saying: "Possibly you are worried wondering what exactly did we accomplish during these past eight months since the atomic energy announcement. Well," he continued – "as a result of research conducted during this period, we have learned how to liberate atomic energy in a reactor on a large scale, that means, we have learned how to build reactors for this purpose." [8]

The dramatic truth of the matter, however, was that nothing had been done about the reactor during that year and, as GEOPE data shows, by April 1952 Richter was still undecided as to what to do. [9]

Bertolo's colorful anecdotes, when he accompanied the author on a tour of the island in the summer of 1979, come to mind. On that occasion, we were standing in the center of the large reactor site when Bertolo, with his characteristic Italian accent, explained: "This is no rock that we are standing on right here, but concrete. Let me tell you how it was: first we dug a huge pit 48 ft. in diameter and 42 ft. deep. We had to use dynamite, of course, as it was all rock. We poured concrete over plank molding down to the bottom till it was 6 ft. thick, so the concrete base of the pit was 36 ft. down below." Changing into a deeper, more secretive voice, he added: "I'm not making it up, it's true. After that, we completed the plank molding all around. We had to cut planks to the very inch, to ensure the roundness of the hole. Imagine, the molding had to withstand the enormous weight of all that huge cement structure that was supposed to go on top. Just as the work was being completed, we suddenly had to stop everything. There was a new order: the pit had to be filled up with concrete! Another change of plans ...! Instructions were that we had to fill it up with cement mixed with the same round pebbles which were to be used for the concrete." Again, his tone changed: "At night, when nobody was looking, we threw in stones, rocks, anything we could find."

In March, Richter had asked GEOPE engineers to prepare plans to continue building the reactor exactly as planned a year earlier; that is, inside the pit, although the building surrounding the pit was to be modified. Richter now wanted to have the walls raised an additional 21 ft. to reach the overall height of 66 ft.

It is interesting to note that the blueprints of this work were signed by Richter at Government House in the presence of Minister Mende on March 31. Mende was obviously trying to corner Richter into a definite plan and avoid future changes. If such was indeed the idea behind the formal procedure set up by the Minister, he had little success: three days later Richter proceeded to modify the plans without the slightest hesitation.

The reactor was now to be built outdoors and Lab # 1 would house the control system. This change was decided on Monday, April 7, and Richter dutifully sent Mende an explanatory note pointing out the causes and advantages of the modification. [10]

There was the problem of filling in the huge pit. GEOPE engineers suggested covering it up with a concrete slab supported by columns. According to a GEOPE technical report, "Dr. Richter decided against such a proposal as it might interfere with the reflection and measurement of 'active rays'". [11] It was then agreed to fill in the pit with very poor concrete and pillars to support the slab of the floor so as to withstand heavy weights.

Sometime later, on April 21, while Richter was making an inspection tour of the site accompanied by Navy Captain Iraolagoitia his brand new counterpart who had replaced Gonzalez "he (Richter) suddenly realized that large amounts of iron were being used while building the skeleton base and body of the columns. This made Richter extremely worried and, explaining that the concentration of iron in certain places would disturb the reflection of active rays, he ordered every piece of iron to be pulled out." [12]

The work was therefore completed without using any iron. The pit was filled up to 9 ft. below ground level with a "poor" concrete mixture for which 9.350 bags of cement were used plus 8.600 bags for the final section of "good" concrete. The filling work was finished by mid July 1952; the 'open air reactor' was never started.

The GEOPE construction company also built several other facilities on the island. Notably, on the first terrace, two large buildings over 4000 square ft. each with walls 45 ft. high which, just as Lab # 1, were plainly visible from the mainland. On August 2, Dr. Richter informed the construction company that a "small" reactor" 33 x 33 x 33 ft. was to be installed in one of those buildings so the walls had to be brought up 6 ft.

In addition, Richter ordered two other completely "dry" labs to be built. One of them, (Lab # 4) had no windows and was built over a double slab with a 5 in. asphaltic treated layer in between. The building was so hermetically sealed that when the final stucco was applied on the inside walls, the plaster never dried. According to a GEOPE report, "the building was heated day and night with wood stoves, to no avail." Richter then changed his mind and in June he ordered large windows (approx. 4.5 ft. wide by 15 ft. high) to be opened up on the walls. A week later he decided they were unnecessary. The window frames had already been ordered to Buenos Aires so they were included all the same, as indicated in a blueprint signed by Richter in July. This was apparently the reason for the large openings which were eventually made by mid September [13].

GEOPE was also instructed to build an office for Richter on one of the highest points of the island, commanding a view of practically all plant facilities. It was built on a big rock 120 ft. above to the back of the large reactor building. The work started in late June. Richter insisted it had to be finished with utmost speed as the office was needed "to welcome President Perón when he comes to visit the island". According to certain witnesses, Richter instructed that the walls of the large reactor building should be brought down (once it was decided the reactor was to be built elsewhere) so as to enjoy a beautiful, unobstructed view from his office. The office was finished on August 26. A two hundred step stairway led to it.

Other minor works were also completed: roads, an emergency pier on the southern shore of the island... That year, some 23.500 cement bags were used between the months of April and October. None of the buildings were ever used except the office, where Richter received the members of the investigating committee in September.

A reading of the final GEOPE report on the works completed on Huemul arouses mixed feelings. On the one hand, one feels incredulity as well as fascination at the record of orders and counter orders which constitute in themselves excellent journalistic material. On the other hand, and more importantly, it produces a grievous sensation of extravagant waste.

Meantime, the resignation of Colonel Gonzalez had been made effective very discreetly, without the news leaking out to the general public. Perón asked him to continue attending the Casa Rosada regularly "in order to avoid the rumors your resignation will surely provoke." Gonzalez and Mende (who took charge of the former's duties during March) managed to maintain a cordial relationship owing mainly to Mende's frankness. Gonzalez appreciated it. Mende explained that all along he had been uncomfortable with Gonzalez' independent style. Too much of a free bird within his own Ministry. It had indeed been so and Gonzalez, now an outsider, could not but agree. [14]

To replace Gonzalez, Perón appointed Navy Captain pilot Pedro E. Iraolagoitia, who had been his presidential aide from 1949 to September 1951. The President placed unlimited confidence in the Captain: Iraolagoitia often accompanied Evita to labor union meetings when Perón was unable to attend. After the failed coup of September 1951, Perón sent Iraolagoitia to the Navy base at Punta Indio, a spot of major conflict. While in this base, the Navy Captain organized a historical naval air campaign which took place in February 1952, establishing the first airmail service to Antarctica with two "Catalina" aircrafts.

Shortly afterwards, while writing a report on his mission to Antarctica, he was summoned by the Minister: "Look Iraola, the President wants to talk to you."

The President informed him that he was to take charge of "the Atomic Agency." Iraolagoitia knew little about the existence of such an institution. He had seen Richter at Government House frequently; he had welcomed Prince Bernhard on behalf of the Argentine government a year earlier, and he had attended the conference at the Defense Ministry for senior ranking officers in early 1950. Together with Capt. Oscar Quihillalt and Capt. Diaz, he had been Navy representative at that meeting where Gamba, Bussolini and even Richter had spoken.

"I've got a problem with Richter; he has turned unmanageable and there has been quite a row, as a result of which Gonzalez resigned." the President explained. "May I have 24 hours to think it over?" Iraolagoitia asked. The former aide was bewildered not knowing whom to ask or where to turn for information on "the Atomic Agency".

Later, Iraolagoitia recalled that once settled in the comfortable office left by Gonzalez at Government House, he frequently heard people speaking of "the headquarters". About a week later Iraolagoitia summoned up enough courage to inquire. The headquarters, he was told, is where the labs are located at the ex Massone building on Libertador Avenue. So there he went. The building was occupied by technical personnel mounting laboratories. "Gamba already had his office there; so had Mallmann. Mallmann was working behind some large, donut shaped spectrometers built by Fabricaciones Militares. The amount of money invested in large equipment was simply staggering. It was most unusual at the time to spend so much money in science." [15]

If it took Iraolagoitia a week to find out about the headquarters of the agency he presided, how could he be expected to adopt a rational decision within 24 hours? Actually, he did not even have 24 hours to think it over. Perón called him again that afternoon: a new commotion had occurred in Bariloche which needed immediate attention. According to a telegram from Richter, there had been a new act of sabotage. An explosion had destroyed a pressure vessel containing a mixture of nitrogen and hydrogen. Richter also asked that two technicians be sent to Bariloche. Iraolagoitia had no choice: he had to take action. His first decision was to send non commissioned officers Borras and Eguireun.

Curiously enough, both Gonzalez and Iraolagoitia started their jobs of looking after Richter's needs under virtually identical circumstances. In October 1949, a short circuit in Richter's lab (which he also described as an act of sabotage) had likewise prompted Perón to summon Gonzalez.

In a way, this new act of sabotage was a blessing for the new head of the Atomic Energy agency: it provided him an excuse to visit Huemul. It was natural for the new administrator to find out exactly what had happened. Were it not for this, visiting the Bariloche Plant would have been tantamount to risking a snub.

A week after having taken on his new post, Iraolagoitia left for Bariloche. Everybody was courteous to him there and he in turn was pleasant with everyone. Richter sent his secretary to pick him up at the airport and take him to the Hotel Roma. Border Police Second Commander Fiscina occupied the room next door. Fiscina, as head of Richter's special guard, was disliked by almost everybody in Bariloche because of his excessive zeal in carrying out Richter's orders, which included detention of civilians. Later, Iraolagoitia remarked he was certain that Fiscina had been planted there to spy on him.

In the late afternoon of Sunday, April 20, 1952, Iraolagoitia enjoyed a magnificent view of the famous island while having tea with the Richters. It was a pleasant evening. Richter recounted in detail the accident which had taken place a week earlier: a cylinder 3.6 ft. high and 1.8 ft. in diameter had broken apart at the bottom with a tremendous noise as the gases inside exploded due to a spark purposely induced between two electrodes. The visitor was amazed that such an accident should be termed 'sabotage' since it is no news that nitrogen and hydrogen in air make an explosive mixture. He refrained, however, from making any comments. "Richter would surely have thrown me out had I dared to disagree," he confided years later to the author.

Next morning, Iraolagoitia visited the island. The group started climbing the zig zag trail which led to Lab #2. Richter insisted on carrying out a demonstration of what had actually happened with nitrogen and hydrogen and using the very same vessel, still torn apart at the bottom, which was lying on the floor. Near the door, a photoelectric cell was connected to a recorder some distance away. Richter picked up the controls and walked outside with his visitor some 60 ft. away from the lab. There, he threw himself to the ground motioning his astonished visitor to do likewise.

Richter pressed the button. An explosion rocked the building forming a dense curtain of smoke and debris. Iraolagoitia could not believe his eyes. Richter walked toward the instrument which had spewed up a few feet of paper recording photocell pulses. He excitedly examined it till he found the explosion signal. Then he wrote: "atomic energy". Iraolagoitia was speechless. "What allegedly had been sabotage the day before, now turns out to be a demonstration performed for my benefit. This chap is absolutely crazy!" he said to himself. [16].

Once the smoke cloud cleared, they walked toward the entrance door to the lab. There was none: it had been ripped away. "Good heavens! Am I supposed to pay for this too?" the brand new envoy thought, not knowing what to make of it all. It was the most peculiar incident, no doubt, that Iraolagoitia had ever witnessed. Meanwhile, Richter was overjoyed.

During the return flight to Buenos Aires, Iraolagoitia wrote a brief report of what he had seen and heard. Though not a scientist, he was a navy aviator and had some technical training. Iraolagoitia recorded at least fourteen different facts that indicated a clearly insane management of the project. Almost three decades later, he still remembered a few: the large number of disconnected equipment; Richter's insistence on using theodolites to lay out cables at Indio Muerto; Richter's comments while walking past the reactor pit that was being filled in to the effect that the steel being used was supposed to avoid disturbance of the terrestrial magnetic field.

Next day, Iraolagoitia got up very early. He knew that the best time to see Perón was at 6:00 a.m. It was Monday, April 28. He marched into the President's office carrying the report under his arm. Perón, though confronted with undisputable evidence, was still hesitant; he was a trapped man. If the evidence were true, then he had been duped.

Iraolagoitia insisted: "Look, sir, I'm only a Navy pilot, I'm not a physicist and I don't know much about all this. You don't have to take my word. But it is urgent that you appoint a committee to conduct a formal investigation."

The New Committee

The scientific visit to Huemul which Gonzalez had proposed in February and now Iraolagoitia was trying to organize was not easy to materialize. According to Iraolagoitia, the delay was due to Mende, who was backing up Richter. ("Every time Mende spoke with Perón, he managed to convince him anew and I had to start all over again"). Father Bussolini, who acted as scientific advisor to Perón, was also in favor of continuing the project.

It was not surprising, that the President was reluctant to believe he had been the victim of a swindle and avoided the inevitable decision. The arguments submitted by Iraolagoitia had some effect however, since by mid May Perón instructed that all foreign equipment ordered by Richter should, upon arrival in Buenos Aires, be sent to DNEA instead of being dispatched to Bariloche. [17]

The President was also facing other problems which might justify his desire to postpone a final decision on this complex atomic adventure. Hortensio Quijano, his partner in the presidential formula, had died recently and the government had to call for new elections. On June 4 Perón was beginning his second term at the Casa Rosada. And more importantly, Evita was now showing the sad effects of her incurable disease and "an ominous feeling which increased with each passing day pervaded the last months of Perón's first presidency. It was the knowledge that his wife was rapidly approaching death. That day, (June 4) was the last time that the Argentines saw her alive." [18] Regardless of how interested Perón was in the Huemul project a parenthesis of mournful respect was observed until late July (Evita died on July 26, 1952).

Mr. Hellmann, according to his own testimony, also contributed to making Richter accept the idea of a probing committee. When Hellmann informed Mende that the last pieces of equipment ordered by Richter would cost about 300 million pesos, the minister - as mentioned earlier was utterly dismayed. Once recovered from the initial shock, Mende asked Hellmann's opinion regarding the probability of success.

"As you know, I'm an electromechanical engineer. I can give you my views as such, not as a nuclear physicist" Hellmann replied. "My opinion is that you should appoint a commission of nuclear experts." "Yes, yes, I know, but Richter refuses to allow anyone inside his lab. Could you try to convince him to accept a probing committee?" the bewildered minister asked, thus underlining the extraordinary influence that Richter exercised over government officials. Hellmann, who had a paid position as advisor to DNEA, left for Bariloche with that purpose. According to his own description of events ("You simply cannot refuse to have a committee of experts visit the

Plant, or there will be no more funds for the project"), he somehow managed to convince Richter. This success, if indeed he achieved it, was short lived.

By late June, new promises were announced from Huemul in connection with a grand experiment that was to take place within fifteen days. On July 31, Colonel Gonzalez, who kept in touch, wrote a family letter to his son who was now in Holland [19]: "Due to recent events (he meant the death of Evita), the wizard managed to save himself. But Iraolagoitia has just told me that next week the squeeze will be on. Unless something unexpected happens, all will be finished by the 15th (of August). The wizard apparently suggested coming to Buenos Aires to talk with Perón, but he was told not to bother. The truth of the matter is that he was coming to berate Iraolagoitia and to accuse him that he lacked formal evidence against him."

To put it mildly, the integration of the visiting committee was not an easy task. Father Bussolini was Perón's firm candidate, though the priest was not a physicist. He had studied astronomy at the La Plata Observatory in the early 40's, "with the purpose of replacing Father Puig as head of the Jesuit Observatory in San Miguel", but Bussolini failed to complete regular courses. "He was good natured and easy going" his professor of Mechanics would recall. "The Jesuits had sent him to Germany to learn the language. Afterwards, he lived in La Plata in a boarding house for students. He used to challenge fellow boarders to walk through the city streets wearing his cassock. He was a fine chap, but ...he knew little physics." [20]

Perón instructed Iraolagoitia to select the rest of the members. Iraola, in turn, relied on his scientific secretary, Captain Beninson. Beninson had studied physics in France, his native country, around 1910. He was not an expert in nuclear matters either.

Gamba, who was appointed deputy director to DNEA in April, was also a firm candidate. In spite of being only 33 years old, he was better equipped than the rest. He had completed post graduate courses in nuclear physics in Illinois, then at the

Poincare and the Radium Institute in Paris, and had worked with radioisotopes. He was not an expert, however, in these subjects. Gamba was a chemical engineer; both in Mendoza and Buenos Aires he had devoted his time to teaching chemical physics and thermodynamics.

As mentioned above, Mario Bancora, an engineer of the University of Rosario had already participated in the first committee. His background included a term of specialized studies in related matters in California and, upon his return to Rosario, Bancora had built a small cyclotron in his laboratory. This had been in truth a noteworthy accomplishment which revealed a creative spirit, and it had rightly impressed both Mende and Iraolagoitia. Bancora had learned electromagnetism the hard (and most effective) way: by dirtying his hands while building magnets, power supplies and radiofrequency circuits. Undoubtedly, his past experience enabled him to evaluate the Huemul facilities.

The fifth member was to be Staricco. According to Bancora, he declined because..."he was afraid of flying." At least a dozen competent physicists could no doubt have been selected for the job from the Argentine Physics Association, but the Association, led by Gaviola, opposed the government.

One day, while discussing the composition of the committee with Perón, Iraolagoitia remarked: "You know, General, there are no Peronist physicists in Argentina". Perón nodded.

There were several scientists at DNEA. The fact that they were not Peronists was noteworthy considering the political atmosphere prevailing at the time in other academic circles, and especially in the educational system of Argentina. This characteristic of DNEA, for which its first directors ought to be credited, produced highly positive results as the institution developed and was a major cause of its subsequent success. Gonzalez, and especially Iraolagoitia, who faced Perón to obtain Ernesto Galloni's appointment, made a special effort to avoid the noxious effects of political discrimination which, unfortunately, was so much in vogue those days at the National Universities.

Yet it was one thing for Perón to allow certain anti-Peronist physicists to work in DNEA, and another to let those physicists stand in judgment of Richter, brandishing a pre established verdict.

Almost by chance, the fifth committee member happened to be Dr. Jose Antonio Balseiro, a key element in this story.

Balseiro's background was similar to that of Gamba and Bancora. After obtaining his doctorate in La Plata in 1944, Gaviola invited him to join the Córdoba Observatory and to work under the guidance of Dr. Beck. Balseiro was one of the first disciples of Beck in Argentina; hence, one of the first young physicists in Argentina to learn Quantum Mechanics. In 1950, he was awarded a British Council scholarship to work in Manchester under Prof. Rosenfeld, where he rounded up a solid scientific training. The scholarship was so modest that Balseiro was forced to leave his wife and child behind.

Neither the rest of the commission members, nor Iraolagoitia himself knew how Balseiro had come to join them in the committee. They were not aware that he had been called back urgently by the Argentine Embassy in London. The reason for this could be traced back to the time Balseiro was a high school student at the Monserrat School in Córdoba, where he had met Silvio Tosello who in 1952 was working for Minister Mende. As a result of this relationship, Tosello suggested to Mende that Balseiro ought to be recalled to Argentina to integrate the committee. Thus, even though Mende opposed any prying into Richter's work, it was ultimately due to him that the scientific figure most capable of coping with the Huemul myth finally became part of the group.

Balseiro arrived in Buenos Aires on July 25. Writing to his son in Holland on August 20, Gonzalez points out: "In order to assuage your doubts regarding the future of the wizard, let me tell you that Iraolagoitia is leaving south next Monday (i.e. August 25), with orders from the General to put an end to the whole show one way or the other." However, a new delay occurred.

Since Richter was on the alert, losing no time he went directly to see Perón. GEOPE technical reports indicate that on August 28 all work on the island was abruptly discontinued. Then, on September 3, "a telegram was received from the Ministry (from Mende) ordering that the works were to be continued." A letter from Gonzalez to his son on that same day illustrates some of the dramatic events the Government had to cope with: "The wizard, in an effort to gain the upper hand, came directly to Buenos Aires to see Perón and Mende. Since the situation was rather confused and Richter had implied earlier that if the 'new gang' (meaning Iraola & Co.) were not dismissed he would be leaving straight for where he had always meant to go, he was placed under surveillance just like on other occasions. So our hero went to visit 'his friends' (the US Embassy) and there he was caught. You can well imagine the commotion that took place then. The fact is that Mende called him on the phone apologizing and suggesting he should return south next morning. That was precisely what he did."

This time, the visit to Huemul was not cancelled but Mende, in order to soften its impact on Richter, insisted on having an entourage of Congressmen, representatives and senators, joining the scientists. The departure to the by now historic Huemul Island finally occurred on Friday, September 5, 1952.

The Veil is Drawn

The 5 scientists and 20 legislators arrived on the island at noon. The weather was glorious: not a cloud in the sky. In the sun, the visitors were comfortable despite the cold breeze blowing from the Cordillera. Richter greeted the visitors with a smile and in Spanish. He was wearing his typical checked shirt, though now with a tie and jacket. The group started their journey up. A short distance from the pier they came upon a plaque in memory of Evita; a few feet up, the security main office, the carpentry shop, the photo lab. Mende and other legislators surrounded Richter. Iraolagoitia, Balseiro and Bancora kept a little distance. The older men, Beninson and Bussolini, dragged behind. They all reached the first turn of the road where the tomb of the Indian chief had been found back in 1949, and walked by the old barracks where the Second Company of Engineers had previously lodged, now used by GEOPE. The first gigantic buildings, still unfinished, were now in sight. Another turn of the road toward the west. The embankments higher up were partially covered with stones. They reached the main area to the left: Lab # 2 enclosed by a fence 9 ft. high with a sentry keeping watch at the door; the power plant in front, Lab # 1 to the right and next to it Lab # 4, where large openings were being made then to install windows. There was nothing to be seen by now in Lab # 1: the pit had been covered up and the concrete slab finished. Not a trace of the fantastic works carried out on that spot, nor of the countless thousands of cement bags buried underneath. Paradoxically, the experts' visit took place at the only point in time when nothing was being done in connection with the large reactor, the center of gravity of so many dreams and promises.

Some group members were by now quite out of breath. Most overcoats were hanging from their backs. Then somewhat inconsiderately, Richter pointed toward the two hundred step path that led to his retreat. Of all possible places on the island, he had chosen to take them up to his romantic lodge on the rocky promontory and there they went.

The view from the top was breath taking. It not only displayed the splendid scenery of the western side of the island, but also beyond the lake, the valley of the Gutierrez river and the majestic Catedral peak. For those who only a few hours earlier had been deep in the frenzied rush of Buenos Aires, this magnificent view was so soothing that they stopped to admire it for a while.

Richter proceeded to expound his scientific ideas. He repeated what he had said at the press conference on March 25, 1951 about the Maxwell law: "A gas at a certain temperature contains atoms travelling at various speeds". He explained how he had managed to obtain a selective distribution to favor the high speeds necessary to unleash a thermonuclear reaction. He added that a mere 2 % of the atoms achieving such speeds was enough to set the mechanism in motion. Balseiro, Bancora and the other members of the experts' committee just listened. Not so Representative Rumbo who, knowing very little physics, engaged in a meaningless discussion with Richter. The exchange became somewhat confused and dragged on. Some of the scientists began to show signs of uneasiness, but fortunately the meeting drew to an end as cordially as it had begun.

Dr. Richter then led the visitors to Lab # 2, his operational center. This was the first and most modest laboratory built on the island approximately 90 ft. long by 45 ft. wide and only 12 ft. high and the only one to be used while Project Huemul lasted. At the time of the visit, the adjoining building lodging the huge induction coil had already been finished. The building inside was separated into various areas by concrete walls 3 ft. thick which stopped short of the ceiling. These walls, designed like a labyrinth, were supposed to act as shield against the radiation produced in the central area where the electromagnet was installed. A battery of condensers and coils was placed next to the door, while the control panel was on the far side: an area of racks full of recording devices and oscilloscopes. There were also large rheostats and gas cylinders, presumably filled with hydrogen.

The center of attraction was in the middle of the polar pieces of the electromagnet. There were two carbon electrodes a few inches apart, cross angled to the axis of the magnet. The polar pieces in the electromagnet had small openings to inject the reactive elements. All this was surrounded though not totally confined by walls with 8 in. holes pointing toward the center of the cross. One of these walls, 6 ft. thick, divided the facility from the control area. There were hoses through two of the holes connected to the gas cylinders. Other minor devices were hanging from the ceiling. A Geiger Muller counter was positioned next to the electromagnet, and a loudspeaker. There was no doubt that the former was there to detect radiations produced by the thermonuclear process, while the function of the latter could not be conjectured. [21]

Actually, what the committee members saw in the laboratory was different from what Colonel Gonzalez had seen when invited to attend a demonstration soon after the February 16, 1951 experiments. In his description, the Colonel had mentioned "a small reactor a cylinder about 9 ft. high and 6 ft. in diameter with cement walls in addition to a spectrograph." It was precisely through this instrument, the spectrograph, that the crucial evidence of success had presumably been obtained: the broadened spectrum lines would have indicated that the temperature needed to initiate a thermonuclear reaction had been attained.

Neither the small reactor nor the spectrograph were in the laboratory when the group of scientists and legislators visited Huemul in September 1952. A year earlier, when Richter had informed Gonzalez about major changes in the lab, most likely he was referring to these. Instead of a concrete cylinder, he now had an electromagnet, and to measure radiation from nuclear reactions he now had Geiger counters.

Richter showed the visitors the electromagnet and then the control panel. The legislators were impressed by the countless devices, their size and complexity. It looked to them like a science fiction movie, as most of them certainly had never seen anything like it, except in the cinema.

During the tour, Balseiro and Bancora worked as a team. They examined the instruments and the way they were connected (or disconnected, as it was later found out in some cases). Bancora kept the details of the lay out to repeat the experiments afterwards. When Richter realized that they were engaged in "espionage", he became furious and accused them of committing a breach of confidence.

Iraolagoitia recalled later that the legislators were mesmerized. When the explosion occurred, some of them fell backwards stumbling over cable grooves on the floor, falling on top of each other. Amazingly, Richter failed to instruct them to protect themselves behind the shielding walls prior to the demonstration. Richter was sitting in front of the control panel and Bertolo, the foreman, a member of Richter's "elite group" and one of his main laboratory assistants, was in charge of connecting the "blades". "And that was not the first time either, I had done it before" he recalled in his simple style, not devoid of a certain sense of humor. "When Richter cried 'Achtung', I, wearing a pair of gloves, had to bring the blades down. All the high voltage was then released. Richter had refused to let us use protection, so when I connected them, sparks flew all over me." Richter, behind a thick wall, handled the rheostats to increase the power across the spark gap.

On that first day of experiments Richter produced an explosion without injecting anything. Father Bussolini, by way of explanation in his report to the President, wrote: "In my opinion (this voltaic arc explosion) was designed exclusively to impress the visiting politicians who are totally unaware of atomic matters." [22]

Lithium hydride was used for the second test. [23] While spouts of hydrogen gushed through flexible metallic hoses in the openings of the electromagnet, the loudspeaker emitted a loud sound which started deep and rapidly reached "a piercingly high note." The hydrogen flared up in the arc and, when mixed with lithium, produced a blazing red flame. [24] "It was an eerie, fantastic sight" Bancora recalled. Vidiri, secretary of Iraolagoitia, was standing next to Richter while he was at the controls and heard him remark mockingly: "Some test, isn't it?" [25]

At full power, in addition to the blazing flame, a roaring sound was heard together with a marked agitation in the recording devices and a high count rate in the scalers. Both the monitoring devices and the scalers were connected to the Geiger counter next to the electromagnet and they all revealed the reception of signals.

Later, Father Bussolini considered in his report that "prima facie", positive results were obtained (in the second test) if the scalers reaction were to be taken as evidence of radiation as well as the graphs obtained during the process." [26]

The group was later taken to the Hotel Pistarini by Lake Moreno, a spot of exceptional beauty. The legislators were satisfied and returned to Buenos Aires on the following morning. Not the experts. Most of them harbored serious doubts as to the theoretical explanations of Dr. Richter, but in addition the experimental demonstrations were very unconvincing. Bancora had brought a calibrated gamma radiation detector from Buenos Aires and during the experiment this device detected nothing, in contrast to Richter's counters.

This inconsistency as well as others were discussed with Richter at the hotel on Saturday afternoon. An issue was the Maxwell distribution law and the temperatures needed to unleash a nuclear reaction. They also discussed a method to control the reaction proposed by Richter during the demonstration. Richter maintained that the process could be controlled by inducing a circular motion on the atoms with a magnetic field a phenomenon known as the Larmor precession –, yet none of the committee members was able to extract a satisfactory explanation on this matter. In any case, Balseiro later made a detailed analysis of this phenomenon and showed that since the experiment was conducted at atmospheric pressure it was impossible for the circular motion even to take place. [27]

Richter offered to carry out a new experiment on Monday. This time heavy water, instead of ordinary hydrogen and lithium, would be used so as to obtain a fusion reaction between two deuterium nuclei (heavy hydrogen). Compared to the hydrogen lithium reaction, the deuterium reaction produces more neutrons. Neutrons can be detected by the radioactivity they induce on other materials. They decided to use indium foils, an element which easily becomes radioactive when exposed to neutrons.

The Richter group remained on the island working all through Sunday in order to have everything ready for the experiment. Father Bussolini praised this fact when describing the activities of those days to the President. He was the one member of the committee who felt increasingly uncomfortable with his inquisitive colleagues. As he was not used to scientific discussions, he felt they were disrespectful towards the head of the Huemul project. Actually, Bussolini mentioned in his report that "skepticism shown on the faces and opinions of the experts' influenced the group of congressmen even before the experiments had taken place on the day of arrival. Thenceforth, the prevailing negative impression was reinforced by the experts' attitudes, which denoted prejudice instead of scientific rigor. If the experts had been fully satisfied, they would not have asked to remain on the island for a few more days trying to solve queries which result naturally from the experiments and which remain to be solved. In my view, the performance of the committee members, which I was later asked to preside, has been politically unwise." [28]

Father Bussolini was right in referring to the skepticism exhibited even prior to the first experiment. In fact, after Richter's presentation at his retreat, both Bancora and Balseiro became convinced of the falsehood of project Huemul. Their conviction stemmed not only from the absence of solid reasoning, but from the vagueness, the errors, the contradictions and the naiveté of Richter's concepts, which swept away any remaining doubts they might have had. They exchanged their thoughts while leaving the shelter. Their whispering comments were overheard by Representative Astorgano, who later told Iraolagoitia: "Those two scientists, the tall one and the fat one, were telling each other: 'If this thing works, I am the king of Siam'". Bancora (the tall one) was present when Iraolagoitia told the author this story and smiled.

The heavy water experiment was carried out on Monday. Eguireun, one of the two non commissioned officers who had arrived in April and who together with Bertolo now helped Richter with his experiments, was in charge of pouring heavy water on the spark gap with "coffee spoons". Once again the roaring sound, the blazing flame, the explosion... but the indium plates did not become radioactive.

Richter reluctantly admitted the negative results of the experiment, but insisted it proved nothing. Bussolini, obviously partial to Richter, stated in his report, "In my opinion, the results may have been negative, but Dr. Richter, was not trying to obtain positive results anyway, since the experiment was merely the outcome of theoretical discussions with the experts."

In view of this, Richter was asked to repeat the experiment of the previous Friday with lithium hydride. While he was busy making the necessary arrangements in the control room, Bancora and Balseiro proceeded to make some checks. First, by means of a radioactive radium sample brought from Buenos Aires they established that the counters in the area next to the magnet were insensitive to gamma radiation. Secondly, while igniting the voltaic arc and prior to injecting lithium hydride, they verified that the counters used by Richter were triggered even in the absence of radiation.

At that point, Richter realized what the two experts were doing and, emerging from behind a shielding wall, he "wrathfully accused them of acting as if he was a swindler. What he ought to do under the circumstances was to throw them off the island." Awkwardly, he also added that "he had been told by Father Bussolini that they (Bancora and Balseiro) suspected he might be staging a fraudulent experiment."[29]

This embarrassing remark almost jeopardized the whole experiment. Father Bussolini had taken sides with Richter as shown in his report. He did not consider himself part of the experts' group: mostly he spoke of 'them' instead of 'us'. In one case he used the first person, "we were called 'Schwindeln' by Richter, swindlers". Bussolini also added in his report that "aside from that particularly strained moment, justifiably so for Dr. Richter, his attitude was always extremely affable and polite. He never refused to enter into any sort of discussion." Further on, even more explicitly: "It is my considered opinion that Dr. Richter is not a fraud as has been implied by the other members of the committee. Dr. Richter is a scientist in the full extent of the word; he is perfectly acquainted with theoretical physics (over six hours of discussion attest to this) and with experimental techniques, not to mention his extraordinary ability for teaching his humble assistants to operate the most complex electronic devices." Probably disturbed and annoyed by the incident between Richter and his colleagues, whom he evidently failed to understand, Bussolini added even more emphatically: "Moreover, in my opinion and as far as Dr. Richter is concerned, none of the committee experts is worthy scientifically speaking of tying his shoelaces, nor could any of them have personally directed an experimental facility such as the Huemul Pilot Plant." [30]

The experiment was carried out in spite of the strained atmosphere. Lithium and hydrogen were injected between the electrodes of the spark gap and a voltaic explosion occurred. Richter's detectors registered the same activity as before; the committee's detectors once again, nothing.

The work of the committee members did not stop there, however. They also visited the lab where physicist Wolfgang Ehrenberg worked. He was a devoted character who lived with his mother and maintained an attitude of respectful admiration for Richter, whose tantrums he occasionally had to suffer. [31]

A year earlier, he had mounted a lab to produce heavy water using for this purpose two ordinary houses in the officers' district along the route to Llao Llao facing the homes of Richter, Jaffke and his own.

While accompanying committee members to the heavy water lab, Richter commented that "in spite of its modest appearance, we have obtained some remarkable results in this facility." Yet when committee members asked Ehrenberg how he determined the enrichment of common water to heavy water, he replied that nothing had yet been done in that direction. [32]

One Verdict Not Enough

All members of the experts' committee but one returned to Buenos Aires with a clear picture of what lay behind the famous atomic project: merely a few well known general concepts mixed with a dose of fantasy; nothing really serious from which positive results could be expected. The exception in the group was, of course, Father Bussolini who together with Minister Mende who had returned to Buenos Aires earlier with Iraolagoitia and the congressmen were deeply impressed by the display of equipment and instruments and by the tone of the scientific discussions, a reaction to be expected from people with no scientific training. They saw things they had never seen before, they heard discussions on subjects they knew nothing about. Surely Richter must know about those things since he had been able to discuss such complex theories and had mounted such sophisticated equipment.

Iraolagoitia was no expert either, but since last April his mind was made up about Richter: he was convinced that Richter was a fabricator. But when it came to facing Perón, it was a two (Mende and Bussolini) to one issue as the rest of the committee members were far less influential. Consequently, the visit's final outcome was still dubious when Iraolagoitia arrived in Buenos Aires. He was worried lest it be impossible to extricate a final decision from Perón. Iraolagoitia confided his worries to his predecessor (Gonzalez), who maintained a vivid interest in the latest developments on the subject. These were then transmitted to his son abroad. "The net result of the experiments was a query. Work will continue, however, until the big experiment he is now proposing actually takes place, though this time it will be in collaboration with Argentine scientists. So you see, it's the same story all over again. Iraolagoitia is thinking of leaving. There's nothing to be done about it. Richter comes first", Gonzalez wrote on September 12, a few days after the experts returned to Buenos Aires. [33]

Records fail to show which Argentine scientists, if any, were in fact to collaborate with Richter. This purported collaboration sounded rather like a sort of appeasement to soothe a feeling of helplessness and disaster. This gesture, however, recalls a humorous incident that occurred during the famous weekend the committee spent in Bariloche. At one time, while engaged in technical discussions, Richter offered Balseiro and Bancora the chance to work with him. Needless to say, both declined the offer. [34]

Minister Mende asked each committee member to submit a technical report in addition to a written personal opinion. Both reports were to be written individually. They were asked not to exchange opinions among themselves before turning in their reports. They submitted them on September 15 together with a general summary jointly signed which stated that "due to lack of scientific evidence, this Technical Committee is totally unable to endorse assertions of such magnitude as those formulated by Dr. Richter..".

Father Bussolini's report, biased toward Richter, undoubtedly contributed to making the general summary less drastic than it might have been. Bussolini, nevertheless, stated that "I would like to suggest the convenience of asking Prof. Richter to clarify the points numbered below", while adding: "should project works continue, I should like to suggest to Your Excellency that in view of the large investments which are to be made, it might be appropriate to appoint not an investigating but a collaborating committee to cooperate in such a momentous undertaking." As this paragraph suggests, the idea of continuing the project and incorporating Argentine scientists was proposed not by Richter, but perhaps by Bussolini. [35]

Bancora and Balseiro submitted the most significant pieces. Bancora reproduced in detail the circuit used by Richter and maintained he had been able to simulate the Bariloche experiments in his lab at the University of Rosario, without using, of course, any of the elements required for thermonuclear reactions such as lithium or hydrogen. The circuit that had been used by Richter was basically none other than the early electromagnetic wave transmitters used by Hertz, Marconi, Duddell and many others in the past. It consisted of a condenser, an induction and a spark gap connected in series; the spark gap, in turn, was connected to a variable electromotive source. This is an oscillatory circuit which serves as a source of electromagnetic waves. Bancora pointed out that these electromagnetic waves not the gamma rays resulting from thermonuclear reactions were responsible for the signals registered on the poorly calibrated counters in Huemul. In addition, Balseiro showed quantitatively that in order to obtain a mere one percent of atoms with sufficient speed to fuse among themselves half of what Richter said were required it was necessary to attain temperatures of 40 million degrees: ten thousand times greater than those produced by the electric arc on Huemul.

Another aspect debated by Balseiro has already been mentioned: he proved beyond doubt the impossibility of achieving any control device or reaction ignition by means of the Larmor precession effect, as Richter claimed. [36]

Certainly, these were not the kind of reviews that Bussolini and Mende would have hoped for. These documents were critical of the work accomplished in Bariloche and were consequently disliked by those who had been involved so deeply in the project. Furthermore, neither Bussolini nor Mendé was in a position to evaluate the actual extent to which these unfavorable opinions invalidated all accomplishments to date and future possibilities. Scientifically they were not knowledgeable enough to understand the technical arguments. These ran parallel to political considerations as two insoluble substances. Such conflicts between scientists and politicians are not unusual. Ordinarily, however, politicians appoint scientific advisors whom they trust. This was not the case, though. Bussolini and Mende were lost.

Faced with the dilemma, the best thing to do was to play for time and get additional data. Nothing would look better than to give the defendant the opportunity to answer the incriminating arguments submitted by the experts.

Richter was summoned to Buenos Aires. He relied, as usual, on the total support of Mende and Perón. This time however, the mien of his hosts failed to show a welcoming expression. The President and his Minister could not help being influenced by the opinions of Iraolagoitia and the experts. Painful as it was, the negative verdicts could not be disregarded altogether. For once, the meeting with Richter was guarded. Possibly by that time the President was already persuaded that the end of project Huemul was inevitable.

That was the last time that Perón and Richter met. The meeting took place on September 25.

Grieved, Richter returned to Bariloche taking along copies of the experts' reports. He had been asked to reply to them as promptly as possible. Richter's response is dated October 11. He took it to Buenos Aires personally, but Perón did not see him. Having no choice, he delivered it to Mende and Iraolagoitia. Gamba, meanwhile, had gone to Europe, so Tossello, who represented Mende, took his place in the group.

In spite of its length, Richter's reply neither breaks new ground nor refutes the objections raised by Balseiro and Bancora but it accuses committee members of confusing the issues. Regarding the estimate made by Balseiro, for instance, showing that it was necessary to reach 40 million degrees to get one percent of atoms above the threshold indicated by Richter, he claims it could also be done with a lower threshold energy; hence, temperatures below 40 million degrees would still be appropriate. However, he failed to make the effort of estimating the value corresponding to his new hypothesis. Balseiro calculated this value afterwards demonstrating that the figures remained essentially the same. Richter also insisted on the possibility of distorting the well known Maxwell law, but neglected to back up his arguments, just as he eluded answering Balseiro's objection in connection with the Larmor effect.

Therefore, once again the verdict was negative. The new report submitted to the Minister on October 16, said [37]: "A successful outcome must be ruled out completely", and, "the assertions made by Dr. Richter are absolutely groundless."

Even so, Bussolini and Mende were still hesitant. Consequently, Iraolagoitia asked Bancora to repeat his Rosario experiments with a circuit similar to that used in Huemul, but in Buenos Aires and in their presence.

The experiment was carried out at the Navy School of Mechanics on Libertador Avenue (in front of the DNEA building) where there was a large electric generator used for anti aircraft reflectors. Bancora connected the generator to a voltaic arc and then to a large transformer used as inductance (equivalent to the induction coil used by Richter). Tosello, friend of Balseiro´s whom Mende trusted, stood in for the Minister at this demonstration. The Geiger counters became activated as soon as the installation was connected, just as had occurred a month earlier on the island despite the fact that no substance had been injected to the arc. The experiment proved that Geiger counters could show activity due to electromagnetic oscillations in the circuit, when not properly calibrated.

This was not enough, however. Bussolini requested a second experiment which was carried out the following day, at which he was present accompanied by "someone from the San Miguel Observatory". Only then did he give in "accepting his colleagues' opinion to the extent that no atomic energy production can be surmised from Richter's experiments." [38]

This was not the end of project Huemul yet. Mende refused to admit that it had been a fraud. Not after all the money invested, all the equipment, all the announcements, and so much at stake...! Gonzalez was no longer there; Iraolagoitia, far from being involved, had been against it since the very beginning; and now that Perón had laid down his arms, Mende was left alone with all the responsibility on his shoulders. If he had been mistaken once, he could not afford to be mistaken twice. If he had to acknowledge that he had been wrong, he had to be certain beyond all reasonable doubt. Apart from Perón, whom out of loyalty he would not leave alone to face the accusations he anticipated, there was nobody else but himself to answer should the atomic project be brought to trial. The extravagant praises that had been lavished on the project by the press all those years, turned now into threatening ghosts hovering over the bewildered minister who had fallen victim to his good faith. Bussolini was with him in spirit, but if things came to the worst, the priest would not have to face a public scandal as he would. There was little comfort to be found, then, in Bussolini's support.

The situation was so complex that it was decided to appoint a new commission which, if need be, was to return to Huemul once more. Somehow it was like starting all over again.

The new committee was made up of Prof. Ricardo Gans and Dr. Antonio Rodriguez. The internationally famous Prof. Gans a German like Richter was working at the time in the Radio Technical Institute (to which Heisenberg had been invited in 1946). Rodriguez, who taught in La Plata, had been a fellow student of Balseiro and had received his doctorate at Edinburgh University under Max Born. Though less numerous, this new committee was well prepared to evaluate a physics research project: both members were solidly trained physicists with the additional advantage that one of them was German like Richter.

Gans and Rodriguez were summoned to Mende's office at the Casa Rosada at 8 o'clock in the morning of October 20. Iraolagoitia explained them what it was all about and handed them copies of the previous committee's reports, as well as Richter's reply. It took them a very short time to size up arguments on both sides and to arrive at a final conclusion. In only two hours they drew up a concise and categorical report endorsing the previous verdict in its full extent. [39]

There was one further instance, however. According to Rodriguez, Perón suggested the possibility of holding a direct confrontation between them (Gans and Rodriguez) and Richter. One can only speculate why Perón would want such a confrontation since he must have known that Richter's chances when confronted with Gans were very dim, especially after Gans had expressed his views on the matter. Probably, it was not so much a question of Perón wanting to give Richter another chance, but rather to confront him with an unwavering Gans who would then play the executioner's role that Perón wished to elude. Then Richter could not say afterwards that he had been judged by 'monkeys up the coconut trees'. (Richter knew perfectly well who Gans was: he turned to him later on for a recommendation to travel abroad [40]).

The confrontation took place a few days later at the Casa Rosada. Richter walked in saying "I am here on behalf of the President." Gans, in his characteristic style and heavily accented Spanish, replied: "Herr Dr. Richter, we are not here on a totally unofficial mission either."

The meeting began at noon and lasted four hours. It was carried out mainly in English with a few splashes of German here and there, whenever Richter lost his temper. "He just insulted you in German", Gans whispered to Rodriguez on one such occasion. Richter tried unsuccessfully to cower behind the shield of secrecy, but the new committee was adamant. A few days later Perón wanted to hold a meeting with them but the resignation of a minister in his cabinet prevented him from doing so. They were received by Mende instead. According to Gonzalez, even then the Minister tried to make the verdict sound somewhat more in accordance to his taste, but the scientists remained firm. The document began: "A detailed analysis shows beyond doubt that there is no experimental or theoretical proof to indicate that any nuclear reaction whatsoever has been attained." [41]. There was no need to return to Huemul: the last word had already been said.

Intervention, Concealment and New Plans

The first explosion of a hydrogen bomb on November 1, 1952, went by practically unnoticed by the men responsible for atomic energy in Argentina, busy as they were during those embarrassing days.

Mende had not made up his mind yet on what to do with Richter or how to wind up project Huemul after such hard work and so many hopes. He was apparently trying to find a way to prolong the situation. He even asked Richter to name a price so as to sell his invention. "Finally, it looks as if Mende will offer Richter a contract to continue working...", Gonzalez wrote to his son. [42]

Yet Iraolagoitia tried his utmost to put an end to the Bariloche activities. On September 24, the GEOPE company had been ordered to stop all work on Huemul. Richter did his best though there was little he could do now to invalidate the order. He travelled to Buenos Aires repeatedly in order to hold meetings with Mende. Among other things, he spoke ill of Iraolaogoitia and tried to get Gonzalez back on the project. [43]

On November 22, while Richter was in Buenos Aires, Iraolagoitia and a group of assistants went to Bariloche placing the island and other Plant facilities under government control. Iraolagoitia frankly admitted being uneasy. "It was a dangerous situation. The island was protected by armed guards with instructions to obey Richter first and foremost." [44]

"Therefore, I went to see (General) Lucero asking him to place the Bariloche garrison commander under my orders. I also took with me a note from Perón. I wasn't sure what the odds were, nor exactly what I would do. What if Fiscina appeared before me barring my way? I headed for Quinchahuala (the residence of the War Minister by Lake Nahuel Huapi) and from there we crossed over to the island."

Commander Fiscina was the first to be removed. Miss Blaha, a loyal and stubborn supporter of Richter, tried to make a stand by blocking the entrance, though unsuccessfully. The laboratories and offices were closed down; the two cars and the piano that the government had presented to the German scientist were confiscated (though the piano and one car were returned later to Richter on Perón's instructions). It was a swift and effective operation, aided by the fact that all work on the island had stopped a month earlier. It was an open secret that something like this was bound to happen any moment. Naturally, there was quite some anxiety, particularly among lower ranking personnel. A typical Bertolo anecdote describes the situation appropriately.

Non Commissioned Officer Eguireun, who had been sent by Iraolaogitia to help Richter a few months earlier, disappeared from the island after the experts' visit to Huemul. His fellow workers wondered what had become of him and Bertolo was naturally worried. When Eguireun had turned up at Lab # 2 to work as a new member of the Richter group under Bertolo, Bertolo realized that Eguireun's hands were not the hands of a mason; therefore, he had to be a spy. "Come to think of it, yes, he was always asking questions about Richter. One day, I just went ahead and told him exactly what I thought about the whole show", Bertolo excitedly explained. "I told him: 'in my opinion, there's nothing in it for Argentina. Whether all this is any good or not, I don't know; I'm a mason, he's a scientist and I cannot judge his work, but it seems to me he is not working for Argentina.' When I told him this, he pestered me with endless questions why this and why that. Somehow I had to justify myself so I told him, 'look, see this pipe over here that he asked me to install? Well, his secretary would come along next asking me how long it would take. I assured him it would take two hours and he replies: 'Ahh, another day without working.' It was like that all the time. If it came to hooking staples, they had to be exactly 25" apart, not 24 nor 26. The 3 ft. thick concrete blocks for shielding turned out to be 1" wider because of the stucco, so we had to tear them down and rebuild them because Richter would not admit the difference. Losing time was immaterial for him. All of this prompted me to think that he wasn't working for Argentina. After saying all this I was scared for they might fire me, but it turned out to be the opposite. Eguireun saved me. He showed up with the intervention and was wearing a uniform. He spoke well of me telling the others I had worked well and was loyal to the country's interests."

Naturally, there were no reprisals, but at the beginning everybody was worried. Many of them like Bertolo continued working for DNEA after the intervention.

Two days after Iraolagoitia took over the island, Richter returned to Bariloche. Both he and his family were authorized to remain at their house in Bariloche until they had had a chance to settle their personal matters. Prieto was appointed administrator and Bancora together with MacMillan proceeded to take an inventory of all the equipment and materials.

The whole operation was carried out covertly to avoid the news leaking out to the public. Considering the volume of activities and the number of workers involved prior to the intervention, it was surprising that for two whole weeks the news about suspension of the monumental atomic project did not reach the press. It was impossible, however, to keep it secret much longer. The New York Times journalist E. Morrow dispatched a two column article from Buenos Aires on December 4 which was published the following day on the front page of The New York Times accompanied by a photo of Perón pinning the Peronist medal on Richter. It was entitled: "Perón's Atom Dream Fades; Director Reported Arrested". The news, of course, was widely reported by newspapers everywhere. Next day, The New York Times again published a brief denial by Iraolagoitia of Richter's arrest. Also, though far less precisely, he referred to the discontinuance of the project. The fact that Richter showed up in Buenos Aires helped to dispel well founded doubts about Iraolagoitia's statements. However, a week later Representative Ravignani of the Radical party among shouts and interruptions from his Peronist colleagues maintained having evidence "that Richter has been thrown out by the army from his Bariloche laboratory". No fearful scandal broke out even then. Among other things, for instance, the powerful illumination of the island which left tourists open mouthed continued just as before. Richter, on the other hand, did little toward curbing the official impression that nothing much had happened. He stayed in Bariloche until February and, as far as the villagers were concerned, his habits remained practically the same: he "never once failed to show up at a 'western'", and he "continued to park his car in the wrong place, blocking the way for the bus from El Bolson." [45]

That summer in Bariloche, Richter wrote a letter to the editor of 'Nucleonics' showing his discontent at a comment that the journal had published on atomic energy in Argentina in its issue of December 1952. Actually, the article was favorable to Argentine atomic development, particularly regarding "the work undertaken by prestigious Buenos Aires physicists", but by contrast left a bad impression on what was going on at Huemul. Richter said nothing new in his reply, but it is interesting to note that he made no reference to the termination of his project, a fact which 'Nucleonics' was unaware of. The episode reveals that Iraolagoitia and Mende were fairly successful in their efforts to keep a low profile on the cancellation of the project Huemul. Of course, such was not the case as far as the people of Bariloche were concerned. According to a tourist's story, in February 1953 "the people of Bariloche indulge in the most varied comments in connection with the atomic project. The hundreds of workers employed on the island who have now been dismissed express themselves in unprintable terms on the subject. As a rule, villagers speak of fraud and extravagant squander". [46]

Antonio Rodriguez recalled going to Bariloche in January accompanied by Iraolagoitia, Balseiro, Gans and others with the purpose of deciding what to do with the facilities. "We wanted both to preserve the image and to do something with all that", he pointed out. [47]

They visited the island accompanied by Juan Roederer, who had been working in DNEA since mid 1951. He had just returned from Europe and was spending his holidays in Bariloche when he happened to meet his colleagues. "Richter was still there, and one of Iraolagoitia's assistants was armed" he recalled, stressing the permanent uneasiness they all felt regarding the nearby presence of the former head of project Huemul. [48]

Once on the island, the physicists in the group could not resist the temptation of connecting the equipment. "We repeated the explosive arc experiment and we checked all the connections" Rodriguez said "Most recording devices were disconnected."

They decided to recommend doing nothing on Huemul because of the cumbersome transportation problem. However, they thought some of the facilities on the stretch of land granted by the Army between the garrison and the officers' housing district could be used. There were a few barracks, some houses under construction and large quantities of bricks. Yet the group explicitly recommended that the place "should not be used to build a school of physics"; an interesting note, no doubt, considering that today one of the best physics institutes in the continent stands on that very site and the man who was to be its main inspirer (Balseiro) was a member of that group.

In what used to be a "high temperature" lab it was decided to mount a cosmic radiation lab, a vanguard subject at the time when large proton accelerators had yet to be developed. They also suggested to use the premises to organize summer schools.

Although the group was against the idea of establishing a permanent Center of Studies, Rodriguez recalled later having discussed with Balseiro that summer the need to develop institutes for advanced learning and research. These were to be completely detached from the political fluctuations which were playing havoc with national universities due to the enforcement of severe ideological discrimination.

This idea though rejected at the time remained dormant for a couple of years (and a couple of summer schools), till it finally bore fruit some time later.

Gaviola Brings his Old Dream Back to Life

Prior to 1949 nobody would have guessed that Bariloche a region of beautiful lakes and the imposing Tronador mountain would someday become a major academic center. It was not the outcome of a plan, for history is often capricious. This makes it even more interesting when analyzed retrospectively. An ambitious plan to transform the Nahuel Huapi area into a pole of national development had wandered aimlessly round the offices of Minister Ezequiel Ramos Mexia at the turn of the century. [49] It was an extraordinary project had it prospered which would have greatly enriched the area and the country as a whole. Unfortunately, this project which had to do with industry and commerce not Physics came to nothing and Bariloche trod towards its destiny as a place for tourism. Things were thus to the day when Richter and his entourage landed in Bariloche a green and blue paradise surrounded by white capped mountains in search of a lonely place to install a secret atomic laboratory. Actually, had Perón not suggested it - interested as he was to populate Patagonia - the group would not have headed south at all. Ultimately, Bariloche remained connected to atomic research and not even the fiasco of Huemul was strong enough to sever those links. DNEA officials might well have decided to bury everything that had to do with atomic energy in Bariloche so as to forget that embarrassing failure as soon as possible. Fortunately, they decided to do exactly the opposite, and to benefit from its ashes as much as possible.

The early beginning of the now prestigious Institute was divided into two stages. The first stage prior to the summer schools began by mid 1953. The leading figure was Enrique Gaviola who, in spite of successive frustrations, still cherished his dream of founding "a local Johns Hopkins University".

Gaviola was then in Buenos Aires working for General Electric. Bancora went to see him with the offer to head the High Temperature Plant. The group which had inspected the installations that summer suggested moving all equipment from the island over to the area where there were a few houses and a small laboratory. The place, known as the High Temperature Experimental Plant, was where summer schools were held later on.

We do not know how much time elapsed between the offer to Gaviola and the XXI Meeting of the Physics Association in La Plata in May 1953. The fact is that by then Gaviola had brought back to life his old dream of a highly competitive training and research center, with his attention focused on Bariloche. On returning from La Plata, he discussed the project with Galloni and González Domínguez, asking them to get him an interview with Iraolagoitia (who was then Director of DNEA).

Two days later, the head of the atomic agency received them in his office together with Captain Manuel Beninson, his scientific advisor. His customary open minded attitude and his wholesome inclination to avoid red tape resulted in a successful first encounter in which Gaviola expounded his ideas on the future Institute. Iraolagoitia asked merely for two days in order to discuss the project with Perón.

Perón agreed, so they met again on May 28. Gaviola wrote a memorandum describing his ideas of the Institute adding as was his habit a draft of its statutes. The memorandum began: "Argentina needs physicists. Top level physicists." His old vigorous style was intact. Over half a decade had gone by since the struggles for the private university had begun, the Radio Technical Institute, the invitation to Heisenberg and the projects submitted to the Senate, but his style remained the same. Cutting remarks not wholly devoid of a certain sense of humor, somewhat exaggerated perhaps, bound one idea to the next. "...there is a deficit of about five hundred physicists in Argentina. It would be erroneous to believe that the gap could be breached by taking five hundred college graduates and giving them PhD's in physics after submitting them to a more or less complex and extended ritual. We would just have five hundred quacks."

Further on he stated: "From the point of view of an original researcher, a physicist starts to grow old at 25, slowly but relentlessly. Boxers and physicists are very much alike in this sense." He then quoted Nobel Laureate William Henry Bragg: "Even if we could expect only fifteen good students per year, we would still be optimistic." [50]

Fifteen was the proposed number of students per year. They were to receive DNEA scholarships. The Institute would have 5 professors only: three physics professors, a chemist and a mathematician. Scholarships for post graduate studies abroad would be granted to outstanding graduates. It was a vast and detailed proposal. It is remarkable how much of it is still alive in the current organization of the Institute, including the student selection process throughout the country aided by a psychologist. Indeed, it was a good piece of work. The proposed resolution giving birth to the Institute had 24 articles, some of them with over half a dozen clauses.

Gaviola submitted those documents to Iraolagoitia on July 18 1953. He certainly would not have committed himself to such tremendous work had he not been persuaded, prematurely perhaps, that the creation of the Institute was a fact. Somewhat imprudently no doubt, and with this conviction in mind, he settled down to write some letters. An invitation to Dr. Horacio J. A. Rimoldi, an Argentine psychologist residing in the US who had earned solid international prestige. Gaviola invited him to resign his post and come to Bariloche claiming that if he himself was prepared to tender his resignation to General Electric, it was sufficient proof of "reliability and stability" to encourage Rimoldi to do likewise. Gaviola wanted Rimoldi to take responsibility for the student selection process. [51] Amazingly, this compromising letter was dispatched on July 20, barely two days after submitting the project to DNEA and even before Iraolagoitia had had a chance to study it. As far as Gaviola was concerned, the task which still needed to be done somehow managing to get the decree through was a mere formality. Once his own part of the work was completed, there was not much else to worry about.

With a similar purpose in mind Gaviola wrote to Manlio Abele in Córdoba, a physicist he had come to respect despite his early association with the Tank group. [52] He wanted Abele as one of the physics professors, the other one was Balseiro.

As could be expected, Rimoldi declined Gaviola´s offer, politely but firmly. He thought conditions in Argentina were not comparable to the position he enjoyed in the US. Abele, on the other hand, showed interest and promised to go to Buenos Aires in order to discuss the matter.

Meanwhile, Gaviola left for Bariloche to examine what modifications or additions were needed for the Institute. Ex Lieutenant Prieto, who had returned to Bariloche and was now in charge of what remained of project Huemul, greeted Gaviola on his arrival. Gaviola inspected the buildings and the houses under construction. There were 26 rooms, each with a bathroom and a kitchen. On the edge of his notebook he wrote "First Rate". There were workshops, a living dining room with a kitchen, troops' quarters and other buildings which could be transformed into labs. Meticulously, he noted the name of each building, what he planned to do with it and what it lacked. Building # 1, was chosen for the laboratories; building # 2, for classrooms and library; building # 3 was to be used for experimental work and research; it needed oxygen, gas and compressed air; building # 4, for unmarried residents and guests, etc. He examined then the collection of instruments that

Richter had left behind: more than one hundred items of major equipment. Gaviola must have been astonished: 2 spectrographs, several recorders with filming cameras, galvanometers, voltmeters and ammeters, low and high frequency generators, several types of oscilloscopes, some of them quite exceptional, photoelectric cells, Geiger counters, photographic and movie cameras and materials.

On his return, Gaviola prepared a report on the "Plant adaptation to the Physics Institute". Some of it was debatable. Students were to live in the houses in groups of five. Bathrooms had to be reformed, with three showers installed instead of bathtubs and bidets. A swimming pool and two tennis courts were to be built. Major modifications had to be carried out in the classroom building. The floor was to be removed and replaced by tiers of seats; a clock tower (Johns Hopkins style) was to be built crowned by an astronomic dome. A good number of partition walls had to be torn down. Troops' quarters were to become a gymnasium after a few slight changes, one being particularly original (at least for the Argentina of those days): the installation of a sauna. One way or another, the list deserved a careful reading, and Iraolagoitia passed it on to Beninson, his secretary, together with the proposed resolution to create the Institute.

A few days later, Gaviola received positive replies from Balseiro and chemist Rodolfo Busch as faculty members for the Institute. Gaviola and Balseiro discussed the project for a few hours; their ideas ran approximately along the same lines. Balseiro, like Gaviola, had been prepared for some time to carry out an undertaking of this nature. Both of them were convinced that a center of studies at that level had to be organized totally independent from the national universities and though their motivations were not identical, they were reasonably close.

Unexpectedly, Abele postponed his trip to Buenos Aires. In a couple of telegrams and letters, he insisted that his duties made it impossible for him to leave Córdoba for the next fortnight or so. Gaviola became worried.

Behind the scenes, other voices began to be heard. F. A. Heyn, the Dutchman who had come to help in starting up the Philips cascade accelerator, allegedly let out an alarming rumor: "The Institute in Bariloche will blow up the universities." Certainly there were quite a few who shared that fear.

Though unofficially, Gaviola learned that his last report had met with some resistance so he decided to tone it down by writing a letter to the head of DNEA on August 23, pointing out that it was not absolutely necessary to have the houses by the lakeside, nor the tennis courts, and that houses need not be for students so it would not be necessary to alter bathrooms, nor undertake several other modifications.

Iraolagoitia repeated once again that he was in favor of the project and, in an encouraging gesture, asked Gaviola not to take on new responsibilities at General Electric. Things, however, were taking too long; waiting for Abele was one of them. Gaviola wanted to begin classes in March, so he was upset as days dragged on to no specific purpose. He began to think that Abele had failed to turn up because of the unfavorable rumors. On September 1, Gaviola wrote to Abele telling him quite frankly: "I'm rather worried because of your absence and your silence. I understand that I shouldn't force you to come to Buenos Aires, but my insistence stems from two major causes: 1. The Captain (Iraolagoitia) has a special respect for you because you are a foreigner. Balseiro, Busch and I are just plain Argentine citizens, natives like himself. 2. You have worked already with lineal accelerators, a subject which interests Iraolagoitia deeply. In my proposal, I have set apart a hall 42 x 48 x 27 ft. which is to be the high voltage lab."

"The Institute will turn out to be what you, Balseiro, Busch, the mathematician (either Calderon or González Domínguez) and I will make of it, provided we all work together. If you are unable to come this week, I shall go to Córdoba on Saturday 5. Losing a year might be fatal for the project, at least as far as I am concerned. "

As a result of this letter, Abele sent two telegrams and finally announced his arrival, but not until Wednesday 16. Gaviola was losing heart; his pride was hurt. Why was he kept waiting if the basic agreement had been reached? But it was not so: the basic agreement as yet did not exist. "Beninson has prepared a negative report he is now enclosing with the file", Balseiro informed him one day prior to Abele's arrival.

The news had the effect of a devastating bomb on Gaviola's harassed spirit. He was not prepared to accept Beninson's opinion. He refused, moreover, to accept that Beninson might question his project. As often happens, his uneasiness stemmed from more causes than one, and several circumstances did not help.

Not without some difficulty, Balseiro persuaded Gaviola to attend a new "summit" meeting but the latter's readiness to reach a reasonable agreement was now dim and the possibilities of success were therefore meager. There are different versions of what reportedly happened on that occasion. Apart from Balseiro and Gaviola, the meeting was attended by Abele, Iraolagoitia and Beninson.

Beninson read his report. He proposed eliminating the first two courses so that the Institute would only offer the final three years of Physics. For Gaviola this was short of a heresy, being as he was intent on the idea of selecting students as early as possible "before they become corrupted by the mediocre conventional education to which students are exposed." This and other subjects were discussed heatedly. What Gaviola afterwards remembered was that Beninson somewhere along the discussion said that Richter deserved a monument for having obtained such large budget allocations. This was the spark that lit the fire. Gaviola rose and left.

Iraolagoitia, on the other hand, while recalling this incident many years later failed to remember that Gaviola and Beninson had quarreled. The remaining impression was that of a difficult personality with 'prima donna' attitudes and extravagant ideas such as "the tower with the weathercock", or the insistence that gas had to be obtained from charcoal because the product of the Gas Company was no good

Unfortunately, once again an outstanding project had come to nothing though there were no important reasons to let it die.

The files contain a draft letter from Gaviola to Iraolagoitia which he may or may not have actually sent, but which summarizes the situation rather well: "I am grateful to you for defending the project. I would have been even more grateful had you spared Captain Beninson and myself all the unpleasantness: spared him the grief he must have felt to attack a good project with bad arguments, and spared me the bitterness of having to hear his report."

Early Activities of a New Stage

By mid 1953, the National Department of Atomic Energy (DNEA) had a sizeable staff of scientists and numerous active research groups. One of those groups was formed around the scientific figure of Walter Seelmann Eggebert, another German refugee who had come to Argentina in 1949 under contract with the University of Tucuman. He had been Otto Hahn's disciple, no less, at a time when Hahn was trying to decipher the enigma of nuclear fission. Seelmann Eggebert knew more about radiochemistry than most people of his time. Though as he has pointed out during the war Hitler considered that building an atom bomb would take too much time, Hahn's laboratory turned to studying how to build reactors with a view to propelling nuclear submarines. Seelmann devoted particular attention to fission products and plutonium production, a new element heavier than uranium of doubtless strategic importance. The Hahn group was then in contact with Werner Heisenberg and Karl Wirtz, authorities on the subject. They worked on the first German reactor, which never reached criticality because the Allies managed to stop the heavy water supply. [53]

The coming of Seelmann Eggebert to Argentina offers a different picture regarding the influence of European immigration after the war in the development of domestic nuclear activities. The Richter case portrays one aspect of that complex history; Seelmann´s illustrates another aspect much more akin to what Gaviola had in mind when he wrote his 1946 memorandum and strove to invite Heisenberg. In this sense, though Seelmann Eggebert's coming to Argentina failed to materialize through the mechanisms that Gaviola had envisaged, its effect was precisely what Gaviola wished to obtain when proposing to attract first rate European scientists.

All nuclear research had been banned in Germany after the war. An Allied group headed by Samuel Gousdmit had occupied the Otto Hahn Institute, which later on was turned into a textile mill. "They took Heisenberg practically as a prisoner and sent him to England" Seelmann said, evoking the days when Gaviola and Beck did their utmost to bring Heisenberg to Argentina.

By 1948, the old Kaiser Wilhelm Institut was reorganized into what nowadays has become the Max Planck Institut. The French occupation had followed and laboratories became annexed to the Commissariat de l'Energie Atomique. Seelmann Eggebert sought to go abroad as a result of the prevailing difficulties to work in nuclear physics. He took advantage of an old contact with Guido Beck to inquire whether South America offered any possibilities. From Beck's point of view, it was like living his own story all over again six years later. He spoke to various people and obtained a contract offer for Seelmann from the University of Tucuman. With the contract in his hands, Seelmann went to see the French authorities requesting a permit to travel to Argentina. But Joliot, Commissariat chairman then, refused because "it was to work for the dictator, Perón." So Seelmann tried something different: he officially changed his place of residence to the US occupation zone. Americans granted permits to go abroad provided contracts were for one year only. With a pair of scissors and a photocopying machine, he somehow managed to change the document and to obtain the final permit. In July 1949, he left Amsterdam in a KLM DC 6, a flight arranged by the Argentine government. Seelmann Eggebert still recollects being afraid of the French in Dakar lest they might arrest him; his journey from Buenos Aires to Córdoba in the "Rayo de Sol"(the Sunray Bus Co.), meeting a sleepy Beck ("he worked by night and slept in the mornings") and his arrival at Tucuman ("already full of Germans").

Seelmann Eggebert had brought with him some instruments from Germany. With that equipment ("next generation to the one used by Otto Hahn when discovering fission") he installed a small nuclear research laboratory (the first in Argentina, perhaps?) and began studying radioactive minerals helped by Violeta Hensey de Gainza. A little later, an Italian chemist came recommending his son. Such were the beginnings of Renato Radicella, who thirty years later became chairman of the Argentine Atomic Energy Commission. He began working in the separation of natural radionuclides of the radium and thorium family. Some samples came from Germany, others from the Córdoba deposits. In 1950, Karl E. J. Wirtz came to visit Argentina invited by Gamba. As a result of this trip, Gamba and Seelmann Eggebert met. "Gamba wanted to have an agency for atomic energy apart from Richter. He suggested that I should prepare a proposal" Seelmann recalled – "I thought immediately of bureaucracy. So, I said to Gamba, "I need big petty cash, and it worked." Seelmann's first contract with DNEA was signed in 1951, in the office of Colonel Gonzalez at the Casa Rosada. At the time, Seelmann was teaching in Tucuman and Mendoza and travelled to Buenos Aires once a month. It was not until 1953 that he moved to Buenos Aires to work full time in the laboratories at Libertador Avenue. His stay in Argentina was short, but his influence decisive. Seelmann returned to Germany in early 1955. By that time, the synchrocyclotron was already in operation, so together with his group of young radiochemists – Gregorio Baro, Josefina

Rodriguez, Juan Flegenheimer and Radicella who had come from Tucuman - they plunged into a wild race to extract as much as possible from that novel machine. Their efforts met with success: in a few months they had discovered a score of new radioisotopes. [54] These results, the first obtained in Argentina in the field of nuclear research at an international level, were part of numerous papers submitted to the First Conference on Peaceful Uses of Atomic Energy which took place in Geneva in 1955.

That group of radiochemists was the forerunner of other groups. The most privileged, with the best and most generous equipment was perhaps the group of physicists. Their first major equipment was the Cockcroft - Walton cascade accelerator, purchased from Philips along with the synchrocyclotron, but assembled earlier. Daniel R. Bes, later the leading nuclear physicist in Argentina, had reasons to remember the inauguration ceremony of the Cockcroft-Walton machine. In 1953, both Bes and Rodolfo Slobodrian (also an internationally reputed scientist) entered DNEA. On their second day at the new job Perón turned up and shook hands with them. They were stunned thinking that the President of the Republic used to go around visiting research centers and greeting scientists. It was not so, of course. Perón had come that day, June 16, 1953, to inaugurate the cascade accelerator, "the most powerful in Central and South America" as reported by The New York Times, capable of producing up to one million four hundred thousand volts to achieve nuclear reactions with proton and deuteron beams. [55] Slobodrian later joined Fidel Alsina, Walter Scheuer and Hugo Lugomirski who were working with the accelerator, while Bes first helped Manuel Bemporad with the mass separator and then Carlos Mallmann, who was mounting two high transmission beta spectrometers. Members of the high energy and cosmic radiation group were the first to use the accelerator in order to gauge their photographic plates with deuteron beam induced radiations; Emma Perez Ferreira, Pedro Waloschek and Juan Roederer were among the first to publish such measurements. Alsina,

Mallmann and Bertomeu had become acquainted with the functioning of this enormous instrument on a trip that Gamba had organized for them to visit a good number of European laboratories. According to Alsina, thanks to that trip they were able to overcome "some 40 to 50 `bugs'" before setting the equipment in operation. This delicate instrument, composed of two science fiction columns almost 30 ft. high, unveiled for Argentina a new scientific as well as technologic field of activity.

Other auxiliary groups were dedicated to building detectors and improving vacuum techniques, while new labs sprung up in electronics, X rays, chemistry, etc. The first pieces of the synchrocyclotron arrived in November 1953. Iraolaogitia requested Galloni to temporarily leave aside his crystallography studies and take charge of assembling this new and far more powerful accelerator.

Several large instruments were being set in operation. As Iraolagoitia remarked: "Never had Argentina spent so much money on scientific instruments". It was the beginning of a new era that was moving ahead somewhat in the dark for lack of an overall plan, but the groups composed primarily of very young people were heading in the right direction, upheld by a stimulating support.

It was not only equipment. There were also trips and training courses such as those benefitting the people who set the cascade accelerator in operation. Roederer was the first DNEA grantee who went abroad in 1951 also as a consequence of Wirtz's visit to Argentina a year earlier, with whom Roederer went to work in Germany. Sometime later Horacio Bosch, another young nuclear physicist, left to specialize at the famous Joliot Curie Laboratory in Paris.

The reactors' group was an outcome of one special course organized in DNEA. It was led by Gamba in September 1953. At the time, there were no reactor specialists in Argentina yet Gamba turned to some highly competent people. That first course attended by seven students [56] was taught by the distinguished mathematicians González Domínguez, Luis

Santalo, Roque Scarfiello and Agustin Duranona y Vedia, in addition to physicists Balseiro and Staricco. This course was an important forerunner of others which took place later on.

A rather unconventional subject that DNEA undertook since its early beginnings was metallurgy. On returning from Bariloche in the summer of '55, Iraolagoitia met Jorge Sabato, who had started working in DNEA shortly before, and conveyed to him his interest in metallurgic research.

"I was under the impression that one had to be a Peronist to enter DNEA" Sabato recalled. A few years earlier he had been ousted from the University for refusing to affiliate to the Peronist party. At that time, he was participating in a seminar together with Oscar Varsavsky, Juan José Giambiagi and Mario Gutierrez Burzaco. "It was Fidel Alsina who took me to DNEA and introduced me to Iraolagoitia. That's how I came to work there."

"By then, there was talk that a uranium pilot plant to be installed in Ezeiza was arriving from Germany, and that we had to make fuel elements for nuclear reactors. Nobody knew, of course, how to make fuel elements. Neither did I, though I had had some experience as a result of my three years with Decker Industries. That's how we started. First we worked next to the synchrocyclotron, then on the first floor, later on in the basement. Finally, we moved over to Constituyentes Avenue where DNEA had some warehouses, and space to build the RA1 (the first Argentine nuclear research reactor). We purchased a few pieces of equipment and settled down in large sheds. There was nothing we couldn't do and most of it from petty cash. We even managed to build concrete slabs from petty cash. The building – Jorge Kittl's masterpiece was made that way." (57)

There was, therefore, considerable activity at DNEA. Nothing like this had ever happened before in Argentina, except perhaps for what Bose had accomplished at the Institute of La Plata at the turn of the century. But after that invigorating experience under the leadership of Joaquin V Gonzalez, neither

Argentine universities nor other academic organizations enjoyed such large budget allocations for research and development in physics (or, for that matter, in any other scientific discipline). In 1947, the possibility of a similar experience had been thwarted when projects for the creation of a National Research Institute - for which a generous sum had been allocated - were abandoned after having been enthusiastically endorsed by physicists and congressmen. Now DNEA made an appearance fulfilling functions similar to those contemplated in the early projects, though differently conceived, without the benefit of thorough analysis, almost by chance, guided gropingly in the dark by the soundly inquisitive spirits of Colonel Gonzalez, Gamba and Iraolagoitia. None of them possessed the essential background to engage in an undertaking of this magnitude, which, moreover, had been born under the shadow of a hoax. A decidedly unconventional and not too healthy start. How come this bizarre, crooked and in the end fruitful development had taken place?

This question has no easy answer, although some elements might be pointed out. The good intentions of its first Directors, for instance, who doubtlessly enjoyed Perón's trust and approval in order to accomplish their tasks. Specifically, they must be credited with a wise and extremely unusual attitude for Argentina of dispensing with whatever political inclination scientists might have had. While universities destroyed themselves because of political persecution, DNEA remained an oasis. "There are no Peronist physicists" Iraolagoitia had told Perón. True, most physicists working in DNEA were not Peronists; yet DNEA welcomed scientists who had been expelled from the universities, making it possible for them to remain in Argentina. In the early beginnings, the men in charge, not being experts in atomic matters might have taken a turn for the worse. But it was mainly due to Gonzalez, Iraolagoitia and Gamba that this was not the case. With considerable tact, Gamba did a superb job in selecting the scientific staff and knew how to organize them appropriately. The quality and non discriminatory policies were probably the seed of an institutional 'mystique' which flourished as years went by.

As might be expected in an atmosphere of serious work and competitiveness, the idea of organizing summer schools in Bariloche fell on fertile soil.

The first summer school was carried out in January and February of 1954 under the leadership of González Domínguez. It offered only one course on Reactors with the collaboration of Santalo and Balseiro.

The task of organizing summer schools such as the first one was fairly easy, particularly since its scope and objectives were modest. Yet it was a job well done, a serious and honest effort, a valuable starting point for atomic research in Argentina and, the first formal activity undertaken in Bariloche in the new era of domestic atomic energy development. Encouraged by the first successful experience, DNEA officials decided to organize a somewhat more ambitious second summer school the following year.

Balseiro headed the second school which took place in January-February 1955. It offered courses of reactors, physics and radiochemistry. In physics, subjects such as nuclear physics, quantum electrodynamics, and electromagnetism were discussed. The first two subjects were organized based on textbooks which were read and discussed by some member of the group randomly chosen each day. Work was intensive and of a good level. Among others, participants in the quantum electrodynamics course were Beck, Balseiro, Carlos G. Bollini and Bes. In nuclear physics, Bes, Mallmann, Juan Peyre, Tito Suter, Santos Mayo, Lucia Lagatta and Slobodrian. The already numerous Seelmann Eggebert group specialized further in radiochemistry using the first experimental results obtained at the synchrocyclotron a few weeks earlier. Abele, Wolfgang Meckbach (who had arrived in Argentina recently) and Kurt Fraenz gave other courses which led to discussing the possibility of constructing an electron linear accelerator. Iraolagoitia was present most of the time. The reactor group was now growing.

A course for Latin American teachers was organized toward the end of the summer with people from Peru, Chile and Bolivia. The summer school as a whole turned out to be a complete success while contributing to shape a veritable scientific community. However, the decision to lay the bases for an Atomic Center and a Physics Institute was its most important result. The idea, which had failed in 1953, now sprang to life.

The Spurning of the Medal

Meanwhile, by mid 1954 the Government had renewed its former interest in uranium deposits. The Executive branch had sent a bill to Congress including uranium as well as thorium among substances in the first category of the Mining Code. This meant that if the law was sanctioned, these minerals would remain under Federal jurisdiction and their exploitation would be subject to legal concessions granted exclusively by the corresponding authority. On the other hand, the Government had begun negotiations with a US company the Atlas Corporation for the construction of a long oil pipeline from Neuquen to Bahia Blanca in addition to a vast program in uranium exploration. Negotiations also included the construction of an atomic plant. [58]

This ambitious contract met countless obstacles raised by the opposition. The proposal was dubbed "the Argentine California", causing the Government's prestige to suffer. Traditionally, the Government had maintained a nationalistic policy radically opposed to foreign involvement in the development of basic domestic industries and strategic mineral exploration. Yet the country was not as rich now as it had been during the first presidency of Perón, and was forced to seek foreign investments. In view of the pressure exerted by the opposition, the Government was eventually forced to abandon the project. Meanwhile, a bill protecting uranium and thorium deposits went to Congress. There it was approved by the Senate and later received the unanimous support of the Lower House. The bill was voted in the 17th parliamentary session of September 1, 1954.

A similar draft bill had actually been discussed in the Senate eight years earlier, in 1946. It had not prospered then due to a constitutional question that was later overcome as a result of the 1949 Constitutional Amendment, stating that mines in Argentina were inalienably and imprescriptibly property of the State.

This law proposal would have been of no particular interest to our story, were it not for the fact that project Huemul was unexpectedly brought to the fore causing a peculiar after effect: Dr. Ronald Richter reappeared in public...demanding to be heard. What he obtained, instead, was a penalty for contempt: five days under arrest in the Congress building.

As stated earlier, Richter had left Bariloche silently and unobtrusively in February 1953, an event virtually ignored by the press. Later the Richter family settled down in a comfortable house in Monte Grande, some 20 miles south of Buenos Aires.

The German scientist showed no animosity at the time. His early years in Monte Grande are remembered by quite a few neighbors still living there. They particularly recall his frequent drives around the plaza in his magnificent Cadillac convertible, his open and easy going ways while sharing a bottle of wine with habitués in bars next to the railway station. Evidently, these testimonies point toward a friendly, good natured, playful Richter who was, moreover, ready to speak Spanish. In short, he lived as an ordinary citizen and member of a community. This style of living suffered an abrupt change in 1954. [59]

On September 1, legislator Ventura Gonzalez of the Chamber of Representatives addressed the audience on the uranium bill. It was a lengthy speech, full of legal and scientific references. Among the latter, he mentioned Antoine Henry Becquerel the discoverer of radioactivity Marie Curie, Ernest Rutherford and others who, like Becquerel, had made significant contributions toward clarifying the incredible properties of these new substances which emitted radiations like magic sources of endless energy. The legislator explained that uranium mines had been liberating such energy since the beginnings of time.

Then, the minority speaker, the Radical Carlos Perette took the floor. His speech was similar to the former both in scope and content, since Radicals were also decidedly in favor of the proposed law. The legislators listened in respectful silence, though actually they were not interested (who would like to hear the same nuclear physics story twice?), until suddenly Perette shook them out of their drowsiness by saying: "Some authors have maintained that uranium is the basic material for atomic processes. Yet in a world shattering announcement, our country stated that thermonuclear reactions could be attained without using uranium."

The speech had taken an unexpected turn. Huemul had not been mentioned for over two long years. Now everybody straightened up in their seats and listened attentively. The Radicals were particularly happy at the opportunity of putting their fingers on a sore spot, as their minority speaker had just done. But where was Perette heading? The Peronists stood in readiness to defend themselves from what they knew to be essentially vulnerable: a costly adventure that had gone to pieces.

Perette recalled names and unpleasant announcements that many felt should best be forgotten. "We do not wish our country to lag behind in atomic research, but we need to know what became of those studies: we want to know why atomic research has been completely ignored in the Second Five Year Plan. Why such a fundamental item has not been considered, when countries involved in the Cold War are constantly fighting one another for atomic predominance and the future applications of this universal tool that we hope Mankind will use to promote peace, fraternity, justice and progress", Perette declared while demanding an official explanation on Huemul developments.

He insisted that there had to be answers to a number of questions which had so deeply involved the prestige of the Nation. Further on, he mentioned the petroleum problem while criticizing the negotiations then currently underway: "A matter of grave concern is the announcement that our economy, and even our independence, may suffer as a result of signing or supporting the petroleum project proposal, submitted to the Government by foreign industrialists over a twenty-five year period."

At this point, Perette was interrupted by the speaker of the House asking him not to digress from the original topic under discussion. So Perette went back to atomic energy. When he finished speaking, the Radicals gave him a standing ovation, handshakes and pats on his back.

Representative Santiago I. Nudelman, a Radical like Perette, addressed Congress next. Once again, a long introduction even more detailed than the former. Any layman reading Congressional Records cannot help wondering whether such display of information served any practical purpose. What followed then amounted to a full scale attack on project Huemul and Richter's public announcements during the time he was responsible for atomic activities. Nudelman demanded explanations. He mentioned international skepticism and recalled certain statements by Perón which had turned out to be totally false. He was even harsher on the subject than Perette. At a certain point in his speech, he was interrupted by Peronist Enrique Labanca who asked him whether the "hypothetical failure" of Huemul made him happy. This seems to have been the first official (though veiled) admission on the possible failure of Huemul. Nudelman replied: "For us, it is always painful when our country is ridiculed and scorned because of our government's lack of formality."

The impetuous legislator got carried away by his enthusiasm. He went as far as stating that a thousand million pesos had been squandered on Huemul an exaggeration that was quoted, among others, by the Physics Association. (This amount was sixteen times larger than what was actually spent). Again, he closed his speech amid a round of cheers and applause.

Mr. Eduardo I. Rumbo then requested the floor. He had been among the legislators who visited the island with the investigating committee two years earlier, and had shown an interest in atomic energy by questioning Richter when the German scientist expounded his ideas on the Maxwell law. He mentioned being pleasantly surprised while visiting the National Department of Atomic Energy laboratories in Buenos Aires. "Over a hundred and fifty scientists are silently working there under the leadership of a distinguished Navy officer: Navy Captain Iraolagoitia." he proudly pointed out. Scathingly, Nudelman interrupted him: "Could our distinguished colleague please inform us what became of the studies, the installations and the large sums of money invested in Huemul, and what eventually became of Prof. Richter, recipient of the Loyalty Medal? "

Rumbo remained calm. He insisted on the importance of atomic energy in the modern world and on the excellent work that DNEA was carrying out. He also made an important announcement when revealing that, according to official reports, Argentina would be having its first atomic plant in operation within the next ten years. [60]

Finally, Rumbo accepted the challenge by openly discussing this extremely irritating subject. He spoke courageously and sincerely. Rumbo was wise to approach the subject only after first having lavished praises on the DNEA people, and not in answer to Nudelman's prodding. Straightforwardly, he said: "Yes, Mr. President, there has been a failure. We do not deny that Richter has failed." Labanca had only admitted to a 'hypothetical' failure. Rumbo's attitude was far more candid, and considering that by and large he was facing an audience accustomed to strict party loyalty, his attitude deserves credit.

"That which occurred to Perón, the doer, is the drama to which all doers are liable: when they turn their heads to look backwards, they see nothing but waste and distress. They find nothing but uncertainty regarding the future of certain peoples and certain schools of thought", Rumbo explained rather confusedly, reaping, nonetheless, a round of applause. He tried to justify Perón as a 'doer' who had welcomed Richter cordially and honestly, as was his habit toward "everyone, regardless of race, political inclination, religion, social standing, knowledge or ignorance", he said, using an attractive figure of speech though in this case not quite fitting. "Actually," he continued, now nearer the actual truth – "Perón accepted Richter's offer out of a feeling of greedy impatience to do things. All this eventually led to a great undertaking which constituted the first footstep in a march that has already been set in motion and ´that will never stop. ´" Encouraged by further applauses, he went on: "This is how it started: through a mistake. Blessed be the mistakes that offer new horizons to the peoples of the world!" (More applauses).

Putting an end to his resonant speech, Rumbo proceeded to tell a story of his inspection tour on Huemul, probably wishing to strengthen his image as a learned man on the subject though the effect was the opposite. He said that he and others had tried to detect the radioactivity supposedly produced by Richter's atomic experiments (the experiments held on Friday, September 5, 1952) by means of a watch with luminous numbers (radioactive, according to Rumbo). "Had there been gamma rays, as we had been told, the numbers on the watch would have turned phosphorescent, yet they did not." So they asked what was the explanation, and the answer (from Bancora? Balseiro?) was that had gamma rays been produced, they would all have been dead. And indeed, Richter's permissive attitude while letting his visitors wander around the experiment to the point of allowing them to expose their watches to atomic radiations, contrasts sharply with the effort spent in building thick shielding walls. Despite the nonsense in his story, Rumbo's conclusion was correct: there had been no radioactivity. "But" he added – "where has this failure led to? A few salaries wasted, no doubt, but what is that compared to the future greatness of the Nation?"

The debate ended amid shouts and discussions while Perette cried from his seat: "Richter ought to give back the Medal for Loyalty at once!"

Next day, on September 2, 1954, the incident was given ample coverage in the local newspapers. It was widely commented by the general public as it was the first time since 1952 that the Government made any reference to project Huemul.

The news upset Richter to the extent that he sent a telegram to Congress demanding a public hearing on Huemul research activities so as to clear up his scientific reputation and to answer the accusation of fraud, over which Peronists and Radicals curiously seemed to be in agreement.

After almost two years of silence, Richter held a press conference announcing he had turned to President Perón. He challenged Argentine experts to divulge the results of his experiments so that the world might judge whether he was a fraud or a scientist. He had waited for "18 months in order to reach a fair settlement of my case with the Government", and now, as the matter had been publicly exposed, he wished to "state categorically that there had been neither errors nor negative experimental results during my tenure as head of project Huemul."

The matter of the telegram posed an interesting problem to the Lower House. Peronists chose to consider the telegram an offense to their corporate dignity and that it should be parried with a charge of contempt.

Radicals, meanwhile, were eager to promote debate of the issue and wanted Richter to state his case. This could be politically explosive for the Peronists, so they resorted to Article 61 of the Constitution. This article stated that no member of Congress may be held responsible, or may be questioned judicially or harassed due to opinions he may have expressed while performing his legislative functions. On the other side, the Radicals proposed creating a five member commission to study the case. A Peronist legislator was of the opinion that if Richter's petition was granted, it might create a dangerous precedent; it would mean that as of then, any tramp could insist on being heard. A heated discussion followed. Perette retorted that the person the legislator had described as "a tramp", had been honored with the Peronist medal which, by the way, he still held. "Moreover" he added – "he would not allow the legitimate concern of legislators in preserving their privileges to be turned into an instrument of censorship, curtailing the right of speech."

Radicals were a minority at any rate and a small minority, at that. The voting was 90 to 8. The opinion which prevailed was that Richter was to be held in contempt and detained for 5 days within the Congress building. The session finally finished on Friday, September 17 at dawn. The police went to fetch Richter at that hour.

Naturally, Richter was furious. His opinion of the Government differed substantially from the kindly comments he had made when journalists interviewed him on the island in June 1951. "I have been arrested in the best Gestapo style", Richter said to a New York Times journalist who managed to interview him at his makeshift cell in Congress that same evening. "The first thing I will do when I get out of here is to hand back the Peronist Loyalty Medal" he promised. [61]

Five days later, he was back at his house in Monte Grande. As of that moment, nothing was to be the same. He could blame the termination of project Huemul on the misguided intentions of a single individual: Iraolagoitia. But the derogatory treatment his case had received in the House of Representatives and his subsequent arrest showed that the Government, all of it, had officially turned its back on him. The bond of loyalty had been severed; he was right in returning the Peronist medal.

The Bariloche Institute

During the second summer school in Bariloche, Balseiro, Juan MacMillan and to a lesser extent Abele, began thinking about revamping the idea of a Physics Institute. In early March 1955, Iraolagoitia went to Bariloche where he held a meeting with the professors in house #13. The basic project was already at hand. The meeting was held primarily to materialize a feeling they all shared and now, they merely had to agree on the finer points. They discussed study plans as well as life styles. As reported by a witness, during the meeting Iraolagoitia expressed some concern about boys and girls living together. "What if a kid is born?" he asked. "In that case, we'll name you godfather" was the answer. Another problem which needed solving was to reach an agreement with the University of Cuyo, an academic institution legally qualified to grant degrees. The Institute was to function as a mixed entity, relying financially on DNEA while academically on the University. A formal agreement was reached between March and August, and no difficulties were encountered thanks to the fluid relationship between Iraolagoitia and Dr. Roberto V. Carretero, President of the University of Cuyo.

The general idea was that the High Temperature Plant would have an area devoted to research and another to teaching. This second area was to be the Institute. "Balseiro was the natural leader to conduct the Institute" Alberto Maiztegui, his friend and collaborator in those early days, recalled.

A different matter was that of conducting the Plant. Iraolagoitia decided to bestow that responsibility on his comrade Captain Oscar Quihillalt. Did this decision cause a certain amount of friction among physicists? Apparently not. In any case, one day Iraolaogitia went straight to Balseiro and told him in advance of this appointment. [62]

Quihillalt was no stranger to DNEA. He had studied Engineering and later engaged in post graduate studies in Sweden between 1945 and 1948. By late 1952, Quihillalt began to show up at DNEA headquarters where he studied shock waves, but in 1955. he was on holidays in Ushuaia "the farthest he could go" recovering from the bitterness of having been by passed for a promotion, when Iraolagoitia happened to call him. [63] Although they had different political views, Iraolagoitia sympathized with Quihillalt's frustration and decided to help by appointing him head of the Plant (which later on became the Atomic Center). Prieto, meanwhile, remained in charge of the administration.

The overall task of organizing the Institute was jointly undertaken by Quihillalt, Balseiro, Meckbach, Maiztegui and MacMillan, with the occasional collaboration of Abele.

Paradoxically, the creation of the Bariloche Institute coincided with the swift decline of the Peronist Government. Violent clashes between Government and the opposition had begun in 1953 with the burning of the Jockey Club, and suffered a marked deterioration when Perón attacked the ecclesiastical hierarchy the following year. Maiztegui recalled that on June 16, 1955, while Navy planes were bombing the Casa Rosada and its environs, they were all discussing the Institute in Iraolagoitia's office.

Despite the serious events taking place then and in the following weeks, the organization of the Institute continued without interruption. Admission exams for the first group of students were taken at the Institute in July, and classes started punctually on August 1. The selection of candidates students who had already completed two years at the university consisted of informal talks with applicants.

Balseiro was responsible for conducting the Institute and teaching a course in electromagnetism; Meckbach was in charge of the laboratory; Mario Foglio taught chemistry; Luis Moretti taught mechanics, and Manuel Balanzat, mathematics. The Bariloche Physics Institute was finally on its way.

When the Peronist government fell in September 1955, Quihillalt was appointed to replace Iraolagoitia, who had recommended him for the post before leaving, and Balseiro assumed total responsibility for both the Institute and the Atomic Center in Bariloche. [64]

Substantial difficulties, both financial and political, were encountered in the course of the following years. Yet the Institute continued to prosper with unparalleled success under the inspired guidance of Balseiro. A new pedagogical experience had been launched in Argentina. According to a student, Balseiro had remarked that the most revolutionary aspect of the new experience was not the full time professors; but rather the style of living, teachers and students together on campus, and the availability of scholarships which guaranteed full time dedication of students.

Arturo Lopez Davalos, a graduate from an early promotion, remembers his teacher affectionately: "From the very beginning, Balseiro maintained an intense rhythm of work solving all kinds of problems each day, teaching the theoretical physics courses within his reach, and planning the various programs to ensure the future development of the Institute."

"Balseiro approached his mission as a crusade to foster the scientific and technological progress of Argentina. To this end he spared no efforts. He was a brilliant lecturer and from his classes - taught nearly always without an aide memoire - it was difficult to guess that he carried such a heavy burden on his shoulders."

"Prior to being confined to bed because of his illness, Balseiro undertook up to three courses simultaneously. In a country with no scientific tradition like Argentina, Balseiro had to lay the groundwork of an institution he envisaged serious and solidly founded."

"Those of us who were privileged to engage in research activities under his guidance, had the opportunity of meeting him under very special circumstances. Due to his illness, in 1961 he was forced to move to Buenos Aires where he lived with his family in Martinez (in the Buenos Aires suburbs). There, he welcomed us as guests in his home to work close to him. We were privileged to have his full attention, while his strength permitted it. "

"Looking back, one still appreciates the originality of the topics he suggested to us. It is distressing to imagine the quality of scientific work he might have accomplished, had he not died at the early age of forty two."

"What I am now saying" Lopez Davalos continued – "may suggest perhaps that Balseiro had a one track personality with science as his sole aim. It was not so. Balseiro had deep religious beliefs and a broad humanistic culture that made him enjoy music, philosophy or biblical history as much as physics. The saying goes that there is always a great woman behind every great man. Balseiro certainly had an admirable companion in his wife Covita. While considering the countless difficulties he had to surmount in order to carry out his magnificent work, to those of us at the Bariloche Atomic Center, Jose Antonio Balseiro demonstrated with his own life how important it is to do the best, whenever you fail to do the impossible." [65]

The Bariloche Atomic Center submitted its first four scientific communications to the 27th Physics Association meeting held in May 1956. Somehow it constituted a symbol: after the painful days of project Huemul, Bariloche had become part of the physicist community. We cannot deceive ourselves, however, nor tamper with historical facts. The Bariloche Institute was far from welcomed by all physicists. When Perón was overthrown in September 1955, the reconstruction of the universities began and with it the struggle to get the best professors. "It was a difficult situation for the recently created Bariloche Institute", Guido Beck recalled. "The Institute and the University of Buenos Aires did not share the same interests. As a result, many felt then that the new Institute served no real purpose. Buenos Aires was actually in urgent need of professors with a good training level and, naturally, the Bariloche Institute only contributed to make this shortage of teaching personnel worse." [66]

For a few years, the problem was critical. Able people who were returning from abroad or going back to academic life after arduous years of political ostracism were strongly in favor of rebuilding university structures in order to accomplish the grand 'take off'. The prevailing atmosphere was the appropriate one. The National Council for Scientific and Technical Research was created in those years under the chairmanship of Nobel Laureate Bernardo Houssay. Under these circumstances, any obstacle on the road to reconstruction was resented and the Bariloche Institute represented exactly that, an unwelcome competition.

An independent witness to this conflict was Prof. Ingmar Bergstrom, who came to Argentina as a "nuclear physics expert" from UNESCO, for a nine month period from 1958 to 1959. Viewed in perspective, his comments are even more valuable. His observations are contained in the report that Bergstrom wrote at the end of his mission during the second semester of 1959. [67]

"After the revolution, (Perón's overthrow in 1955) the situation was such that CNEA (DNEA became CNEA in 1956) ended up with a huge budget, large amounts of equipment and over one thousand employees. In this sense, the School of Sciences (at the University of Buenos Aires) constituted an almost perfect vacuum. It was only natural for those in charge of reconstructing the School to single out immediately the most outstanding feature of present day science in Argentina: the great potential of CNEA and the void in the universities."

Bergstrom, who trained the first nuclear physics groups both at the Buenos Aires School of Sciences and at the Bariloche Institute, later observed with remarkable good judgment: "What a temporary visitor perceives is what might be achieved if the past is forgotten and the universities and CNEA collaborate with one another. There are people on both sides "pathologically" against each other. Many people from CNEA still believe the myth that the University of Buenos Aires cannot change (and they are wrong). Likewise, some people at the universities simply refuse to forget what happened during Perón's regime and therefore will have nothing to do with CNEA. While living in the past, they are "contributing" to the future of Argentina only by thinking and talking: that is a passive, or I should rather say a destructive exercise. Fortunately, there are also in both places open minded people who realize that the important thing is the future of the country; not the petty personal or historical prestige."

"The extreme solution sponsored by many is to close down the Bariloche Institute. From the point of view of Argentine science, this would be tantamount to a national catastrophe", Bergstrom added. Fortunately, this "solution" never materialized and, as Beck pointed out, the Bariloche Institute served to establish a healthy academic rivalry between the institutions.

"Undoubtedly, to a certain extent the Bariloche Institute posed difficulties and delayed the development of the Buenos Aires Department of Physics. What Buenos Aires may have missed however, was amply recovered later as a result of this high level rivalry. Proof of this is the successful current development of the Department of Physics. What Balseiro at his model Institute was able to establish as minimum goals for university teaching, the University of Buenos Aires was forced to strive for, and indeed, the University not only reached these goals, but it surpassed them. I have always considered this angle of the problem as a major contribution of the Bariloche Institute." [68]. This was written by Guido Beck in 1962, on occasion of the premature death of his disciple Balseiro, when the Bariloche versus Buenos Aires conflict was practically over due to the accelerated development attained in spite of all odds by the Buenos Aires University. The 1966 university disaster was still in the future. When that fateful incident occurred, the convenience of having preserved the Bariloche Institute was underscored once again. [69]

In his report, Bergstrom also remarks: "Bariloche results are surprising. The development of solid friendships among students in Bariloche will be of major importance in a few years from now, when these students reach key positions throughout the country. This youth has something which I cannot find in people of my generation: a collective way of thinking, which is absolutely essential for the future development of Argentine science."

In time, the Institute acquired an international reputation based on its particular style, its high level of teaching and its research groups (metals, low temperatures, theoretical physics, ionic beams, linear accelerator and others) which gradually became strengthened by contributions of domestic and foreign scientists. It was, in fact, the combination of teaching and research that produced such excellent results, as had been pointed out many years earlier by Gaviola and others. This combination happened to mix harmoniously in Bariloche.

Meanwhile, Gaviola had remained annoyed with CNEA since that fateful meeting in September 1953, when the first project to build a Physics Institute in Bariloche had crumbled. After the downfall of Perón, his views were publicly exposed in various articles, arguments and criticisms that Gaviola wrote for the magazines Esto Es and Mundo Argentino. [70] His writings were usually aggressive, a mixture of absolute truths and exaggerations which gave his words a dangerous, merciless edge. Naturally, they were not devoid of humor; he knew extremely well how to use words. But the breach between Gaviola and CNEA grew deeper than ever before.

It seemed as if this gap were irremediable. Fortunately, it was not. In 1961, Quihillalt, chairman of CNEA, sent Gaviola an invitation to visit Bariloche. A few months later, Gaviola offered himself to replace Ricardo Platzeck in the teaching of a course during the summer of 1962, and by the end of that year, he donated several books to the Institute.

Some months later Carlos Mallmann, who succeeded Balseiro at his death as head of the Institute, wrote to Gaviola thanking him for the donation, and offered him a chair at the Institute. Within a few days, Gaviola not only accepted the offer but referred to the Bariloche Institute as "actually the only School of Physics (in Argentina)." [71]

Gaviola began his period of residence in Bariloche in 1963. Significantly, this was also his last post before retirement in

1982. In 1963, Beck, who had been in Brazil since 1951, also returned to Bariloche. This is a coincidence that cannot be overlooked: Gaviola and Beck, the two founding fathers of modern physics in Argentina were reunited, of all places, in Project Huemul's territory, twenty years after their initial meeting in Córdoba, where their crusade had begun. Balseiro, the disciple sadly gone, was the bridge between then and now crossing over Huemul.

Under the leadership of Balseiro, the Institute of Physics had grown to measure up to international standards. It was the best realization of Gaviola's dearest dreams. The old warrior, never to be satisfied, must have felt gratified.

* * * * * *

<u>Above</u>: Scientific committee members discuss the agenda with R. Richter. From left to right: O. Gamba, R. Richter, M. Beninson (with beret partially hidden), J. Balseiro, another unidentified person, M. Báncora and Father Bussolini.

<u>Below</u>: Richter, scientists, congressmen and others in their way to visit the laboratories. *Courtesy of M. Báncora*

Above: Climbing 200 steps leading to Richter´s cabin on the island´s highest vantage point.
Below: O. Gamba, J. A. Balseiro, M. Báncora and Father Bussolini listen to Richter, while R. Mendé, Minister of Technical Affairs attentively follow their reactions (below).
Courtesy of M. Báncora

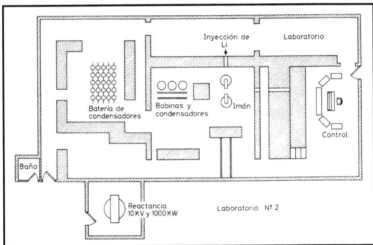

Above: Magnet used by Richter when the Scientific Committee visited the laboratories in September 1952. *Courtesy of M. Báncora*

Below: Layout of Lab 2. The control room is on the right hand side. To the left, separated by a 6 ft thick shielding wall is the reaction zone at the center of a large magnet. At this point hydrogen gas and lithium powder were combined while a powerful electrical spark was discharged between two electrodes. Other elements were coils and condensers.

Navy Captain Pedro E. Iraolagoitía, Secretary General of CNEA and Director of DNEA between April 1951 and September 1955. He resolutely canceled Huemul Project in November 1952.

Dr. José Antonio Balseiro, in his desk at the Bariloche Institute of Physics (today Balseiro Institute). Balseiro was the leading member of the Scientific Committee that evaluated Richter's work in late 1952. In 1955 he helped to organize the Institute in Bariloche where he was Director until his untimely death in 1962. *Courtesy of A. López Dávalos*

Second Summer School in Bariloche in January and February 1955. The decision to create the Physics Institute was taken during this School. From left to right, first row: Elsa Rosenwasser (looking back), Lara, Tito Suter, Mrs Munczek, Lucía Lagatta, Meckbach's son. Second row: Jorge Cosentino, Rodolfo Slobodrian (partially hidden behind Rosenwasser), Daniel Bes, Mario Foglio (partially hidden behind Lagatta), Wolfgang Meckbach and Mrs. Meckbach. Third row: Hernán Munczek, Sonia Nassif, Pilar Reyes (looking down), Mario Schoenfeld (partially hidden behind Bes), Juan Peyre, Rubén Norcini and Santo Mayo. *Courtesy of M. Foglio.*

Enrique Gaviola and his wife Elena in their house in Bariloche (Km 5 of road to Llao-Llao), February 1976. Gaviola was the first to propose in 1953 the creation of an Institute of Physics using the facilities left by Richter in the mainland facing Huemul Island. However, the initiative soon came to a dead end in part due to Gaviola´s inflexibility during discussions with Iraolagoitía and advisers. It was revived later in 1955 by Balseiro and others.

Lab 1. The big reactor (see Chapter 3 and picture there in) was built here. Later Ricther decided its demolition and ordered to dig a hole of similar dimensions (40 ft diameter, 40 ft deep) meant to build the reactor underground but then he changed his mind once more and send the crew to fill in the hole with gravel, cement and sand. This was observed with astonishment by Iraolagoitía when he visited the island upon taking charge of CNEA in early 1952 and contributed to persuade him to convene a scientific committee to evaluate Richter´s work. *Pictured is from 1981.*

Lab 4 was never used. It was finished shortly before the end of Project Huemul. The top picture shows how it looks since 1973 when the Peronists returned to power and covered with black paint the chart of expenses "wasted" (sic) in Project Huemul posted after the fall of Perón in 1955 as seen in the insert below. The chart´s head line reads: "Total cost of Project Huemul" and exhibits the expenses incurred in "Constructions" (about U$ 10 million of 1955); "Scientific instruments and machinery" (U$ 2.5 million); "Salaries" (U$ 2 million); "General expenses" (U$ 2.5 million) and "Spent without any benefit" (U$ 17 million). *The picture in the insert by courtesy of M. Frugoni and A. Mariscotti.*

Ronald Richter in 1982 in his house in Monte Grande in the outskirts of Buenos Aires. *Courtesy of Edgar Sánchez*

After Huemul Argentina made progress in atomic energy. Key to the early developments were Philips CW electrostatic accelerator (top left) and the powerful Synchrocyclotron (top right). Both machines were acquired after Prince Bernard met Perón in April 1951. Another historical development was the inauguration of the first nuclear reactor made in Latin America, in 1958 (left).

NOTES TO CHAPTER 5

[1] Unless specified, most material in this section is based on documentation kindly provided by Colonel E. Gonzalez to the author. (Author's file)

[2] Interview with Ruth Spagat on February 7, 1978 and Gonzalez' report to Perón (ref. 1).

[3] The New York Times, February 20, 1952.

[4] Report of Inquiry Commission headed by Prof. Teofilo Isnardi, Casos de la Segunda Tirania, Vol I, Integracion, Buenos Aires, 1958.

[5] Interview with Eng. H. Hellmann, May 1, 1980.

[6] Ibid. 5

[7] GEOPE, Public Works Co. Report dated February 23rd, 1953, addressed to the "Head of the High Temperature Experimental Plant's Technical Office." Other information quoted in this section has been obtained from the above mentioned report.

[8] Mundo Atomico, Year III, number 7, 1952, and various December 12, 1951 Argentine newspapers.

[9] According to the GEOPE Report (ref. 7), there were still other changes and modifications introduced by Richter in connection to the large reactor.

[10] Ibid 7.

[11] This expression brings to mind the matter of the "terrestrial rays" on which Richter wanted to write his doctoral thesis. It is appropriate to quote the testimony of Dr. Kurt Sitte, who kindly shared with us his recollections of his years in Prague, when he was Richter's fellow student: "I distinctly remember meeting Ronald Richter during my early student days at the University

of Prague. I happened to sit next to him in our small theoretical physics classroom. It impressed me deeply when once, during a recess, Richter furiously began jotting down all kinds of weird signs and symbols, oblivious of everything around him. I was a beginner at the time, and it all seemed extremely sophisticated to me. I believe he was in his third year then. He appeared to be an impetuous student, though somewhat introverted. He rarely participated in informal discussions or other activities with fellow students. My admiration for Richter began to fade in the following years when meeting him in more advanced courses and seminars. Richter did not shine there; the limits of his technical abilities and his small capacity for criticism particularly self criticism became increasingly evident. His attendance to classes became erratic and the progress of his studies practically stopped. Sometime later, while I was assistant to Prof. Fürth in the Experimental Physics Department, Richter tried to interest us in a fantastic project. He had read in a magazine (not a scientific magazine, of course) about the discovery of a mysterious radiation the "terrestrial rays" which emanated from the center of the Earth and caused all sorts of fabulous effects. This is what he wanted to investigate. He was terribly excited with the idea and it was very hard to dissuade him (I don't really know that we did), by pointing out that the 'evidence' he quoted was spurious, or worse, and that the whole thing was utter nonsense. In the end he agreed to do his doctoral thesis on a more conventional subject which had to do if I remember correctly with the application of barrier photocells in measuring X rays. I had nothing to do with the supervision of that work, so I have no first hand knowledge of it. He eventually got his degree anyway, though shortly after he left the validity of his results was questioned. Consequently, Felsinger was asked to repeat the experiments and, indeed, some discrepancies were found."

[12] Interview with Admiral Pedro Iraolagoitia, on August 28, 1979. Other information in this section on Iraolagoitia's performance corresponds to the interview held on this date.

[113] The openings can be seen even now surrounded by half finished stucco. In this large building known as Lab #4, it is interesting to note a detail of historical significance: after the downfall of Perón in 1955, the place was used as an exhibition hall for the instruments used on Huemul and to describe Richter's experiments. Facing the entrance on the wall at the back, a large sign about 24 ft. by 9 ft. conveyed the following information on the cost of project Huemul: "Amount of pesos spent in constructions: 35 million; in equipment, almost 10; in salaries; 8, in overhead expenses, another 10 million." The last line read: "Amount of pesos spent to no benefit whatsoever: $ 62,428,729.82" (About 17 million dollars of that time). Eighteen years later, when Perón came back to power in 1973, the sign was painted over in black and that is how it stands now: a sort of huge blackboard, a testimony to the political intolerance of Argentines on either side.

[114] CNEA actually reported to the Ministry of Technical Affairs, but Gonzalez regarded this institution as his own territory. In the same manner that Gonzalez had resented Richter's independence, Mende resented Gonzalez'.

[115] Ibid. 12.

[116] Other people shared this same view. One of them was Edward Teller, the 'father of the H Bomb'. In 1956, Gordon Dean, who was chairman of the Atomic Energy Commission in 1951 and had been so upset by Perón's announcement (see The Announcement), was invited by the then Captain Quihillalt, president of CNEA, to visit Argentina. Richter, who was then living in the vicinity of Buenos Aires, requested an interview with Dean. The meeting took place at the Plaza Hotel. "Richter walked in and told me that nobody understood him and that he wanted to go to the States. I told him to send me his papers and I would see what could be done about it", Dean told Quihillalt. Six months later, Quihillalt went to the States and met Dean. Dean told him he had given Richter's papers to Edward Teller who had returned them with a note which said: 'On reading the first line of Richter's papers one would think he is a genius; on reading the second line one comes to the conclusion that he's

nuts.' Manfred Von Ardenne arrives at a slightly different conclusion in his autobiography: "My experience with this person (Richter) was unfortunate. I had to dismiss him quite soon despite the shortage of personnel because of the war. He used to mix fantasy and scientific facts in such a way that his work could not be relied upon." Von Ardenne also recalls that "I had already heard by 1943 that Richter wanted to turn light nuclei into helium by applying discharges to high current gases". While acknowledging that Richter was moving in the right direction in this respect, Von Ardenne felt that the way he acted was "unworthy of a scientist: Richter used to introduce theoretical speculations as scientific facts and through the expediency of presenting a deceitful picture of the situation, he tried to obtain funds for his experiments.". Still another informed opinion on this matter belongs to Prof. R. Fürth, who supervised Richter's thesis in Prague. In a letter to Peter Alemann, he stated: "My personal opinion is that Richter is a moderately gifted scientist, with an excess of imagination and not enough self criticism." The author is grateful to Admiral Quihillalt for the description of his talks with Gordon Dean.

[17] Letter from Colonel Gonzalez to his son, dated May 11, 1952. (Author's file)

[18] Felix Luna, "Argentina, de Perón a Lanusse" (Argentina, from Perón to Lanusse), Biblioteca Universal Planeta, Barcelona, 1972.

[19] Letter from Colonel Gonzalez to his son, dated July 31, 1952. (Author's file)

[20] Interview with Fidel Alsina, February 1, 1979.

[21] The generally accepted version is that Richter used acoustic energy from the loudspeaker as a contribution toward increasing the temperature of plasma. This is an utterly nonsensical proposition, considering the small value of such a contribution. However, when the author interviewed Richter in 1979, he offered a different explanation: he had used sound to measure, not to increase, the temperature of the plasma since, as he said then, "the speed of sound is proportional to the

square root of the temperature of the medium through which it travels", which is correct. However, this method is quite impracticable in such a non homogeneous medium. Furthermore, a pulsed sound source would have been required which, according to Dr. Balseiro's testimony to the 1955 Investigating Committee, was not the case (see ref. 24). When the author pointed this out to Richter during the interview, he showed not the slightest indication of being annoyed and, acknowledging that it was indeed so, and simply changed the subject. Also during this interview, Richter repeated his well known assertion that it was unnecessary for him to attain extremely high temperatures. Among other ideas, he mentioned the injection of deuterium into a vessel until one achieves extraordinary pressures. At the very limit, "a plasma will be formed and atoms will fuse". When the author pointed out to him that there is no vessel or compressor in the world capable of withstanding such pressures, he replied: "That is my secret."

[22] Report by Father Bussolini to Perón dated September 15, 1952. (Author's file)

[23] According to Bertolo's testimony on the Committee's visit, and more specifically on this particular experiment and the use of lithium: "I was in charge of connecting the blades. I recall that at the first boom! while the 20 Peronist congressmen scrambled away as fast as they could, Balseiro and Bancora asked for more and he (Richter) began getting nervous: 'I can give you an atomic facility, and you, what can you offer me?'. 'That is precisely what we are expecting from you', they told him. Then they stopped. All the lithium spilled on the floor had to be cleaned up with a vacuum cleaner. Lithium produced short circuits in the vacuum cleaner. It exploded on me afterwards, and people thought it was atomic energy, but it was only those dirty carbon brushes."

[24] Ibid. 4. The "eyewitness" in this reference was Balseiro, as can be inferred from the quotation on page 260 of Balseiro's technical report, indicated in the preceding page.

[25] As told by Vidiri to Iraolagoitia and by the latter to the author.

[26] Ibid 22.

[27] Interview with Mario Bancora on August 28, 1979. On the question of the Larmor precession, see Balseiro's report and ref. 4.

[28] Ibid 22.

[29] Testimony by Balseiro to the Investigating Committee after 1955. See ref. 4.

[30] Ibid 22.

[31] On one occasion, Richter threw him violently out of the Plant. Ehrenberg was forced to leave with his mother for Buenos Aires on very short notice. Sometime later, Richter called him back again and Ehrenberg returned and continued working on the project.

[32] This observation was taken from Balseiro's report. Yet it is important to underline a virtually unknown fact: Ehrenberg, in collaboration with Jaffke, published a scientific paper on heavy water enrichment that eventually turned out to be the only scientific result ever to be published in connection with project Huemul. The work was published in Z. angew. Physik 5 (1953) 375, an almost unknown German journal, quite difficult to find nowadays. (The author is obliged to Dr. Walter Davidson, National Research Council, Canada, for his efforts in providing him a copy of the journal). The paper describes the results obtained in Bariloche regarding enrichment of water into "heavy water" (D_2O) through the fractioned distillation method. The authors state that Dr. Richter had encouraged them to undertake this work. They also claim partial success in achieving a certain degree of enrichment though they admit that results were insufficient to make this method competitive when compared to the fractional electrolysis method. From a technical point of view, the work has certain shortcomings such as: quoting some "approximate" values ('zirka' in the German original); failing to evaluate or to mention the errors involved; the fact that experiments were not carried out starting with

natural water but with already enriched water; and finally, the absence of references to other related works. It should be pointed out that neither of the above mentioned methods can be applied to industrial production of heavy water. The author is grateful to Dr. Andres Kreiner for helping him to analyze this work.

[33] Letter from Colonel Gonzalez to his son, dated September 12, 1952. (Author's file)

[34] Interview with Mario Bancora, August 28, 1979.

[35] Ibid 22.

[36] Balseiro's report, made available to the author by his son Dr. Carlos Balseiro. (Author's file)

[37] Ibid. 4

[38] Ibid. 4

[39] Interview with Dr. Antonio Rodriguez, January 5, 1981.

[40] Ibid 39.

[41] Ibid 4.

[42] Letter from Colonel Gonzalez to his son, November 16, 1952. (Author's file)

[43] On September 21, 1952, Colonel Gonzalez wrote to his son as follows: "There's not much to tell around here except that I met Mende the other day. He asked me to tell you that he wishes to receive, as soon as possible, any publication that might be of interest to Argentina such as criticisms, articles on the government, etc. published abroad. We also discussed the "colo" (madman in slang). They must come to some sort of conclusion about his future in a meeting to be held with Pablo (Perón's name in disguise) next Thursday. The Marx Brothers five have already submitted their report unfavorable, as was to be expected. In my opinion, however, it is not final, it says that this is an old story, apart from being expensive, etc., etc. In short, nothing new. Mende also told me that the "colo" had sent word through a trustworthy friend that he wanted me back on the job as a condition to continue working, heaping all kinds of praises on me, and speaking evil of Ira. Evidently, the guy is crazy." Gonzalez, who in 1943 had collaborated in the creation

of the Information Service, was always conscious of security norms. In his letter to his son in Holland (who was working at Philips), he chooses to disguise the names of real people under fairly obvious forms: the "colo" is Richter (loco, which means crazy or insane, read backwards); "Pablo" is Perón and "the Marx Brothers five" are the five members of the Investigating Committee who visited Huemul. "Ira", of course, is Iraolagoitia. (Author's file).

[44] Ibid 12.

[45] From an article entitled "Desde Huemul" (From Huemul), signed by 'A Visiting Reporter', published in 'Nuevas Bases', the official newspaper of the Socialist Party, on February 20,1953.

[46] Ibid 45.

[47] Ibid 39.

[48] Interview with Juan Roederer in April 1983.

[49] Bailey Willis, "El Norte de la Patagonia - A History of the Hydrological Studies Commission, Public Works Ministry, 1911-14". Published by the Agriculture Ministry, National Parks and Tourism Bureau, Argentina, 1943. The author is grateful to Alberto Boselli for having brought this book to his attention. The book describes an ambitious project sponsored by Minister Ezequiel Ramos Mexia at the beginning of the Century, aimed at transforming the Nahuel Huapi area into an industrial and commercial development pole.

[50] Report by Gaviola dated July 18th, 1953. The Bariloche Atomic Center Library.

[51] Letter from Gaviola to Rimoldi, July 20, 1953. The Gaviola File, Bariloche Atomic Center Library.

[52] Correspondence with Manlio Abele, Bariloche Atomic Center Library.

[53] Interview with Seelmann Eggebert, May 17, 1982.

[54] Dutch physicist A. H. W. Aten's contribution in connection with the early days of the synchrocyclotron should be emphasized, as well as the use the Seelmann group had previously made of the cascade accelerator in operations since July 1953. Baro and Flegeinheimer, who had the privilege of

living that fascinating adventure, recall that: "...in those early days when there were no labs, no neutrons, no accelerators, and only one or two home made Geiger counters which had come down from Tucuman or from Otto Hahn's old equipment, Seelmann was already training us in the separation of nuclides derived from thorium and uranium minerals. The range of nuclides our group was able to obtain increased fantastically when the cascade accelerator was set in operation in 1953. The first artificial nuclei, wholly produced and measured in Argentina, were obtained on July 17 of that year. Neutrons were abundant, though not as much as we desired. Since we already had a few kilos of purified uranium from minerals, fission nuclides began showing up right away. Actually, the whole nuclear chart was our hunting ground in those days, and we were just about in time. The table in the April 1953 issue of 'Review of Modern Physics' constituted our bible then; it showed a thousand radioactive nuclides, many of which carried uncertain or erroneous information. With Mallmann we used to make lists of new nuclides which might be of interest to all of us. Almost sixteen months went by between the inauguration of the cascade accelerator and the synchrocyclotron: time enough to whet our appetite for radiating with deuterons and then passing on to more exciting things. Prof. Aten's assistance from the Amsterdam Nuclear Research Institute was of fundamental importance. He had first arrived in Argentina in October 1953, and used to give us talks on his extremely broad radiochemical experience with the Amsterdam synchrocyclotron, whose twin brother - ours - was then under construction." (see '25 años' [Twenty five Years] Mario A. J. Mariscotti, Editor, Dept. of Physics, CNEA, 1979, NT 23/81, Buenos Aires.)

[55] The New York Times, June 17, 1953.

[56] The students were: Carlos Buchler, Unrico Koppel, Clara Mattei, Eduardo Nasjletti, Emilio Roxin, Cesar Sastre, and Esteban Vagi.

[57] Interview with Jorge Sabato, August 31, 1979. Sabato apparently suggested to Balseiro the possibility of undertaking physics of metals in Bariloche. "Balseiro told me that I was out

of my mind, that he absolutely refused...however, that's how physics of metals started in Bariloche." Iraolagoitia had asked Sabato to start thinking about developing metallurgy. Balseiro, being aware of this and suspecting that Iraolagoitia wanted metallurgy to be undertaken in Bariloche, erroneously came to the conclusion that in Sabato's mind physics of metals and metallurgy were the same thing. Sabato felt differently, however. He believed that metallurgy should be developed right next to industry. He therefore convinced Iraolagoitia to start it in Buenos Aires. The person who actually started physics of metals in Bariloche was Gunther Schoeck, an outstanding Austrian specialist. According to Sabato, Schoeck came to Argentina as a result of a dish of spaghettis. 'While in Birmingham in 1958, an Englishman came along recommending Schoeck as candidate because he wanted to ski (in Bariloche). I invited him to my house and told my wife to prepare a dish of spaghettis with sauce: if the chap could handle the spaghettis, then he was the ideal candidate for Argentina.' That was how he eventually came to Bariloche."

[58] The September 6, 1954 Financial Section of The New York Times carried the following headlines: "Argentina Awaits Odlum's Plan for Atom Powered Electric Plant". Then it said: "Buenos Aires paper reports installation would use only domestic uranium. Oil, pipeline deals also under way." Mr. Floyd Odlum was the American industrialist who negotiated these contracts with Perón. He was president of the Atlas Corporation and in an ample package deal, he offered to invest dollars in Argentine petroleum and uranium deposits. The agreement was covered again in the Financial Section of The New York Times on September 16, 1954.

[59] When the author visited Monte Grande in February 1979 to interview local people, all who had known Richter in his 1953/54 extrovert style believed he had left Monte Grande in the mid Fifties. None of them knew that Richter was still living there. Mr. Guillermo Rodriguez, a former bus driver, offered a vivid description of Richter sharing a bottle of wine with other habitués in some bar facing the plaza near the railway station.

[60] Actually, 20 years went by before Nuclear Power Plant Atucha I began its operation. Yet the first research reactor RA-1 began operating four years later, in 1958, and the RA 3 for radioisotope production was inaugurated at the Ezeiza Atomic Center in 1967.

[61] The New York Times, September 18, 1954.

[62] Interview with Dr. Alberto Maiztegui, December 12, 1980.

[63] Interview with Adm. Oscar Quihillalt, December 12, 1980

[64] Balseiro exercised total control of the Bariloche Atomic Center from 1955 to 1957, until Captain Cabrera became head of the Center (though not of the Institute). Balseiro became head of the Atomic Center again a couple of years later.

[65] Arturo Lopez Davalos, Newspaper Rio Negro, Special issue on the Bariloche Atomic Center, December 13, 1980. Dr. Lopez Davalos, an outstanding student of Balseiro's, became Director of the Atomic Center and of the (now) Balseiro Institute in 1986.

[66] Guido Beck, Ciencia e Investigacion [Science and Research], number 4, Vol. XVIII, April 1962.

[67] Ingmar Bergstrom, "Project Number 5 for Argentina", Final report to UNESCO Headquarters, 1958.

[68] Ibid 66.

[69] A reference to "The Night of the Long Sticks", when the police violently broke into the premises of the School of Sciences of the University of Buenos Aires, in June 1966. General Juan Carlos Ongania had just overthrown the constitutional Government presided by Dr. Arturo Illia and taken office. Many professors were wounded and many more arrested. Over 80% of the School faculty tendered their resignation (including the author), thus interrupting the remarkable progress accomplished in those years, especially in connection with the level of teaching and research in physics, chemistry and meteorology.

[70] Enrique Gaviola, "Esto Es", number 96, week of October 18 to 24, 1955, page 26; "Mundo Argentino", December 14, 1955; "Mundo Argentino", December 21, 1955.

[71] The Gaviola File, Bariloche Atomic Center. Gaviola was exaggerating, of course. He was resentful then of the Buenos Aires School of Sciences. Consequently, he chose to ignore the major contribution toward training scientists that the School had made during all those years (including the author). Yet we have used this reference to emphasize the fact that Gaviola, indeed, became reconciled with Bariloche, hence with CNEA, and so "the peace was restored."

Epilogue

The Secret of Huemul

On February 16, 1951 Ronald Richter informed Capt. Gonzalez Jr. that positive results had at long last been obtained. Five weeks later, those results led to one of the most spectacular scientific announcements in history: controlled thermonuclear reactions had been produced.

Despite its momentous importance, the experimental evidence on which the announcement was based was never disclosed. What exactly happened on that day? What moved Richter to conclude that he had achieved a chain thermonuclear reaction? The answer to this question - key to the whole project - remained unknown for almost thirty years. In search of an explanation, in the winter of 1980 the author interviewed Mr. Heinz Jaffke.

Jaffke, Richter's long time friend and assistant had been in charge of taking data on that memorable day and, at the author's request, he kindly agreed to review the instrumental details of the experiment. As described in chapter Project Huemul, Richter had installed his first reactor, a 9 ft. high- 6 ft. diameter cylinder, and a spectrograph with a photographic plate to record the spectrum of the atoms 'burnt' in the spark gap at the center of the cylinder. A spectrum, as seen on a plate, is an irregular sequence of vertical lines produced by the radiation emitted by the hot atoms. The sequence in itself is characteristic of the radiating elements.

In Richter's experiment, the photographic plate moved upward while the powerful electrical discharge took place, recording the spectrum as the experiment progressed. Temperatures above the fusion reactions threshold (some million degrees) should alter the spectrum. Richter employed the spectrograph with this purpose, that is, to detect the occurrence of fusion temperatures by looking at the spectrum of the reacting elements. In this respect the spectrograph was used as a sophisticated thermometer.

"The sliding mechanism that pulled the plate upwards was not working properly" Jaffke said to the author – "occasionally when moving upwards the plate went into a slanting position."

On February 16, 1951, the plate was immediately developed and taken to Richter. Jaffke indicated that while crossing the lake with the results of the day, he examined the plate and noted that the lines were not fully straight but at some point they showed a deviation from vertical.

"When Richter saw the plate with the lines shifted, he became very excited and said that this was the signal of success" Jaffke recalled "Although I am not a physicist, and could not ascertain the full meaning of the experiment, it seemed to me that the fact that the lines of the spectrum were not vertical was due to the defective sliding mechanism of the spectrograph. I suggested the convenience of repeating the experiment, but Richter refused."

Jaffke's description is striking. His understanding that the curved lines were due to an instrumental defect was correct while Richter's interpretation that they were due to the high temperatures of the plasma in the electric spark gap, was not because it is not a shift but a broadening of the lines which results from a hot plasma with atoms moving in all directions. Richter was so carried away by his enthusiasm that he not only disregarded further checks (as required in all scientific research) but he made a gross mistake in considering a shift to be the proper answer to what he was looking for. He was so convinced of this that he explicitly said so in the press conference of March 25, 1951 (see "The Press Conference", in chapter Crisis and note 1 in that same chapter).

This was the secret of Huemul. Lack of knowledge of basic physical processes and irresponsible refusal to check experimental results further, led Richter to involve the Government and the Nation in the sensational announcement of March 24, 1951.

*****

List of acronyms

AEC	US Atomic Energy Commission
AEG	German General Electricity Co. established in 1930´s in Argentina.
AFA	Argentine Physics Association (Asociación Física Argentina)
BA	City of Buenos Aires.
CEO	Chief Executive Officer.
CNEA	Argentine Atomic Energy Commission (Comisión Nacional de Energía Atómica) created in May 1950.
DC	Direct electrical current.
DNEA	National Department of Atomic Energy (Dirección Nacional de Energía Atómica). Created in May 1951. In 1956 became the "new" CNEA.
DNIT	National Department of Technical Research (Dirección Nacional de Investigaciones Técnicas). Created in June 1950.
GEOPE	German construction company, contracted by Richter after SACES left.
GOU	Group of United Officers (Grupo de Oficiales Unidos). Driving force behind the 1943 coup that eventually brought Peron to power.

HAMAC Co.	A company created by Heriberto Hellmann after AEG was confiscated in Argentina after WWII. It supplied Richter with heavy equipment.
ID	Identification.
INVAP S.E.	A technological company, created in the 1970´s as a spin-off of the Bariloche Atomic Center.
LNEA	National Atomic Energy Laboratory (Laboratorio Nacional de Energía Atómica), created in 1951 as Richter´s Laboratory in the PNEA.
MIT	Massachusetts Institute of Technology.
PNEA	National Plant of Atomic Energy (Planta Nacional de Energía Atómica). Created in 1951. It was Richter´s official institution for Project Huemul.
RA1	First Argentine nuclear research reactor. Inaugurated in 1958.
SACES	Italian construction company that worked in Huemul after the Army Engineering Co. left the island.
UNESCO	United Nations for Education, Science and Culture Organization,
UNW	United Nations World magazine.
US, UK	United States, United Kingdom
WW I, II	World War I and II.

Chronology of Major Events

1906	Creation of the La Plata Institute of Physics.
1917	Gaviola begins studies in La Plata with R. Gans
1921	Gaviola goes to Germany, first to Göttingen, then to Berlin.
1928	Gaviola works at Johns Hopkins with Robert Wood.
1929	Gaviola works at Carnegie Institute with Merle Tuve and Larry Hafstad.
1930	Gaviola returns to Argentina as Professor at the University of Buenos Aires.
1938	Discovery of fission by Hahn, Meitner and Frisch.
1939	Gaviola travels to the US to supervise the construction of the mirror for the new 60" Córdoba telescope (July).
1943	Guido Beck arrives in Argentina (May).
1943	Military coup led by General Farrell and Colonel Perón (June).
1944	Creation of the Argentine Physics Association (September).
1945	First Gaviola´s initiatives to create a private university.
1945	Atomic bomb, Hiroshima and Nagasaki (August).
1946	E. Condon publishes article denouncing military censorship (April).
1946	Gaviola publishes its "Argentina and the Atomic Age" memorandum (May).

1946	Peron takes oath as President (June 4).
1946	Heisenberg accepts coming to Argentina (November).
1947	Proposals for a National Institute for Scientific Research, discussed in the Senate.
1947	First article by Mizelle in New Republic, on Perón´s atomic plans (February).
1947	Second article by Mizelle (March).
1947	Kurt Tank arrives in Argentina (December).
1948	Ronald Richter arrives in Argentina and meets Perón (August).
1949	Construction works start in Huemul Island (July).
1950	Richter and his wife move to Bariloche (March).
1950	Perón and Evita visit Huemul Island (April).
1950	Concrete poured into the Large Reactor molding (May).
1950	Creation of CNEA and DNIT (May).
1950	Mónica Richter is born in Bariloche (July).
1950	Richter exchanges letter with Mr. Sforza of the US Embassy in Buenos Aires
1951	Peron- Richter announcement that controlled thermonuclear reactions at a technical scale have been achieved.
1951	Prince Bernhard visits Argentina and offers Philips technology (April)
1951	Prof. Bakker meets Richter and offers Synchrocyclotron (May)
1951	Creation of DNEA
1951	Prof. Thirring publishes critical opinion on Richter´s works in UNW (May).
1951	Synchrocyclotron purchase order is signed (June).

1951	Lyman Spitzer gets U$S 50,000 grant from AEC to develop Sterallator (July)
1951	Richter's press conference: Argentina seeks industrial partner to exploit new atomic process (December).
1952	First review committee cancelled at the last minute (February).
1952	Gonzalez resigns and Iraolagoitia takes charge of CNEA (March)
1952	Peron initiates second term as President (June).
1952	Evita dies (July).
1952	New review committee visits Huemul; issues negative reports (September).
1952	Gans and Rodriguez meet Richter and issue last negative report (October).
1952	Iraolagoitia takes over the laboratories in Huemul and closes them (November).
1952	First thermonuclear explosion in the US (November).
1953	Richter leaves Bariloche with family and moves to Montegrande (March).
1953	Gaviola proposes creation of an Institute of Physics in Bariloche (May).
1953	Cockcroft-Walton accelerator is inaugurated in Buenos Aires (July).
1954	Richter is detained in the Congress building for 5 days (September).
1954	Synchrocyclotron is inaugurated in Buenos Aires (December).
1955	Second summer school in Bariloche (February).
1955	First courses start in the new Bariloche Institute of Physics (August).

1955	Coup de Etat ends Peron´s second presidency (September).
1955	Quihillalt becomes president of CNEA (October).
1956	DNEA becomes CNEA
1958	First Argentine research reactor is inaugurated

Name Index

CPSIA information can be obtained
at www.ICGtesting.com
Printed in the USA
FSHW011110270119
55290FS